The Failing Distance

The
Failing
Distance

THE JOHNS HOPKINS UNIVERSITY PRESS

THE AUTOBIOGRAPHICAL

IMPULSE IN John Ruskin

BY JAY FELLOWS

BALTIMORE AND LONDON

This book has been brought to publication with the
generous assistance of the Andrew W. Mellon Foundation.

The Johns Hopkins University Press, Baltimore, Maryland 21218
The Johns Hopkins University Press Ltd., London

Library of Congress Catalog Card Number 74-24374
ISBN 0-8018-1671-8

Library of Congress Cataloging in Publication data
will be found on the last printed page of this book.

For Frances and Otis Fellows
and Lisa Andrus,
who were there on Cyprus Avenue

Preface

Ruskin's books, his articles, his lectures are not enclosed. They are like his rooms, which always have views. The last period does not mean that a subject has been concluded. He organizes his world, at least at first, in an angelic "collective aspect" that is outside of sequence. There is nothing final. His works are as open-ended as the distance he takes for food. Like unstable water, eddying digressively as if to imitate the processes of an overwrought mind, material spills from work to work. Empty pages are original models for the space of his world, and he fills those pages in the same way that, "cramming and ramming," he fills space. If he is dependent upon distinctions, fences, devices of separation, those devices are, in part, created in order that they may be transgressed. But the transgression is the work of an outlaw who is preparing for his own unhappy end, unaware that the movement over borders, or the insistence upon playing all the perceived roles, of using up all the pages and all the space, of seeing, finally, St. Paul's from both ends of London Bridge, perhaps even at the same time, is the act of someone who will eventually find himself without options, with no empty containers, and with nowhere to go. The transgression is the work of someone who will, after all the boundaries have been outraged, find the approach to the "mosaic" of homogeneity and simultaneity, which is the final condition of the organic vision, horrifyingly claustrophobic—a prison. But the work spills and blends, like cursed water that will be blessed before it is forgotten.

And because of the spillway, the organic nature of the entire body of his work, I have avoided the perpetual identification of specific works. Instead, I have identified a work either when it seemed necessary for the sake of clarity or in order to make a distinction between public writing and private writing, a distinction that is important because it bears on the reticence or assertion of the first person, the way in which he chooses either to hide or reveal himself, and the problem of audience, whether the material has been adopted and refracted for public engagement or the autobiographical confrontation of a writer acting as an audience for himself. Although my instincts are to view a body of literature—Ruskin's more than most—in its "collective aspect," as if, removed from serial progression, it were alive, autonomous, all portions occurring simultaneously, I have attempted, though with few references to dates, to proceed with what I hope to be a tactful regard for sequence, beginning close to the beginning, ending at the end, with the concluding passage of *Praeterita,* which is also a new opening, the discovery of a new distance, an "openly golden sky," and, in the middle, dealing with the "nothing but process" of Ruskin's Third Style, a style that has neither beginnings nor endings. Attention to sequence is perhaps necessary because Ruskin, though almost always contradictory, establishes his precarious sanity on an aesthetics of windows and doubleness, undergoes striking changes in his attitude towards himself, as he creates and explores his landscape and examines the tenses that he has available to him. Essentially, he begins at the vantage point and ends at the focal point. He begins in the present and ends in a middle-distance of memory and calculated forgetfulness that is somewhere between a fictional past and an infernal present.

There are scattered references to Ruskin's madness, the profound disequilibrium of an extraordinarily sensitive mind attempting to avoid the consequences of what his Desiring Eyes have seen: a world of "bloody carcases," a "green tide" filled with floating corpses, the Spectral Vision of collapsing spaces, of "World Collision." But as I am largely writing about Ruskin's relation with his first person, his notion of autobiography, I have myself avoided dealing with the exterior events of Ruskin's life—his biography that has been treated so well by E. T. Cook and Alexander Wedderburn in the lengthy and detailed series of introductions to the Library Edition. At times I have dealt with the biography of Ruskin's mind, and find myself greatly indebted to both R. H. Wilenski, who has sympathetically charted the disequilibrium of Ruskin's consciousness, and John D. Rosenberg, who has shown the essential sanity and enormous humanity of the man. Still, I have written more about autobiography than biography, although Ruskin's autobiography is itself close to biography, and I have involved myself with the design that emerges from a text that is, of course, hardly separate from biography—a design that, while not recording Ruskin's movements in and out of madness, nevertheless suggests the nature of some of the pressures responsible for those movements.

About pressures and autobiography, this book is at the same time about landscape, the shifting structure of a world created out of both perception and imagination, fact and fiction, and the way in which Ruskin situates himself in a world, or, more accurately, "worlds," that are both infernal and paradisiacal. But this presents a problem. For Ruskin, aspiring towards the condition of a whole self, is in fact nothing of the kind. He assumes a "biped" stance towards his worlds. Obsessed with doubleness, he is at once the reticent, pseudonymous Kata Phusin of the early *The Poetry of Architecture,* who would annul himself in recessional space, and an intruding first person who would make his foreground presence noisily known. Often many selves, each with idiosyncratic preoccupations, Ruskin, with both public and private attitudes, is at least two selves. Despite the organic nature of his work, a work that knows no bounds and refuses to be contained, and the distaste he expresses for the division and tyranny of the aesthetics of the Renaissance frosts, as well as the Industrial Revolution's serial and specialized assembly line, he privately requires distance and options rather than unity, surprise rather than recognition, and discriminations rather than any union but a Marriage in Cana.

The problems of situating a contradictory self in worlds of shifting landscape is examined by the exploration of what I have called the "autobiographical impulse," by which I mean any desire for the emergence of the first person from a condition of voyeuristic invisibility, from an optical system without a sense of self, to a condition of density and opaqueness. It is an emergence that can take the form of self-conscious response to either claustrophobic tense—a confining present—or claustrophobic space, with Ruskin "face to face" with the "costermonger's ass" of Rembrandt; or the movement from pseudonymity to performance, which is the acting out of what has been seen by Ruskin's selfless Desiring Eyes. The autobiographical impulse, beginning as a reflexive, spatial heresy of mirrors, as opposed to the orthodox space of windows, ends in a triumph of tense and memory, the triumph of a new sequence and a new distance that masters a recessional space that has failed.

In order to get a sense of the shape of the book, as if aided by the kind of aerial perspective of which Ruskin seldom approved, perhaps a summary would be helpful—a summary that necessarily cannot take into account significant contradictions and rather complicated transitions. This book, then, attempts to establish Ruskin's initial optical bias: he can (and "may," which is at least as important) always see—though touching, as the tactile expression of a reluctant self, is an entirely different matter. What is required, most of all, is a separation between an optical self and the observed landscape—a distance in which the heretical, though compelling, autobiographical impulse can be lost. Seeing, Ruskin explores his world; as he does so, he translates those perceptions into language. And filling blank pages with urgency, he also fills his world, as description and identification give dimension to landscape. Yet what was once new and nothing, now becomes too much: the *horror vacui,* leading to an initial delight in plenitude, becomes a horror of claustrophobia. The instincts for separation are frustrated. Further, landscape, seen and obsessively described with a refraction that is distinctly Ruskin's own, becomes itself autobiographical. Claustrophobia and autobiography conspire unhappily in reflexive space.

Still, there are the eyes, and a transcendent far-sightedness. Distance is sought as a version of separation. Foreground, the landscape of claustrophobic autobiography, is anathema. To annul an increasingly apparent self that he would avoid meeting in its all too characteristic expressions of vanity and dogmatic assertion, Ruskin seeks vistas. Highly idiosyncratic, he nevertheless sees himself as a man of the times. Writing the history of landscape (among many other things) in *Modern Painters,* Ruskin writes his own autobiography: once, in a condition of Greek immanence and his own childhood, animated foregrounds of "vitality" and "nerves" were entirely pleasing. But in a condition of transcendence, in which the only animation is the false animation of the "pathetic fallacy," there are mountains, backgrounds and distances. Space has opened up, become recessional. And Ruskin moves into that recessional space, first with his eyes, and then by travelling to the Alps. But the penetration of space, if it is a journey that is finally taken and not simply talked about, requires a return trip, unless one is prepared to perform the difficult task of living in the distance. Space, rather than being happily recessional, is at least incipiently reflexive. And any chronicle of the return to foreground is a disagreeable form of autobiographical confrontation, almost like a guilty narcissist stealing a glimpse in a mirror.

In any case, the depth perspective, coming or going, is a private perspective. Yet Ruskin, learning as he explores, begins to take the horizontal perspective into account, the panorama that includes such extra-aesthetic public considerations as architecture (no longer exclusively "poetic") and economics. With Ruskin, both landscape—what is focused upon by the selected or inevitable perspective—and time work in a kind of complicated coordination. At its simplest, the distance is at first the future and later, when there is no more future, the past; and the foreground, as well as the peripherally inclusive spaces of panorama, are versions of the present. Incorporating panorama, Ruskin considers the necessity, if one is to be responsible, of a tense of living immediacy, a present tense that is as "vital" as Greek or childhood landscape. Bringing the present tense to panorama, he consolidates his perception of an overweening social consciousness. But public concerns and private needs begin to merge, and the public "living present" gives way, at times, to a private and digressive tense that is initially as apparently irresponsible and bitterly playful as the "living present" is somber and public-spirited.

Yet, as if in the end public spirit might have the moral obligation of taking over private realms, the public present causes private problems. Highly parenthetic, with various syntactical voices speaking among themselves, the syntax of the private present is cannibalistic: the "outside" is turned "in," while Ruskin, as an aggressive parenthetic territory digesting the "outside," establishes a syntax of defense against not only the panorama of inclusion, which is a claustrophobic dimension of the present tense, but also against a failing distance, which is also a failing future. Style now reflects, if not the early enthusiastic exploration and charting of recessional space, at once protection against the loss of separation and release from a panoramic perception that can be more maddening than infuriating. Distance vision gives way to myopia, the future to the present. And the syntax of the private present is an early version of autobiographical indulgence, of the writer's speaking freely about his first person without fearful premeditation.

If the private present offers release from panoramic perception before a diminishing future, the failing distance becomes not so much a failure, without apparent remedy, as an assault. What were, in *Modern Painters,* white lights of the distance—vanishing points in the Infinite where the optical self might lose that heretical autobiographical impulse—now become lights of an inverted perspective, closing in on Ruskin, his first person existence as an autobiographical "I." Basically, stereoscopics become pseudoscopics. The distance, like Ruskin's cannibalistic and parenthetic syntax, is turned "outside in." Both sight and sound assault Ruskin's defenses. He would be blind. He will stuff cotton in his ears to keep what is closing in on him from his senses. The man who began *Modern Painters* because of an antagonistic review in *Blackwood's Magazine* of Turner's painting of Juliet and the "mysteries of lamplight and rockets," virtually becomes the *Blackwood's* reviewer, as Ruskin, himself under spatial, temporal, and aural assaults, attacks Whistler's "Falling Rocket"—as if by doing so he could reclaim, or at least protest aginst, his failing distance.

Simply—too simply—Whistler's "Falling Rocket" is Ruskin's failing distance. Less aphoristically, with a world infernally organized about an inverted perspective, which would bring autobiography home before the autobiographer's readiness, Ruskin finds fireworks that are equivalents of claustrophobic focal points or mirrors—the light "in front of" darkness instead of "behind," like those paradisaic vanishing points of infinity—entirely infernal. And his present self, without distance or future, had been, as the *Blackwood's* reviewer, despised—not a fit autobiographical subject for one who no longer has the options of losing himself in recessional space, and for whom claustrophobia means an autobiographical confrontation between selves that, without the necessary sense of separation, the autobiographer, as well as his unfriendly subject, would choose to avoid.

For a while it is possible to escape into the proximate, what is close at hand. He determines to make the foreground livable by seeing only what he wants to see, hearing only what he wants to hear—a performance of limited perception that is not always easy ignorance. He will disregard both inclusive panorama and the distance that is rushing in upon him. And he will do this by concentrating upon what is narrowly and immediately before him. He will create a nest for himself. The remedy can only be temporary. Yet there is another solution with more endurance, just as there is another distance that, like all distances, exists to be used up, employed: in fact, the new solution is the new distance. And the new focal point is the old self— the old self, "peeled" and filtered (made more presentable) for the occasion of autobiography, and seen not claustrophobicly but at a new distance, almost telescopicly.

Essentially, Ruskin takes the past as a fresh mnemonic distance. And if he cannot either write autobiography or discover a first person worth talking about in the present tense, he can at least write an autobiography of the past, where there is an old self, a younger Ruskin who, if he had the opportunity, would doubtless attack his autobiographer as he had the *Blackwood's* reviewer. Efficacious autobiography is the result of warring selves. And the success of this war is dependent upon not writing the subject into the autobiographer's present. Autobiography, then, need not be prompted by its conspiracy with claustrophobia, and, for a while, before the madness and silence of the last eleven years of Ruskin's life, time—mnemonic time, as a kind of resurrected separation—solves some of the problems of an old distance that has failed. Yet the failure has occurred only after the distance has been occupied and travelled through, forwards and backwards. Its use is its abuse, which is finally no failure at all but the binding and blending of all things. With Ruskin, failure is, at least in the apparent end (or even before it, in the "nothing but process" of the middle) almost always fortunate, as it is in the "lucent verdure" of the Hampton Court Maze. But that is for later, and the transformations of labyrinths.

I want to thank Louis Cornell, Michael Riffaterre, and Carl Woodring, all of whom read my manuscript, and offered early suggestions that helped give it final shape. Further, I would like to express my debt to Georges Poulet, Richard Poirier, and J. Hillis Miller for immediate inspiration from afar. And to Laurence d' A. M. Glass, Van Morrison, Sean Sculley, Jane Shaw, and Sigrid Spaeth, I wish to express special thanks for help and friendship in lonely places. Finally, I want to thank John D. Rosenberg. He knows why; he knows the debt.

Fairfield Beach, Connecticut
July, 1974

Contents

The Failing Distance

CHAPTER I

The Desire of the Eyes

THE CAMERA LUCIDA AND THE OPTICS OF INTERVENING SPACE

Before all else, Ruskin, encyclopedic in interests and composed of multiple selves to accommodate those interests, is, as a highly complex system of vision, an optical self. At first avoiding variations of the reflexive movement towards autobiography, which he sees as a regrettable and heterodox impulse of the age, an age of self-consciousness and vanity, Ruskin is a voyeuristic optical self with no interest in indulging in any variety of self-portraiture. He is determined to avoid corporeality. Seeing all, Ruskin will himself be invisible. As far as anyone will know, he will not exist. But he will be watching, a spectator removed from the action. Even his verbal entrance into the public world beyond the enclosed walls of his Herne Hill garden is, as Kata Phusin, the author of *The Poetry of Architecture,* tentative, pseudonymous. Still, verbal visibility, the introduction of the first person on the page, is always to be easier for Ruskin than spatial visibility, which is either intense awareness of self in confined space, the face to face confrontation with a mirror, or performance beyond the page.

Invisible, Ruskin's optical self incorporates fundamental and antithetical aspects that are, by turns, humanized and dehumanized, feeling and unfeeling, inclusive and exclusive. Yet before division, Ruskin's essential identity is a single optical self that allows him, first, to explore the landscape of his world, and, in the process of exploration, to come to know his own idiosyncratic requirements for an entirely visual affiliation with that perceived landscape; and, second, to translate this affiliation, the spatial organization between self and world, into a relation between self and the interior topography of consciousness and memory, which will be intensely resurrected when he has run out of both landscape and future tense. Sight is memorable in a way that words are not, which is why Ruskin, at first determined to avoid autobiography, is reluctant to show himself. He wants a highly visible and memorable landscape to be perceived by an invisible and forgotten optical self. Almost from the beginning, emerging from his Herne Hill garden, he understands that he requires a selfless world, a world large enough to either hide himself or lose himself. He will search for a vanishing perspective.

Ruskin's major sensory preoccupation, if not the reason for it, is apparent in a letter to Mrs. Cowper-Temple that alludes to Ezekiel 24: 16: "The worst of me is that the Desire of the Eyes is so much to me! Ever so much more than the desire of the mind."[1] His Desiring Eyes permit him to approach without touching, to involve himself on his own terms, terms that require distance between self and the object of that desire. If the Desiring Eyes were to overcome the distance of separation, all that would be left is either claustrophobic autobiography, a painfully intense awareness of self in confined space, or a retreat into the long perspectives of memory.

Failing to detect either a desiring mind, or heart, in his readers, Ruskin uses the color of the heart to attract their eyes by the "actual printing of my pages blood-red—to try if I could catch the eye at least, when I could not the ear or the heart" (xxix, 469). At first, neither Ruskin's heart nor his ears can be appealed to any more than those of his readers. Yet always, the desiring eye can be attracted, caught. Despite Ruskin's later gastronomic preoccupations—his need, as the Supper Guest of his diaries, to taste, possess, and ingest the "outside"—the way to his evasive heart, if not those of his readers, is less through the alimentary canal than through his prized optical system.

Manipulated more by his Desiring Eyes than his desiring mind, Ruskin meets a personification of his optical self in a dream that, transporting him to Verona, "or some place that was and wasn't Verona," finds the optical

---

[1] *The Works of John Ruskin,* edited by E. T. Cook and Alexander Wedderburn, 39 vols., Library Edition (London, 1903–12), xxxvii, 153. References to this edition will appear in parentheses after all quotations from the works.

self engaged in emblematic behavior that wins Ruskin's praise: "Met an Englishman, who said he 'had been staring at things.' I said I was glad to hear it—to stare was the right thing, to *look* only was of no use."[2] The ability to stare is dependent upon the condition of the staring self's optical system. Throughout the body of Ruskin's work, but especially within the privacy of diaries that are written, essentially, to no audience but a later self—the ideal audience of autobiography—the chief concern of the shadowy figure behind Ruskin's various selves is apparent. Without the public accommodation that renders Ruskin both invisible and silent, there emerges a history of the eyes, or, more accurately, an ocular autobiography of the staring self, which even spills over from those diaries to the semi-public, epistolary writing of the early *Letters to a College Friend*. Beyond the reflexive complaints of the diaries, the writer talking to himself in the form of a reader, those letters indicate an extreme sensitivity to optical shifts:

As for myself, I am better, though my eyes are still weak; nothing but a little roughness left of my affection of chest; and my eyes are better, though, as you may imagine, they have had a great deal to try them; (i, 433)

I have got a decent number of sketches, forty-seven large size and thirty-four small, but even then my eyes hinder me; (i, 453)

I was much tempted to begin botany among the ruins of Rome, but I found it did not suit my eyes at all, and gave it up; (i, 457)

a day lost with me is lost indeed, and I cannot work double tides before or afterwards, owing to the weakening of my eyes. (i, 494–95)

But the more personal ocular autobiography, without the accommodating refraction of an audience, is more to the point. Even as a young man, with the future extending before him like the vistas he admires, Ruskin is obsessed with the problems of endings. Yet blindness is more threatening than death: "I thanked God for giving me a few more such hours and scenes, while my sight is still so far perfect" (*Diaries,* p. 94). For the staring self, sight is life, and the optical end, which is the end of everything, is always near: "my failing sight plagues me, I cannot look at anything as I used to do, and the evening is covered with swimming strings and eels" (viii, xxvi). If sight, more than food, is the substance of life, sight is still dependent upon the stomach: "Attack of sight failure after breakfast, caused, I doubt not, by two eggs at tea on Thursday . . ." (*Dia-*

---

[2] *The Diaries of John Ruskin,* selected and edited by Joan Evans and John Howard Whitehouse (Oxford, 1956–59), p. 685. References to the diaries will appear in parentheses after the quotation as *Diaries,* followed by page number.

ries, p. 1124). Still, to improve the self, optical perception, not gastronomic ingestion, must be improved: ". . . if my eyes were but as they used to be, what a different creature I should be" (*Diaries,* p. 355). Nevertheless, the condition of "used to be" is an optical paradise that cannot be regained because it never existed. The decline of the eyes is a fiction manufactured out of excessive concern.

Late in the ocular autobiography, the staring self is still awaiting the end of vision. But Ruskin's complaints continue; he is concerned that his "eyes are quite dark" (*Diaries,* p. 904). He notes the "sense of failing eyes always oppressing" (*Diaries,* pp. 906–7). And he feels his "eyes weak and quivery . . . and can see nothing now in any darkness" (*Diaries,* p. 907). Yet despite the lamentations, as late as 1883, even as he fights for his precarious sanity, he is pleased to mock his earlier concerns: "I must warn you of the total and most mischievous fallacy of the statements put forward a few years ago by a foreign oculist, respecting the changes of sight in old age. I neither know, nor care, what states of senile disease exist when the organ has been misused or disused; but in all cases of discipline and healthy sight, the sense of colour and form is absolutely one and the same from childhood to death" (xxxIII, 387).

If, finally, Ruskin, with his optical obsessions, is troubled occasionally by "eyes swimming a little in the bad way" (*Diaries,* p. 1130), he is still able to "see the blue lines [of his diary]. D. G." (*Diaries,* p. 1134). Furthermore, his distant focus is as efficient as his proximate focus: "Then I saw rosy dawn, and now the 'white mountain,' above long laid calm morning mist, as clearly with my old eyes as when I was twenty-one" (*Diaries,* p. 1149). With varying degrees of intensity and directness, the staring self's ocular autobiography charts the performances of an optical system responsible for Ruskin's most characteristic kinds of activities: not only the exploration of, and affiliation with, the exterior world, but also the establishment of perspectives or spatial organizations that are later internalized. And like that other, larger autobiography, which is at once more inclusive and more censored, *Praeterita,* the ocular history of the staring self ends with a vision of peace that includes all portions of the observable world: "I see everything far and near, down to the blue lines on this paper and up to the snow lines on the Old man—a fine wreath along his ridge on 30th May—as few men my age" (*Diaries,* p. 1128).

The staring self, shaping the very relation that Ruskin establishes with his world—and beyond relation, the nature and structure of that world—is created out of contradiction, the need for "doubleness," for options—a way out. Organized about antitheses, the staring self says one thing in order to establish the groundwork for later opposition. Its consistency is in its anticipated inconsistency. To announce is good, but to contradict is better.

Ruskinian dogma, the pronouncements of a highly visible self, is undercut, though somehow not cancelled, by antithetical statement that is pronounced with an assurance equal to the original. This is not merely a matter of change of mind, but something far more complex. The result is an architecture of the mind that would achieve the stability of opposed flying buttresses. In *Modern Painters* III, as his vision becomes increasingly inclusive, incorporating disparate material, he points out: "the more I see of useful truths, the more I find that, like human beings, they are eminently biped; and, although, as far as apprehended by human intelligence, they are usually seen in a crane-like posture, standing on one leg, whenever they are to be stated so as to maintain themselves against all attack it is quite necessary they should stand on two, and have their complete balance on opposite fulcra" (V, 169).

To turn the imagery of stance to the organizing principle of optics, Ruskin, in the guise of the staring self, like most "useful truths," is "biped." It is as if, visually, he has the equivalent of "complete balance on opposite fulcra," or better, eyes for opposing requirements. Ruskin's eyes, like both his truths and his feet, offer alternatives. One set of optical components, creating the balance of anticipated contradiction, is dehumanized, unfeeling, and entirely invisible—invisible, beyond the normal reticence of the optical self, in that it is without the inclination towards sympathetic identification. And without the desire to become visible even in sympathy, those optical components would attain the dispassionate precision of a camera lucida: "The sight of a great painter is as authoritative as the lens of a camera lucida . . ." (XXXIII, 387). And Ruskin compares his own affective responses with that same camera lucida: "In blaming myself, as often I have done, and may have occasion to do again, for my want of affection to other people, I must also express continually, as I think back upon it, more and more wonder that ever anybody had any affection for *me*. I thought they might as well have got fond of a camera lucida . . ." (XXXV, 457).[3]

The *locus classicus* of Ruskin-as-lens, of one capable of a response no more affective than that of the Camera Lucida, is the passage in *Praeterita*, concerning the Carlyle correspondence: "I find at page 18 this—to me entirely disputable, and to my thought, so far as undisputed, much blameable and pitiable, exclamation of my master's: 'Not till we can think that here and there one is thinking of us, one is loving us, does this waste earth become a peopled garden.' My training, as the reader has perhaps enough perceived, produced in me the precisely opposite sentiment. *My*

---

[3] The camera lucida, which is used by Ruskin as a kind of shorthand for objectified observation, is an optical instrument that may be attached to the eyepiece of a microscope. The camera projects the image of an external object on a sheet of paper, for purposes of tracing.

times of happiness had always been when *nobody* was thinking of me . . .''
(xxxv, 165). Shortly afterwards, he continues: "My entire delight was in
observing without being myself noticed,—if I could have been invisible, all
the better. I was absolutely interested in men and their ways, as I was
interested in marmots and chamois, in tomtits and trout" (xxxv, 166). No
subject for future autobiography, this version of Ruskin, approaching the
invisibility of the voyeur—"observing without being myself noticed"—is the
quintessential, uninvolved optical self-as-Camera-Lucida, whose special
modes of perception and affiliation, limited and unreflexive, are troubled by
nothing more affectively demanding than what Ruskin, in a different
context, calls "lenticular curiosity" (xxvi, 115).

To understand the Camera Lucida, its vantage point must be examined,
the phenomenology of its living, if dehumanized, space. The vantage
point—the immediately surrounding space of the Camera—is not large
enough to be sociable, affective space. Fundamentally, it is a solipsistic
space, a space for only one person, and that person's tangible existence is
entirely problematical: "A small chamber, with a fair world outside: —
such are the conditions, as far as I know or can gather, of all the greatest
and best mental work. At heart, the monastery cell always, changed sometimes, for special need, into the prison cell" (xxix, 464). Or the unsociable,
solipsistic space may be a portion of a larger, ostensibly social room: "a little recess, with a table in front of it, wholly sacred to me; and in which I
remained in the evenings as an Idol in a niche . . ." (xxxv, 39).

As opposed to Ruskin's underlying requirements for vistas, recessional
space, a *horror vacui* is involved in the camera self's need for enclosed living
space, which must be fully occupied and controlled by that dictatorial but
invisible self. Barely existing, the Camera feels no need for the vanishing
perspective. Simply, there is nothing to lose. Reflexive space closes in only
on a single transparent lens. The mirror reflects nothing. And because of
that, nothing is too small. The problem with Ruskin's rooms in Verona and
Venice is their size: "It pours rain, and the big room is in confusion" (*Diaries,* p. 915); "I think the big rooms, and sense that I can't stay in them,
put me out greatly (*Diaries,* p. 909). Yet at Oxford, in enclosed, manipulative space, creating a foreground that is livable precisely because it is
shallow and narrow—a foreground for proximate focus—Ruskin finds no
problem: "Just a day to spend in my nest here" (*Diaries,* p. 892). The shift
from the small rooms of Herne Hill to the large, uncontrollable spaces of
Christ Church disorients the Camera Lucida aspects of the self: "The
change from our front parlour at Herne Hill, some fifteen feet by eighteen,
and meat and pudding with my mother and Mary, to a hall about as big as
the nave of Canterbury Cathedral, with its extremity lost in mist, its roof in
darkness, and its company, an innumerable, immeasurable vision in
vanishing perspective, was in itself more appalling to me than appe-

tizing . . ." (xxxv, 194). The "vanishing perspective" that creates and organizes Ruskin's open spaces, his world of vistas and recessional space, is "appalling" in enclosure. With Ruskin, nothing vanishes "inside," and to pretend that it does predicts the inverted perspective's turning of the "outside in," an inversion that brings the panic of spatial, "face to face" confrontation. He describes the ideal "space and splendour of domicile" (xxix, 464) of Sir Walter Scott—whose biographical fragments in *Fors Clavigera* by an empathetic Ruskin are anticipations of Ruskin's own autobiography—as "a small parlour on the ground floor of the north side of the house, some twelve feet deep by eleven wide; the single window little more than four feet square, or rather four feet cube, above the desk, which is set in the recess of the mossy wall . . ." (xxix, 463).

Yet Scott, even according to Ruskin, is not Ruskin, and biography is not autobiography, but preparation for it. Scott's "space and splendour of domicile" is Ruskin's with a difference. The Camera's inhabitable vantage point is not the self-enclosed exitless space of Scott, whose "workroom is strictly a writing-office, what windows they have being designed to admit the needful light, with an extremely narrow vista of the external world" (xxix, 463). Instead, from a vantage point of filled and catalogued space—the space of the curator—the Camera requires an opening, a window. What is needed, finally, is interior, controllable space that also has a view—an optical exit: "I'm horribly sulky this morning, for I expected to have a room with a view, if the room was ever so little, and I've got a great big one looking into the Castle yard, and I feel exactly as if I was in a big modern county gaol . . ." (xxxvii, 236). Without the visual release that, as we shall see, Ruskin, facing a "costermonger's ass," fails to find in Rembrandt, interior space, no matter how large, is a space of imprisonment. Without a way out, the autobiographical inversion of Ruskin's original vanishing perspective is prefigured. Enclosed space is both the foreground and background of a reticent first person.

But everywhere the architecture of escape abounds. Searching for vanishing perspectives, Ruskin will always find a way to the outside. "Letter 69" of *Fors Clavigera* is about windows: ". . . setting myself in the corner of a carriage next the sea, for better prospect thereof" (xxviii, 690); "None of the three ever looked out of the windows at sea or shore" (xxviii, 691); "They both read papers all the way to Warrington. I was not myself employed much better; the incessant rain making the windows a mere wilderness of dirty dribblings . . ." (xxviii, 691). Finally, Ruskin resorts to comic strategy: "The train to Ruabon was crowded, and I was obliged to get into a carriage with two cadaverous sexagenarian spinsters, who had been keeping the windows up, all but a chink, for fear a drop of rain or breath of south wind should come in, and were breathing the richest compound of products of their own indigestion. Pretending to be anxious about the construction of the train, I got the farther window down, and my body well out of it; then put it only half-way up when the train left, and kept putting my head out without my hat . . ." (xxvIII, 693). For the Camera Lucida self, the vantage point is only habitable when it may be left, either optically, through prospects, or actually. Confining space, holding both vantage and focal points, requires an exit—the alternatives and extensions of optional space.

The exit-as-prospect, in which the focal point is distanced, offers a view of several things. For the Camera Lucida, the most interesting view is the world of society, which is an alternative to the small rooms and solipsistic space of the Camera's vantage point. Predictably, the Camera does not require active engagement with people: ". . . I hate society in general. I have no pleasure, but much penance, in even the presence of nine out of ten human beings" (I, 456). Impelled by the same timidity that transforms the early first person into Kata Phusin, the Camera's entrance into society is reluctant, if not pseudonymous. Instead of shaking hands, he will write letters: "I do not look to my correspondence as a duty to be performed, but as the best mode of entering into society, because one talks on paper without uttering absolute truisms to fill up a pause . . . without being subjected to any of the thousand and one ills and accidents of real conversation. Therefore if I like a friend at all, I like him on paper" (I, 456). The paper friendships of the Camera, answering limited affective requirements from a virtually invisible self, are tenuous, with the characteristic intervening space—this time epistolary rather than optical—between friend and Camera. Ruskin would prefer either to observe or write than touch. Intimacy, without claustrophobia, is impossible. Attachment requires distance: ". . . the thoughtful reader must have noted with some displeasure that I have scarcely, whether at college or at home, used the word 'friendship' with respect to any of my companions. The fact is, I am a little puzzled by the speciality and singularity of the poetical and classic friendship. I get, distinctively, attached to places, to pictures, to dogs, cats, and girls. . . . Without thinking myself particularly wicked, I found nothing in my heart that seemed to me worth anybody's seeing; nor had I curiosity for insight into those of others . . ." (xxxv, 424).

As an instrument of objectification, the Camera Lucida is without emotions to exercise: ". . . I had nothing animate to care for, in a childish way, but myself, some nests of ants . . . and a sociable bird or two . . ." (xxxv, 37). The result of atrophied affections, beyond epistolary friends, is a strange cast of characters: "Sorry to bid him goodbye. I wish Vesuvius could love me, like a living thing; I would rather make a friend of him than of any morsel of humanity" (*Diaries,* p. 166). A curious series of confrontations occur in April, 1875, at the Crystal Palace: ". . . played with automaton. Drew a game and contested another close—pleased with myself";

"Up to Crystal Palace, and played three good games with automaton"; "Automaton beating me badly" (*Diaries*, pp. 841–42). The Camera has found a friend capable of matching its own affective requirements.

But the Camera's final attachment is not for the Crystal Palace's cunning, though dehumanized, automaton. Curiously, the enduring affection of a Camera that would be invisible is a visual affection, an affection for something that is only to be seen. It is a complementary affection of opposites. The invisible confronts the visible: "Men are more evanescent than pictures, yet one sorrows for lost friends, and pictures *are* my friends. I have none others. I am never long enough with men to attach myself to them" (x, 437, note). But pictures, the best friends the objectified Camera self has, are even more than friends. Pictures, Turner's especially, are life itself: ". . . the exquisite pleasure that every new one gives me is like a year added to my life, and a permanent extension of the sphere of my life" (xiii, xlviii). Furthermore, the Camera is certain that the artist of those paintings that extend life has an affective involvement no greater than its own. From the Camera's point of view, the artist is incapable of sympathetic identification: "You must be in the wildness of the midnight masque—in the misery of the dark street at dawn . . . without ever losing your temper so much as to make your hand shake, or getting so much of the mist of sorrow in your eyes, as will at all interfere with your matching of colours; never even allowing yourself to disapprove of anything that anybody enjoys, so far as not to enter into their enjoyment. . . . Does a man die at your feet—your business is not to help him, but to note the colour of his lips . . ." (iv, 388).

The Camera Lucida's attachment to objects or friends that can be engaged in an optical or epistolary mode underlines the psychic requirements for an intervening space, a distance between a removed vantage point, where a loss of all self but lens has occurred, and the focal point of affection. The Camera can only have intimacy with distance. Separated, the two are also inseparable. And like Ruskin himself, the Camera will have it both ways: a tenuous physical presence, the presence of a polished lens, in a small room of unsociable space, as well as a focal point outside a room that would be claustrophobic if it contained both vantage and focal point, a room that would require opaqueness of the Camera, a sense of density and bulk. But the Camera will have no autobiography. There is always the window, the room with the view.

The Camera's reliance upon sight is not only the result of having "nothing animate to care for . . . but myself, some nests of ants," but also of the early substitution of observation for performance. As a child, separated from what he saw by the strictures of attentive parents, Ruskin derived his pleasure from "merely watching." His existence is entirely optical: "I was not allowed to row, far less to sail, nor to walk near the harbour alone; so that I learned nothing of shipping or anything else worth learning, but spent

four or five hours every day in simply staring and wondering at the sea,—
an occupation which never failed me till I was forty" (xxxv, 78). In a more
complicated passage, discerning a political truth of Tory bias, he gives a ra-
tionale for his reluctance to exchange his position at the detached vantage
point, his position of invisibility for the performance required at the focal
point. Preferring the audience's role to that of the actor, he feels "that it was
probably much happier to live in a small house, and have Warwick Castle
to be astonished at, than to live in Warwick Castle and have nothing to be
astonished at . . ." (xxxv, 16). Failing to have any impulse to dramatize
the focal point, to activate what it sees with some portion of a self that
hardly exists, the Camera, separated from potential activity by an intervening distance, willingly sacrifices the active engagement of the self at
the focal point to a dehumanizing and exclusive mode of apprehension.
Like the great painter, who notes the color of the dying man's lips, the
Camera Lucida, choosing to look at Warwick Castle rather than live there,
does not bring the vantage point to the focal point, does not allow itself,
even for a moment, to be the observed performer rather than the passive observer. Finally, a Camera that is virtually lifeless would rather look than
live. But then, for Ruskin, sight is life, if only the mirror can be avoided.

THE MORAL RETINA AND THE OPTICS OF AFFECTION

But just as "useful truths" are "biped," so the staring self, consistently inconsistent, has two eyes with different focuses. And it is as if those eyes,
perceiving differently, perceive with a variation of stereoscopic vision. Yet
they do not so much see from slightly different vantage points as they see in
different ways. This double vision does not result in depth perception, although that is to come later. Rather, there is a difference in the affections of
observation. Instead of yielding the third dimension, the difference yields
the complexity of antithesis: the objectification of the Camera Lucida is opposed to a sympathetic involvement with what is observed. Though neither
the Camera Lucida nor its opposite touches or performs, their only similarities are the similarities of contrast. The Camera's opposite announces:
". . . you will emancipate yourself from any idea that artists' sketches are to
be mere camera-lucidas, mere transcripts of mechanism and measurement.
It is of no consequence to any mortal that there is a cottage eighteen feet
high by twenty-five broad . . . but it is—or may be—of some interest to
know that there is a piece of secluded cottage feeling by Coniston Water, or
that such a character is peculiar to the cottages of the Lakes" (i, 422).
    The bias against lenses, which is a bias against the dehumanized
precision of the Camera Lucida, indicates dissatisfaction with a science

guilty of a form of ocular hybris: "The pleasure of modern science is the pride of seeing more by instruments than common people can with the naked eye" (xxii, 510). The manipulation of the staring self can become excessive: "David's astronomy with the eyes, first rightly humbles him,—then rightly exalts;—What is man that Thou so regardest him—yet, how Thou has regarded! But modern astronomy with telescope first wrongly exalts us, then wrongly humbles" (xxix, 28). The notion of ocular hybris, caused by "lenticular curiosity," allows Ruskin to speculate playfully on not merely the altitude of the optical self, exalted or humbled, but also on the transformation of someone like the staring self into an optical mutant:

> We are now, so may of us, some restlessly and some wisely, in the habit of spending our evenings abroad, that I do not know if any book exists to occupy the place of one classical in my early days, called *Evenings at Home*. It contained, among many well-written lessons, one under the title of "Eyes and No Eyes," which some of my older hearers may remember, and which I should myself be sorry to forget. For if such a book were to be written in these days, I suppose the title and the moral of the story would both be changed; and, instead of "Eyes and No Eyes," the tale would be called "Microscopes and No Microscopes." For I observe the prevailing habit of learned men is now to take interest only in objects which cannot be seen without the aid of instruments; and I believe many of my learned friends, if they were permitted to make themselves, to their own liking, instead of suffering the slow process of selective development, would give themselves heads like wasps', with three microscopic eyes in the middle of their foreheads, and two ears at the ends of their antennae. (xxvi, 114)

The implied comparison between traveling and various kinds of observation is instructive: seeing what comes within the range of the unaided eyes is similar to spending "Evenings at Home." On the other hand, the ocular hybris involved in moving beyond the normal area of vision suggests a transcendence of the eyes, a concern for what lies beyond lensless vision, and an eagerness to sacrifice the home, the foreground, even the room with a view, for distant landscape. Ruskin attacks those lenses which, bringing the "knowledge that modern science is so saucy about," bring knowledge of what is removed from the environs of the self: "—having invented telescopes and photography, you are all stuck up on your hobby-horses, because you know how big the moon is, and can get pictures of the volcanoes in it!" (xxvi, 262) But, for those with Empedoclean instincts, there are volcanoes other places than on the moon: ". . . you never can get any more than *pictures* of these while in your own planet there are a thousand volcanoes which you may jump into, if you have a mind to . . ." (xxvi, 262). As the telescope allows transcendent travel, carrying the self away from "Evenings at Home," to the remote volcanoes of the moon, the foreground volcanoes of the earth threaten to swallow that far-sighted observer.

Spending his evenings not at home but in Venice, Ruskin, in "Letter 75" of *Fors Clavigera,* makes the same emphatic, if inconsistent, point. He will bring the "here" to the "now." He will join space and time in absolute immediacy. There will be no distances: "I have nothing to do, nor have you, with what is happening in space (or possibly may happen in time), we have only to attend to what is happening here—and now" (xxix, 60). Ruskin, his very existence organized about distances, is not so much giving advice as writing fiction, a fiction that will be elaborated upon until it is finally transformed into the autobiography of *Praeterita,* a fiction of nonexistent evenings spent in a nonexistent home. Still, the assumption behind both potential observation and movement is that the focus of attention should be immediate, at least within the field of lensless perception. One should stay home, in a room with a view. But that room must not have a telescope.

Yet proximity, immediacy of concern, is not necessarily a solution to the problem of ocular transcendence. The microscope, while not focusing on distant points—the volcanoes of the moon, say—nevertheless creates the functional equivalent of transcendence. After a point, there is no distinction between the distant and the near, the large and the small. Magnified, discriminations fail: "In old times, then, it was not thought necessary for human creatures to know either the infinitely little, or the infinitely distant; nor either to see, or feel, by artificial help" (xxvi, 115). The "entertainments of scientific vision" that the microscope presents are absurdly unappetizing: "fleas mostly and stomachs of various vermin; and people with their heads cut off and set on again . . ." (xxiii, 329). And if "*all great art is delicate,* and fine to the uttermost," Ruskin understands that all that is "rightly pleasing to the human mind is addressed to the unaided human sight, not to microscopic help or mediation" (xxxiii, 346). While for the "proper study of any good work in painting or drawing the student should always have in his hand a magnifying-glass of moderate power" (xiv, 408), the emphasis is on a power that is only "moderate."[4] The areas for the observer to explore are, essentially, those that can be seen with the "natural focus of sight," "unmuzzled by brass or glass" (xxxiv, 64–65), or unencumbered by the "three microscopic eyes" of the optical mutant.

The bias against "brass or glass," which results in the outlawing of

---

[4] Ruskin distinguishes between magnifying glasses and microscopes. He writes to a "Rose Queen": "Look at the crystals with your subjects when they have time, using a common magnifying glass. I send you one for yourself, such as every girl should keep in her—waistcoat pocket! always handy. And this is a very solemn last word for to-day: never use a microscope. Learn to use your own two eyes as God made them to see His works, as He made them, for Queens and Peasants too" (xxx, 346).

optical areas, is part of what Ruskin sees as an important stance against prevalent modes of observation: "All living artists contradict whatever I say; and you see what fatal impediment that puts in the way of my use to you" (xxii, 508); "you will hear a separate theory from every art professor in Europe, and every one of their theories, however disagreeing among themselves, are in unison of opposition to me. I am alone against all the host of them" (xxii, 508). For if Ruskin is certain that "the food of Art is the ocular and passionate study of Nature—ocular, especially as opposed to microscopic," it was argued by living artists and European professors of art that, on the contrary, "the food of Art is a telescopic, scalpellic, and dispassionate study of Nature" (xxii, 508). What Ruskin was attacking was the idea of an exclusive and mechanical optical system, which is as reductive as the vivisection in the laboratories at Oxford that gave Ruskin an excuse to resign from the Slade Professorship. Attacking the "entertainments of scientific vision," Ruskin attacks a "great physiologist," Professor Huxley, who "said to me the other day . . . that sight was 'altogether mechanical.' The words simply meant, if they meant anything, that all his physiology had never taught him the difference between eyes and telescopes" (xxii, 194–95).

Ruskin is making a distinction between, on the one hand, the use of the eye as an "imperfect and brutal instrument," which may be "vivid with malignity, or wild with hunger, or manifoldly detective with microscopic exaggeration, assisting the ingenuity of insects," and, on the other hand, the eye as an instrument of "noble human sight, careless of prey, disdainful of minuteness," which becomes "clear in gentleness, proud in reverence, and joyful in love" (xxii, 208). The optics, which the great physiologist calls "altogether mechanical" are, "far from being the perception of a mechanical force by a mechanical instrument," actually "an entirely spiritual consciousness, accurately and absolutely proportioned to the purity of the moral nature, and to the force of its natural and wise affections" (xxii, 208).

The personification of this inclusive mode of perception can be opposed not only to the Camera Lucida, but also to an unmechanical, exclusively optical process that leads Ruskin to speculate on the optics of the rattlesnake: "What sort of image . . . is received through that deadly vertical cleft in the iris; through the glazed blue of the ghastly lens?" (xxii, 200) Like the Camera Lucida, the "rattlesnake retina," which does not receive light and images as part of "an entirely spiritual consciousness," is antithetical to the optical equipment of Ruskin's theoretic and imaginative faculties—optical equipment that is dependent upon "the intellectual lens and moral retina, by which, and on which, our informing thoughts are concentrated and represented" (iv, 36). The "intellectual lens and moral retina"—"the lens faithfully and far collecting, the retina faithfully and inwardly receiving" (xxii, 513)—obtain a different order of image and information from that received by the "rattlesnake retina." The theoretic faculty is informed by no mere Camera Lucida's lens, or "deadly cleft in the iris" of a rattlesnake's eye. An inclusive faculty, it is distinguished from an aesthetic faculty that threatens to degrade perception "to a mere operation of the senses, or perhaps worse, of custom; so that the arts which appeal to it sink into a mere amusement, ministers to morbid sensibilities, ticklers and fanners of the soul's sleep" (iv, 35–36).

The self as Moral Retina, attending to the charted landscape that comes within the scope of "unaided human sight," is not guilty of the "lenticular curiosity" and ocular hubris of "brass and glass." But this does not mean that the Moral Retina is without ambition. What the Moral Retina is attempting is nothing less than the creation of a visual mode of perception, a birth of Desiring Eyes, that will be synthetic rather than "scalpellic," passionate rather than "dispassionate," humanized rather than dehumanized, and, finally, religious rather than narrowly scientific or anatomical.

In a much-quoted passage, Ruskin reduces complexity to gnomic simplicity by amplifying the function of the optical system: "Hundreds of people can talk for one who can think, but thousands can think for one who can see. To see clearly is poetry, prophecy, and religion,—all in one" (v, 333). The birth of the Desiring Eyes requires a new, public awareness: ". . . every man in England now is to do and to learn what is right in his own eyes. How much need, therefore, that we should learn first of all what eyes are; and what vision they ought to possess—science of sight granted only to clearness of soul; but granted in its fulness even to mortal eyes: for though, after the skin, worms may destroy their body, happy the pure in heart, for they, yet in their flesh, shall see the Light of Heaven, and know the will of God" (xxii, 207). A minister of the eyes, Ruskin interprets the Beginning to fit the needs of his allegory of optical birth: "you are to remember still more distinctly that the words 'fiat lux' mean indeed 'fiat anima,' because even the power of the eye itself, as such, is *in* its animation" (xxii, 194). As the eyes undergo an enlargement of faculty and function, the vision becomes a vision of coalescence. And the self as Moral Retina becomes a self with other physiological and anatomical considerations: ". . . if the eye be pure, the body is pure; but, if the light of the body be but darkness, how great that darkness!" (xxii, 200)

Hardly exclusive, the Moral Retina, pure and bathed in light, is connected with the central portion of anyone's anatomy that Ruskin had attempted to appeal to directly and unsuccessfully. Agony is best understood verbally through ink that is the color of blood. Always, the heart of the matter is approached through the Desiring Eyes: ". . . according to the clearness of sight, is indeed the kindness of sight, and . . . the noble eyes of

humanity look through humanity, from heart into heart, and with no
mechanical vision. And the Light of the body is the eye—yes, and in happy
life, the light of the heart also" (xxii, 201). From the anatomical, Ruskin
moves to the extra-anatomical, from heart to soul: ". . . the eyes of man are
of his soul, not of his flesh" (xxii, 513). And again: "You do not see *with*
the lens of the eye. You see *through* that, and by means of that, but you see
with the soul of the eye" (xxii, 194). Vision is elevated from a mechanical
to a religious operation by ecstatic language:

> Sight is an absolutely spiritual phenomenon; accurately, and only, to be so de-
> fined; and the "Let there be light," is as much, when you understand it, the
> ordering of intelligence, as the ordering of vision. It is the appointment of
> change of what had been else only a mechanical effluence from things unseen to
> things unseeing,—from stars that did not shine to earth that could not
> perceive;—the change, I say, of that blind vibration into the glory of the sun
> and moon for human eyes; so rendering possible also the communication out of
> the unfathomable truth, of that portion of truth which is good for us, and ani-
> mating to us, and is set to rule over the day and night of our joy and sorrow.
> (xxii, 195)

The movement is from the lens outside, through the retina within,
"faithfully and inwardly receiving," to the soul. The process of regression is
a process of inclusion. The shaping aspect of optics, retreating from outside
to inside, incorporates more as the distance between the object of the Desiring Eyes and the eyes themselves becomes greater. The widening spiral
of optical involvement is evident in all areas, from the expansion of visual
function to include heart and soul, to the thing perceived. The necessary
enlargement of the focal point helps explain another ingredient of the
Moral Retina's antagonism to "brass or glass," the dehumanizing lenses of
the Camera Lucida and binocular camera:

> Flowers, like everything else that is lovely in the visible world, are only to
> be seen rightly with the eyes which the God who made them gave us; and
> neither with microscopes nor spectacles. These have their uses for the curious
> and the aged; as stilts and crutches have for people who want to walk in mud,
> or cannot safely walk but on three legs anywhere. But in health of mind and
> body, men should see with their own eyes. . . . The use of instruments for exag-
> gerating the powers of sight necessarily deprives us of the best pleasures of
> sight. A flower is to be watched as it grows, in its association with the earth,
> the air, and the dew. Dissect or magnify them, and all you discover or learn at
> least will be that oaks, roses, and daisies, are all made of fibres and bubbles;
> and these again, of charcoal and water; but, for all their peeping and probing,
> nobody knows how. (xxxv, 430)

Enlarging the focal point, Ruskin is attempting to include the context—

what, surrounding the perceived object, the flower, is connected to it by "association with the earth, the air, and the dew." As opposed to the "lenticular curiosity" that magnifies the perceived object out of context, this awareness of the peripheral is an optical version of the topographical immanence—the landscape of "nerves"—that Ruskin discusses in the "Of Classical Landscape" chapter of *Modern Painters*. There is a sense of interrelation that exists not only between the focal point and its context, but also between the observer and the observed. Optics suggests separation, the distance between the Desiring Eyes and the object of affection. Yet the optics of the soul, of the Moral Retina, are an optics of participation and involvement in a world of animation and immanence, a world from which nothing has withdrawn.

Simply, the affections of the Moral Retina are not those of the Camera Lucida. Both spiraling outwards towards the inclusion of the peripheral context about the focal point, and establishing a relation, albeit optical, between self and that context, the Moral Retina, though neither performing nor touching, is engaged in a form of affiliation—a form that, with antecedents, anticipates Vernon Lee's "empathy" and Theodore Lipps' "einfuhlung." Apparent in Turner, this involvement, which is part of the capacity of the Moral Retina, is a component of greatness: "Throughout the whole period with which we are at present concerned, Turner appears as a man of sympathy absolutely infinite—a sympathy so all-embracing, that I know nothing but that of Shakespeare comparable with it" (xii, 370). But the sympathetic affiliation with a perceived object is dependent upon a loss of selfhood—an impulse of Desiring Eyes away from autobiography and towards either the pseudonymity or invisibility that forms a significant design in Ruskin's work.

With its vantage point of solipsistic space and its tentative, epistolary entrance into a despised society, the Camera Lucida, existing only as a lens with paper friends, is a self without a self, a self without substance. It has nothing of consequence to lose, and, losing nothing, its affiliation with the perceived object is merely a fiction. But the Moral Retina, with its enlarged, optical capacities, its heart and soul, can, losing itself, engage in sympathetic affiliation. Yet the act of sympathetic affiliation is reflexive. The Moral Retina, penetrating the perceived object with intense, if not "all-embracing," sympathy, finds the lost, sympathetic self reinforced in the process of an "utter forgetfulness of self" (xii, 370): ". . . on the one hand, those who have keenest sympathy are those who look closest and pierce deepest, and hold securest; and on the other, those who have so pierced and seen the melancholy deeps of things are filled with the most intense passions and gentleness of sympathy" (iv, 257). Ending in the ocular immanence of an inclusive, synthesizing vision—a vision that exists happily in lensless immediacy—the Moral Retina's affections permit sympathetic affiliation with "vital beauty." And beauty that is "vital" is beauty perceived by the "unaided human sight." To be magnified out of context by "lenticular curiosity" is to be destroyed. The life of sight is dependent upon coherence and connection. It is not an optics of vivisection. The affections of the Moral Retina are expressed in that "keenness of the sympathy which we feel in the happiness, real or apparent, of all organic beings . . ." (IV, 147).

SIGHT: PROSPECTIVE AND RETROSPECTIVE

Ruskin's eyes are desirous. His concern with optics is obsessive. But, beyond his own private chronicle, the history of the eyes is a history of neglect: ". . . the faculty of sight has been virtually despised by every leader in education, its sensibilities not only uncared for, but insulted; and the pleasures derivable from it usually narrowed into the lazy perception that roses are pleasingly red, gold attractively yellow, diamonds conspicuously bright" (XXXV, 628). And this neglect has occurred, apparently, despite the eighteenth century's self-conscious interest in sight—an interest that can be traced through the "blind men" of Molyneux, Locke, and Berkeley, who proliferate until the "blind man" becomes a stock figure of the eighteenth century,[5] even surfacing, as we shall see, in Ruskin, a hundred years later.

Language has been elevated at the expense of sight. Ruskin's support of the pre-Raphaelites' revolutionary attention to visual detail—"they will draw either what they see, or what they suppose might have been the actual facts of the scene they desire to represent, irrespective of any conventional rules of picture-making" (XII, 322)—comes over fifty years after Wordsworth's *Advertisement* and *Preface* to the *Lyrical Ballads*. Along with the elevation of language, there has been the elevation of the ear. Words and the ear have conspired against the eye: "You know we have hitherto been in the habit of conveying all our historical knowledge, such as it is, by the ear only, never by the eye; all our notion of things being ostensibly derived from verbal descriptions, not from sight" (XVI, 91). But the time of the eye is upon us, or shortly will be. And the eye will retrieve and store information: "Now, I have no doubt that, as we grow gradually wiser—and we are doing so every day—we shall discover at last that the eye is a nobler organ than the ear; and that through the eye we must, in reality, obtain, or put into form, nearly all the useful information we are to have about this world" (XVI, 91).

[5] For a discussion of the blind man in literature, see Kenneth Maclean, *John Locke and English Literature of the Eighteenth Century* (New Haven, 1936), pp. 106 ff. Also see Marjorie Hope Nicolson, *Newton Demands the Muse: Newton's Optics and the Eighteenth-Century Poets* (Princeton, 1966), pp. 82–84.

With the time of the eye, there will be the art of the eye. Ruskin, who, as we shall see, in his intense sympathetic affiliation with the "vital beauty" of landscape, takes topography for autobiography, assumes that the visual arts will become more important than the verbal precisely because of a new landscape awareness that belongs not only to himself but the century:

> . . . as the admiration of mankind is found, in our times, to have in great part passed from men to mountains, and from human emotion to natural phenomena, we may anticipate that the great strength of art will also be warped in this direction; with this notable result for us, that whereas the greatest painters or painter of classical and medieval periods, being wholly devoted to the representation of humanity, furnished us with but little to examine in landscape, the greatest painters or painter of modern times will in all probability be devoted to landscape principally; and farther, because in representing human emotion words surpass painting, but in representing natural scenery painting surpasses words, we may anticipate also that the painter and poet (for convenience' sake I here use the words in opposition) will somewhat change their relations of rank in illustrating the mind of the age; that the painter will become of more importance and the poet of less . . . . (v, 330)

But seeing comes before painting, and seeing is itself no simple matter. On the one hand, not only is "the truth of nature . . . not to be discerned by the uneducated senses" (iii, 140), but also "sight depends upon previous knowledge" (iii, 144). To observe, one must have a history of observation. Sight requires a past. Illustrating this, Ruskin considers an example of childish vision:

> . . . if a child be asked to draw the corner of a house, he will lay down something in the form of the letter T. He has no conception that the two lines of the roof, which he knows to be level, produce on his eye the impression of a slope. It requires repeated and close attention before he detects this fact, or can be made to feel that the lines on his paper are false. And the Chinese, children in all things, suppose a good perspective drawing to be as false as we feel their plate patterns to be, or wonder at the strange buildings which come to a point at the end. (iii, 144)

But, on the other hand, to see what "He Himself paints" requires precisely this childish vision. The eye, if not ignorant, must at least be as innocent as the eye of a child or a blind man suddenly granted sight: "The whole technical power of painting depends on our recovery of what may be called the *innocence of the eye*; that is to say, of a sort of childish perception of these flat stains of colour, merely as such, without consciousness of what they signify,—as a blind man would see them if suddenly gifted with sight" (xv, 27, note). Visual education is a form of regression, a peeling off of reflective, associationist, and mnemonic layers that shape the perceived objects in a way that is unsupported by the evidence of the retina: ". . . a highly accomplished artist has always reduced himself as nearly as possible to this condition of infantine sight" (xv, 28, note). Yet if Ruskin's observer must at once educate himself in order to "draw the corner of a house," and uneducate himself in order to become that blind man suddenly given "infantine sight," at least it is apparent that imprecision and visual convention, unsupported by actual observation, must be avoided for Ruskin's blind man to become his staring self.

The instincts for visualization have been slighted. Because language gets in the way of sight, words in the way of objects, language must be put in its place. But it is special kind of language that creates the problem. To read is to be blind. But hearing animates language. If the "eye is a nobler organ than the ear," the ear nevertheless transforms a dead medium into one that is alive. Simply, the eye should not be wasted on language: "Our eyes are now familiar and wearied with writing; and if an inscription is put upon a building, unless it be large and clear, it is ten to one whether we ever trouble to decipher it . . ." (x, 133). And if the church is a book, Ruskin prefers illustration to language: "I have above spoken of the whole church as a great Book of Common Prayer; the mosaics were its illumination. . . . The walls of the church necessarily became the poor man's Bible, and a picture was more easily read upon the walls than a chapter" (x, 130).

Yet the problem is not entirely one of language that is written rather than spoken, the eye as opposed to the ear. More acccurately, it is a matter of speed—the ratio of time to language. Ruskin plans to have script taught in his St. George schools that "will take from half-an-hour to an hour for a line" (xxix, 486). As opposed to this script that approaches stylized illustration is the print that is manufactured and multiplied by the "present fury of printing" (xxix, 483), a language that, instead of appealing to the eye, as Ruskin hopes his blood-red print will, deadens the responses of an overworked retina.

Essentially, the change in the "ordinary school discipline" will be to make the pupils "remember more," by reading less (xxxix, 449). We are back to the Hermetic memory systems of Alexander Dicson and Giodorno Bruno, and what amounts to the creation of an interior musem instead of a library, a museum of the mind, from which information, locked in images instead of language, can be retrieved. Coming close to this position, Gaston Bachelard, in *The Poetics of Space,* suggests that memories are locked not in duration, the sequence of language, but in sight and space: "Memory . . . does not record concrete duration, in the Bergsonian sense of the word. We are unable to relive duration that has been destroyed. We can only think of it, in the line of an abstract time that is deprived of all thickness. The finest specimens of fossilized duration concretized as a result of long sojourn, are to be found in and through space. The unconscious abides. Memories are motionless, and the more securely they are fixed in space, the sounder they are."[6]

Like Dicson before him, in his *De umbra rationis,* Ruskin, recalling the *Phaedrus* of Plato and the interview between Thamus and Theuth, the inventor of writing, supports Thamus's view that writing is a "quack's drug for memorandum," which leaves "the memory idle" (xxix, 483). With Ruskin, to see clearly is to remember. The eye, avoiding the written word, its responses alert, is the organ of memory. The highest form of cognition, called "Conception," is the "knowledge of things retained in . . . visible form":

> Some facts exist in the brain in a verbal form, as known, but not conceived; as, for instance, that it was heavy, or light, that it was eight inches and a quarter long, etc. . . . Other facts respecting it exist in the brain in a visible form, not always visible, but visible at will, as its being of such a colour, or having such and such a complicated shape: as the form of a rose-bud for instance, which it would be difficult to express verbally, neither is it retained by the brain in verbal form, but a visible one: that is, when we wish for knowledge of its form for immediate use, we summon up a vision or image of the thing; we do not remember it in words, as we remember the fact that it took so many days to grow, or that it was gathered at such and such a time. (iv, 229)

Unfairly to himself, Ruskin contrasts his own dependency on the "quack's drug for memorandum" with Turner's mnemonic ability: "I myself . . . have written down memoranda of many skies, but have forgotten the skies themselves. Turner wrote nothing,—but remembered it all" (xxix, 483). A form of "dream-vision," Turner's memory is his imagination. His composition is an "arrangement of remembrances summoned just as they were wanted, and set each in its fittest place. It is this very character which appears . . . to mark it as so distinctly an act of dream-vision; for in a dream there is just this kind of confused remembrance of the forms of things which we have seen long ago, associated by new and strange laws" (vi, 41). Both memory and imagination are dependent upon an optical system that focuses on the unforgettable—what Ruskin, talking about Turner, calls the "first vision": ". . . whenever Turner really tried to *compose,* and made modifications of his subjects on principle, he did wrong, and spoiled them; and that he only did right in a kind of passive obedience to his first vision, that vision being composed primarily of the strong memory of the place itself which he had to draw; and

[6] Gaston Bachelard, *The Poetics of Space* (New York, 1964), p. 9.

secondarily, of memories of other places . . . associated in a harmonious and helpful way, with the new central thought" (VI, 41).

Turner's "dream-vision" is past-tense sight, a past-tense sight that is the equivalent of distant vision. Images, undisturbed by an updating in the present tense, are locked safely in the depths of memory. Turner does not revisit. To do so would be to annihilate a mnemonic distance that is as necessary to the clarity of "first vision" as the distance between vantage and focal points is to the survival of Ruskin's staring self. The intensity of Turner's "first vision" suggests a nostalgia for origins that may be perceived with the purity of Ruskin's optically reborn blind man, a purity uncorrupted by the inevitable layers of association. The "first vision," which is a central vision, remains unforgotten: ". . . he seems never either to have lost, or cared to disturb, the impressions made upon him by any scene,—even in his earliest youth. He never seems to have gone back to a place to look at it again, but, as he gained power, to have painted and repainted it as first seen, associating with it certain new thoughts or new knowledge, but never shaking the central pillar of the old image" (VI, 42). The "first vision" is made memorable by the strong visualizing instincts that fix the original observation into Bachelard's "fossilized duration."

But Ruskin, without Turner's facility for locking images in memory, occasionally employs language—the "quack's drug for memorandum"—instead of image, in a form of "fossilized duration," as if language, a debased medium, could be elevated into sculpture. He will complain that the "frosts" of the Renaissance "acted first . . . in leading the attention of all men to words instead of things . . ." (XI, 127), yet at the same time he will use words as objects, creating a spatialized language. As Mario Praz points out in *Mnemosyne,* Ruskin's description of St. Mark's—"'Cleopatra-like, 'their bluest veins to kiss' '" (X, 82–83)—like Winckelmann's description of *Belvedere Torso,* and Pater's *Gioconda,* is a version of Hazlitt's attempt to employ criticism as a verbal equivalent to the thing perceived.[7] Ruskin's description is no "quack's drug for memorandum," but a substitution of words for things. With Ruskin's verbal architecture, no memory is needed: the verbal architecture becomes the thing perceived, the "first vision," and not a recollection of it.

Yet the spatialization of language—a strong instinct—is not the rule. And the "quack's drug for memorandum" does not, in great artists, displace memories that are like museums, or

> vast storehouses, extending, with the poets, even to the slightest intonations of syllables heard in the beginning of their lives, and with the painters, down to

---

[7] Mario Praz, *Mnemosyne: The Parallel between Literature and the Visual Arts* (Princeton, 1967).

minute folds of drapery, and shapes of leaves or stones; and over all this unindexed and immeasurable mass of treasure, the imagination brooding and wandering, but dream-gifted, so as to summon at any moment exactly such groups of ideas as shall justly fit each other: this I conceive to be the real nature of the imaginative mind, and this, I believe, it would be oftener explained to us as being, by the men themselves who possess it, but that they have no idea what the state of other persons' minds is in comparison; they suppose every one remembers all that he has seen in the same way, and do not understand how it happens that they alone can produce good drawings or great thoughts. (VI, 42)

But Ruskin is not talking about himself, the storehouse of his own memory. If Ruskin's optical faculties are of the first order, his memory cannot imaginatively retrieve "first vision," locked into memory by sight, with the consistency of Turner.[8] As if to make up for what is hardly an inadequacy, he uncharacteristically turns to performance. He acts out the mnemonic process, substituting not words but objects for images. As a curator by proxy of his St. George's Museum at Sheffield, which he considers making his home—taking up residence in the "vast storehouses" of an architecture that is neither cerebral nor verbal—he becomes an allegorical figure for the "dream-gifted" imagination, "brooding and wandering."[9] Without Turner's memory, Ruskin participates in his version of Turner's imaginative process by storing and retrieving objects that are catalogued in conventional ways. It is as if he would make his memory a museum, his images objects. It is as if he would solidify his world in the same way as he would spatialize his language. Invisible himself, Ruskin will make his world dense.

Yet despite the emerging density of his world, sight rather than touch is still the best way to apprehend a world in which distance is a necessity. And despite the cataloging of objects, which is memory made concrete, memory, as retrospective sight, is an extension of his means of apprehension. To see is to remember. But further, to remember is to see. As George Poulet says, speaking of the mnemonics of Joubert: ". . . to remember is also to render visible and expressible—thanks to the perspective of memory—a temporal depth which is analogous to the spatial depth."[10]

---

[8] This is not to suggest that Ruskin is either without a sense of "first vision" or the means to retrieve it: ". . . my early impressions have been invincible by later ones, however grand. Matlock is still Matlock to me, soar the cliffs of Lauterbrunnen never so high, Skiddaw still Skiddaw, however well I love Mont Blanc" (XXXV, 620). Still, the act of retrieving "early impressions" is not often informed by a creative imagination as intense as Turner's.

[9] The actual curators, first at Walkley, then at Sheffield, were Henry Swan and William White.

[10] Georges Poulet, *The Interior Distance* (Ann Arbor, 1964), p. 79.

The process is reciprocal. Prompted by Desiring Eyes that are both edu-cated—dependent upon "previous knowledge"—and "infantine"—uncor-rupted by association—sight fills the mnemonic space of "vast storehouses" with "first visions" in preparation for the recall of the "dream-gifted" memory—a recall of perceived images that is itself a form of visualization, a retrospective sight.

Still, what is not yet apparent is that the eye, nobler than the ear, is also more explosive—that the eye, forced back upon itself before a failing distance, can be an instrument of infernal perception. The staring self, trap-ped within the prison of the autobiographical impulse, would be Ruskin's blind man, unblessed by sight and the vision of what is later to become Rembrandt's "costermonger's ass." And memory combined with language, which is the "quack's drug for memorandum" that Ruskin attempts to turn into the "fossilized duration" of verbal architecture, can rearrange the failing distances perceived by Desiring Eyes that are both noble and in-fernal. But that is for later. Now, the distance has not failed, language is transformed into space that is still available, sight, perceiving objects in space, fixes "first visions" that will later be felicitously recalled in a process that is itself a form of visualization, and the eye is nothing if not noble.

CHAPTER II The Occupation of
Space:
Varieties of Enclosed
Landscape Experience

TANGIBLE TIME AND ELBOW ROOM:
USING NOTHINGNESS

The kind of world Ruskin inhabits is dependent upon the staring self's optical equipment, its affective requirements and antipathies: the topography that Ruskin is attracted to, and that he constructs in verbal miniatures, is dictated by his means of apprehension. That the world of the staring self should be landscape is not surprising. We recall Ruskin's notion that the painter and the poet will shift in importance because "the admiration of mankind is found, in our times, to have in great part passed from men to mountains." More specifically, the staring self's preoccupation with landscape is consistent with the increasing importance that the "picturesque," as a "mode of vision,"[1] plays in forming the topography of the eighteenth century. Speaking of the interrelation of the visual and the picturesque, E. H. Gombrich points out that "nature could never have become 'picturesque' for us unless we, too, had acquired the habit of seeing it in pictorial terms."[2] The picturesque sensibility was not one that pleased

[1] Richard Payne Knight, as quoted in Wylie Sypher's *Rococo to Cubism in Art and Literature* (New York, 1960), p. 83.

[2] E. H. Gombrich, *Art and Illusion: A Study in the Psychology of Pictorial Representation* (New York, 1960), p. 315.

Ruskin. He was troubled by Turner's *Liber Studiorum,* done in competition with Claude's *Liber Veritatis.* But the landscapes of Claude lie immediately behind both the landscapes of Turner and Ruskin, just as the landscapes of Thomson, Mallet, and Savage lie immediately behind those of Wordsworth. And the picturesque, lapsing occasionally into the sentimentality of "calendar art," is after all to be seen.

Because of the reciprocal influence between sight and landscape—an influence like that between sight and memory—the Desiring Eyes offer Ruskin his most characteristic mode of affiliation with his world, a world that has been selected, at least partly, precisely because of the "desire" of his eyes. But at first, with the exploration of Ruskin's childhood world, which is the miniature world of the garden at Herne Hill, the distance between vantage and focal point is merely incipient. Simply, enclosed space is livable. Windows are a pleasure rather than a requirement. "Inside," the child has no sense of the "outside." Distinctions have not occurred. The individuation between self and world, not needed, has not been fully made. The affective problems that will only permit visual affiliation are no more than potential.

Still, even in enclosed space that is livable, touching—which overcomes limited distance—is not allowed: "The differences of primal importance which I observed between the nature of this garden, and that of Eden, as I had imagined it, were, that in this one, *all* the fruit was forbidden . . ." (xxxv, 36). But if he cannot touch, neither does he require the vistas and rooms with a view of the later staring self. The dimensions of the Herne Hill garden—"seventy yards long by twenty wide" (xxxv, 35–36)—do not inspire ambition within Desiring Eyes. Yet the limited space is not the claustrophobic sealed space that becomes a dimension of unsought autobiography. It is a space that is enclosed by walls that are paradisiacal, benign—the "walls of Eden" (xxxv, 37).

In this world that cannot be touched, but which is without the distance of windows and vistas, the child has no alternative but to employ a proximate focus for affiliation and exploration: "I was only interested in things near me, or at least clearly visible and present" (xxxv, 104). Assuming that this attention to what lies near the self is characteristic of children in general, Ruskin nevertheless notes that "it remained—and remains—a part of my grown temper" (xxxv, 104). The proximate focus is not merely a focus of necessity. Later, when his world is enlarged by the introduction of a recessional space uncontained by Edenic walls, Ruskin will still employ that same private focus with solipsistic delight. But in this "little domain," where the climate "in that cycle of our years, allowed me to pass most of my life" (xxxv, 36), scrutiny of the immediate is virtually the child's only mode of apprehension. He is living in a world without distance, a world in miniature. All the same, by examining small things carefully, he is able to magnify them. He sets "all the faculties of heart and imagination on little things, so as to be able to make anything out of them he chooses." "Confined to a little garden" and without either an intervening distance or the need for it, the child does not locate his consciousness of himself "there," in the sense of Mario Praz, who is speaking of "telescopic" structure, but "here,"[3] with an "acorn-cup" that, like a cornucopia, can bring forth a treasure. Instead of thinking about a background he has never seen, he thinks about the foreground. He locates himself "here."

Just as his Edenic topography is organized by the child to answer beginning requirements—essentially, the examination of what lies closest at hand—so the child, with some notion of going about first things first, examines tenses that are most immediate. In the beginning of his process of exploration, there is no past tense for a child without a history. But even the future, which lies before him in the way that the distance soon will, is shunned. He will not look ahead: "I already disliked growing older,— never expected to be wiser and formed no more plans for the future than a little black silkworm does in the middle of its first mulberry leaf" (xxxv, 103). Living in the foreground, he further determines to live in the present. Enamoured of immediacy, he will combine "here" with "now." As he later says, but is unable to do, we "have only to attend to what is happening here—and now" (xxix, 60). He will do without distance and without either a sense of the past or the future:

> . . . I remain in a jog-trot, sufficient-for-the-day style of occupation—lounging, planless. . . . I am beginning to consider the present as the only available time. . . . I spend my days in a search after present amusement of what I have not future strength to attain . . . . (i, 435)

> I was very sorry that my aunt was dead, but, at that time, (and a good deal since, also,) I lived mostly in the present, like an animal, and my principal sensation was,—what a pity it was to pass such an uncomfortable evening— and we at Plymouth! (xxxv, 71)

> So far as I have myself observed, the distinctive character of a child is to live always in the tangible present, having little pleasure in memory, and being utterly impatient and tormented by anticipation: weak alike in reflection and forethought, but having an intense possession of the actual present, down to the shortest moment and least objects of it. . . . (xx, 249)

The present tense, like the spatial "here," can be magnified by proximate attention: ". . . possessing it [the shortest moment], indeed, so intensely that the sweet childish days are as long as twenty days will be . . ." (xx, 249). Yet the present tense, "tangible" and capable of intense possession, is,

---

[3] Mario Praz, *Mnemosyne: The Parallel between Literature and the Visual Arts* (Princeton, 1967), p. 163.

unlike the equivalent topography, almost tactile in its apprehension by the child. Unable to touch the fruit of the enclosed garden, he touches what the Desiring Eyes cannot see. It is as if he can only touch the invisible. Seeing what is "here," he touches what is "now."

"Tangible" time is not the dimension of the alienated staring self who, dependent upon intervening distance for optical survival, would prefer to touch nothing at all. Instead, it is the dimension of a garden inhabitant who, without spade, wants to touch what is "here" as well as what is "now," but cannot. At Herne Hill, Ruskin's urge "to dig a hole" is "blighted" (xxxv, 426): "I was extremely fond of digging holes, but that form of gardening was not allowed" (xxxv, 59). Later, at Denmark Hill, as the circumference of the child's enclosed world enlarges, the opportunities increase for something other than the "contemplative philosophy" (xxxv, 426) of a staring self. The child begins to get his hands dirty: "Sometimes, in the kitchen garden of Denmark Hill, the hole became a useful furrow, but when once the potatoes and beans were set, I got no outlet or inlet for my excavatory fancy or skill during the rest of the year" (xxxv, 426).

Thwarted by rules that result in the "contemplative philosophy" of optics, "excavatory fancy" becomes a preoccupation with the adult. Still requiring windows, he is determined to do more than merely look. He will make a gesture in the direction of engagement, performance. At the least, he will get his hands dirty, and, in the process, develop an aesthetics of the spade: "Even digging, *rightly* done, is as much an art as the mere muscular act of rowing; it is only inferior in Harmony and time. On the other hand, the various stroke and lift (in soft and hard ground) is as different in a good labourer from a tyro as any stroke of oar" (xx, xliii). Ruskin participates in road-digging with his Oxford class, the "Hincksey-Diggers," both "here," in person, with his gardener, David Downs, and "there," from afar, by a kind of epistolary proxy. Digging by letter, which is digging with clean hands, he employs minute descriptions that create a verbal involvement that would seem to have it both ways—engagement with distance. From Genoa, he writes James Reddie Anderson: "When, after crossing the ferry, you turn to the left in the lane under the hills, you come presently to a place where the road is depressed in front of a cottage, which has beautiful old steps going up to its door: and this depression in the road is usually full of stagnant water, or otherwise offensive. I want this to be first filled up and levelled and the road made good over it, with a drain beneath to carry the hill drainage clear" (xxxvii, 89). His "excavatory fancy" finds outlets that are large, as well as small. He plans to save the Alps by digging:

> I will take a single hillside; and so trench it that I can catch the rainfall of
> three average years at once, if it came down in an hour (that's exaggeration, for

the rush would carry all before it). But I will so trench it (as they say) that I can catch any rainfall without letting a drop go to the valley. It shall all go into reservoirs, and thence be taken where, and when, it is wanted. When I have done this for one hillside, if other people don't do it for other hillsides, and make the lost valleys of the Alps one Paradise of safe plenty, it is their fault—not mine. But, if I die, I will die digging like Faust. (xxxvi, 567)

"Digging like Faust" and, at the same time, demonstrating the "gospel of labour," Ruskin, among other things, is involved in a form of objectification, which combats, by active engagement, the self-consciousness that is to become a form of unwanted autobiography. Touching something other than himself, he loses a sense of himself. But digging, Ruskin is not creating holes, vacancies, which at this time are anathema. Rather, road-digging is road-filling: "I want this to be first filled up and levelled and the road made good over it. . . ." Vacancy has been a problem for Ruskin from the beginning. In an early letter to his father, the child says: "Really, Sir, I think the drawing room, withdrawing room or room into which I withdraw to draw, owes all its beauty to your presence. We have sat in it two nights, and the vacancy of that chair, I say, made the room appear vacant, and the absence of that conversation made conversations flat. Return, oh return from thy peregrinations . . ." (xxxvi, 5). The youthful word-play attempts to fill the vacancy of the absent father. The act of filling is an act of unwitting autobiography. Later, as the present tense turns into a tense of consciousness, the mind becomes a prison. But at first, before the world of tense and space has become the topography of Ruskin's consciousness, before he has filled up all empty containers with what he has to offer, a vacant room, which is like a mind without a memory, is the prison from which that mind attempts to escape: "I believe the notion of fixing attention by keeping the room empty, is a wholly mistaken one: I think it is just in the emptiest room that the mind wanders most; for it gets restless, like a bird, for want of a perch, and casts about for any means of getting out and away" (xvi, 89–90). Empty spaces, which are the spaces of potential, are intolerable. He will bring potential into the "jog-trotting" present in an automatic act of realization. There is no sense of conservation: ". . . because I do not like leaving a blank for its name, I put 'Fair-ladies' for it in the letter . . ." (xxvii, 532); ". . . the blankness of the fascade having been, to my mind, from the first, a serious fault in the design" (xvi, 216). Anything empty inspires self-expression, submerged autobiography, intrusion, without self-consciousness. With empty space everywhere, self-expression does not have to be regarded. Space is not reflexive, and there are no mirrors.

Yet images of vacancy, of the abyss, pile up to create a plenitude of nothingness: "the abyss of time" (xxxvi, 364); "the fathomless abyss of time and space" (xxxvi, 367); "its abysses of life and pain" (xxxvi, 380).

Empty space is as much a threat as it is potential for unreflexive self-expression. Often, there is too much abyss and not enough self: ". . . the abyss of utter confusion produced by modern science in nomenclature, and the utter void of the abyss when you plunge into it after any one useful fact . . ." (xxv, 20). Establishing a hierarchy of artists by their choice of subjects, Ruskin considers depriving those who represent "brutalities and vices (for the delight in them, and not for rebuke of them)" of any rank at all, and then decides that, instead, they require a hierarchy in a minus category—a "negative rank, holding a certain order in the abyss" (v, 49). And at times, Ruskin's diction becomes an incantation to infernal Nothingness: "vacant in invention, void in light and shade, a heap of cumbrous nothingness, and sickening offensiveness, is of all its voids most void in this . . ." (IV, 101). A new title for the third volume of *The Stones of Venice* occurs to him: "I almost wish I had thought of Isaiah xxxiv. 11 before fixing the title of the third volume. I think the 'Stones of Emptiness' would so precisely have fitted the Renaissance architecture" (x, xliv). Proliferating, absence is everywhere. It is as if Nothingness were self-generating: ". . . and I've nothing to do and I can't think of anything to think of,—and the sea has no waves in it—and the sand has no shells in it—and the shells—oyster shells—at lunch had no oysters in them bigger than that [drawing of oyster-shell with small oyster] in a shell—and that won't come out!" (xxxvII, 570–71)

The *horror vacui* brings about the remedial furnishing of a world. Theoretically, to fill a void that horrifies is to create a world that will not. But it may also fill up a distance that is necessary for the optical affiliation of the staring self. Touching and seeing are not sympathetically coordinated. In any case, plenitude, which is "numerical superiority," is at first an uncomplicated good. Praising Turner's "expression of the infinite redundance of natural landscape," Ruskin notes that Turner has "always on the average twenty trees or rocks where other people have one, and . . . wins his victories not more by skill of generalship than by overwhelming numerical superiority" (vi, 353). What amazes Ruskin about Turner's living space, which is an architectural version of his mnemonic space, is the quantity it contains:

> I have just been through Turner's house with Griffith. His labour is more astonishing than his genius. There are £ 80,000 of oil pictures, done and undone. Boxes, half as big as your study table, filled with drawings and sketches. There are copies of Liber Studiorum to fill all your drawers and more, and house walls of proof plates in reams . . . .
>
> Nothing since Pompeii so impressed me as the interior of Turner's house; the accumulated dust of forty years partially cleared off; daylight for the first time admitted by opening a window on the finest productions of art buried for

forty years. . . . It is amusing to hear dealers saying there can be no Liber Studiorums—when I saw neatly packed and well labelled as many bundles of Liber Studiorum as would fill your entire bookcase, and England and Wales proofs in packed and labelled bundles like reams of paper, as I told you, piled nearly to ceiling. . . . (xiii, xxvi–xxvii)

Turner's house is another version of ideal space, a half-way house between the "storehouses" of the mind and museum—what the St. George's Museum at Sheffield might have become for the allegorically "dream-gifted" Ruskin. "Piled nearly to the ceiling," Turner's house is a model of the plenum, of space that is wisely used simply because it is used. Employed, space is necessarily benign.

Predictably, the fear of Nothingness extends to economics: "A national debt . . . is a foul disgrace, at the best" (xxviii, 428). He despairs of many of the readers of *Fors Clavigera,* for whom an economic vacancy, which is a debt, may be a store: "My readers, however, will even yet . . . be unable to grasp the idea of a National Store, as an existing possession. They can conceive of nothing but a debt;—nay, there are many of them who have a confused notion that a debt is a store" (xxviii, 428). But Ruskin proposes to combat that economic void, just as he does other kinds of absence: "I . . . will set aside some part of my income to help, if anybody else will join me, in forming a National Store instead of a National Debt . . ." (xxvii, 377). Or again: ". . . each of us laying by something, according to our means, for the common service; and having amongst us, at last, be it ever so small, a National Store, instead of a National Debt" (xxvii, 14). Collectively, St. George's will do what Ruskin proposes individually: "But there is one public fact, which cannot be debated—that the nation is in debt. And the St. George's Company do practically make it their *first,* though not their principal, object, to bring *that* state of things to an end; and to establish, instead of a National Debt, a National Store" (xxviii, 639). Ruskin's National Store, contributing to the aesthetics of the plenum, would counteract the persistent incantation to Nothingness by sheer "numerical superiority."

But quantity, if the acquisition of it is an economic impulse, is an impulse complicated by Ruskin's notion of usable "Wealth." Beyond an employable Wealth is surplus. And surplus, past mere plenitude, is a condition that reduces to less than nothing. It is one of those "minuses" that Ruskin, in *Unto This Last,* describes as having a "tendency to retire into back streets, and places of shade,—or even get themselves wholly and finally put out of sight in graves . . ." (xvii, 91). An economic *horror vacui* results that is a void of excess. Too much is less than nothing. In *Munera Pulveris,* Ruskin discusses his notion of "Illth," which, compared to the plus of real Wealth, is a retiring, backstreet minus. "Illth," retiring by advancing towards parody, achieves its backstreet position by exaggerating Wealth: "A man's power over his property is, at the widest range of it, fivefold; it is power of Use, for himself, Administration, to others, Ostentation, Destruction, or Bequest; and possession is in use only, which for each man is sternly limited; so that such things, and so much of them as he can use, are, indeed, well for him, or Wealth; and more of them, or any other things, are ill for him, or Illth" (xvii, 168).

Still, the impulse to fill space, to create a plenum, is everywhere evident. "Illth," bringing complication to economics, does not intrude generally until plenitude brings repletion. Ruskin's "instinct for teaching" is, among other things, a desire to occupy space, which is to say employ potential. Prompted by "no more sense of duty than the tide has in filling sandpits," he takes "an inexplicable but strongly instinctive pleasure in the filling of empty heads and hearts, as if they were so many bottles, like to be broken for having nothing inside, or cells or a honeycomb too hollowly fragile" (xxxv, 629). And like the teacher, the artist must fill space. Unable to compete with the infinite variety of nature, the painter can at least "give us a lesser kind of infinity. He has not the one thousandth part of the space to occupy which nature has; but he can, at least, leave no part of that space vacant and unprofitable. . . . And if he will only give us all he can, if he will give us a fulness as complete and mysterious as nature's, we will pardon him for its being the fulness of a cup instead of an ocean. But we will not pardon him, if, because he has not the mile to occupy, he will not occupy the inch" (iii, 333). Awed by Tintoretto's industrious occupation of space, Ruskin decides "to calculate the number of feet square he has covered with mind in Venice; there are more than 4000 square feet in three of his pictures . . ." (iv, xxxviii). But if Tintoretto occupies enormous quantities of space, it is Turner who demonstrates "that universal command of subject, which never acts for a moment on anything conventional or habitual, but fills every corner and space with new evidence of knowledge . . ." (iii, 489).

A typographical model for the vacuum, for absolute vacancy, is the blank page. The "snowy couch of paper," upon which all manner of interesting thoughts might have "blackly rested" (xxxvi, 3), is an affront: "It's a pity to leave that nice half-sheet empty" (xxxvii, 146). But it is an affront that is easily remedied by the young Ruskin, whose verbosity in the face of Nothing can make language claustrophobic. He writes his father: "You will be smothered under a mountain of words. . . . You will groan under the weight of lines, the sea of rhymes, which I shall load you with on your return" (ii, xxxiii). The impulse is away from concentration, towards a centrifugal diffusion that is like the water painted by Turner, in which "the heaven is all spray, and the ocean all cloud" (iii, 570). The flow of words is unrestrained: "I would write a short, pithy, laconic, sensibly concentrated, and serious letter, if I could, for I have scarcely time to write a long one. . . . I would roll on like a ball, with this exception, that contrary to the usual laws of motion I have no friction to contend with in my mind, and . . . have some difficulty in stopping myself" (xxxvi, 4). Ruskin's father attempts to provide that friction by constricting the size of the burgeoning *Modern Painters*: ". . . my father says I must keep to the same size as the other volume—floorer no. 2. My mother asked if I were not getting diffuse—floorer no. 3" (*Diaries*, p. 258). But the friction fails, and Ruskin's father cannot impede his son's explosive and discursive industry, which, taking advantage of any opening, employs all empty space as if it were time that might be wasted: "He writes verse and prose perpetually, check him as we will" (i, xxvii). Yet if later, as Ruskin writes *Modern Painters,* his father wants to restrain his "mountain of words" that threaten to preclude an ending with collateral, horizontal swelling, at first his father encourages him to write in bulk by paying a shilling for each filled page (i, xxvi). With a future that is an untapped resource and a recessional space "outside" Edenic walls that seems to be able to swallow all things in its vanishing perspective—a perspective that can be as cannabalistic as the "abyss of utter confusion"—the young Ruskin is more interested in speed than the friction of qualification. At this point, he is still unconcerned about the "present fury of printing." Language is cheap but good. He will assert himself in the face of Nothing. But the bulk, the density, will be on the page, not where he stands. His father is amazed by the "fury" of his writing: "I have seen production of youth far superior, and of earlier date, but the rapidity of composition is to us . . . quite wonderful. He is now between fourteen and fifteen, and has indited thousands of lines" (i, xxvii).

The obsessive concerns that shape the frictionless aesthetics of bulk and diversity, requiring Ruskin to replace unoccupied space with the occupied space of manipulative, typographical models, and necessitating his consideration of a National Store to replace a National Debt—these concerns are impelled by attitudes surrounding a tradition that, extending back through Bruno, the Schoolmen, and finally to Plato, has religious ramifications: to occupy space with bulk and diversity is to imitate the infinite variety of the Divinity.[4] Operating elegantly in the shadows of this tradition, Robert Fludd might be speaking for either the zealous and excavatory Ruskin, whose spadework on the Hincksey road is the creation of a prosaic plenum, or the youthful Ruskin who, lamenting the absence of his father from the "withdrawing room or room into which I withdraw to draw," might be prefiguring a nineteenth-century lament of an even more

---

[4] See Arthur Lovejoy, "Romanticism and Plenitude," in *The Great Chain of Being* (New York, 1960), especially p. 295.

significant withdrawal: ". . . *Christus implet omnia,* Christ *filleth all things.* Whereby we may perceive, that all plenitude is from the divine Act, as contrariwise Vacuity is, when the formal life is absent from the waters, and this is the reason that *Vacuum* or *Inane* is held so horrible a thing in Nature."[5]

Seeing first, no more than an optical system, Ruskin is now determined to touch, and, touching, fill. There are, after all, precedents.

Yet Ruskin digs like Faust, instead of filling like Christ, and, without Christ's divinity, the act of digging or filling can become a problem. To touch is to use up space, the distance of vistas that are so important to the object of Desiring Eyes. Again, sight and touch are at odds, just as language and vision are. And although he does not suffer from a variation of John Stuart Mill's fear that all the musical combinations may be used up, he is nevertheless aware that the act of filling, as opposed to the static occupation of space, requires vacant space—"that magnificent blank" (xxxvii, 38) which may inspire the observer with its potential, rather than horrify him with its Nothingness. Discriminations are made. The problem of quality is introduced. To fill is not enough: space must be filled well. Ruskin becomes jealous of model space, which is typographical space: "How one hates the direction for taking up such quantity of room, as if it thought itself of such mighty importance" (xxxvi, 3). Yet the problem is as large as it is small. Instead of being the offending void of a hole in the Hincksey road that has to be filled, space becomes something of value, whether it is a sheet of paper, magnificently blank with nothing but potential, or the earth, which is now in its "third, or historical period," when "the valleys excavated in the second period are being filled up, and the mountains, hewn in the second period, worn or ruined down. In the second aera the valley of the Rhone was being cut deeper every day; now it is every day being filled up with gravel" (xxvi, 118). The direction on the letter is the equivalent of the gravel unworthily filling the valley of the Rhone.

Vacant space, in this historical period of geological filling, is no longer an affront. It is no longer an abyss in which to rank those obsessed with "brutalities and vices" for their own sake. Instead, it is a dimension of privilege that allows the self extension and exploration. In the same letter in which he complains to his father about the letter's "direction" taking up too much space, Ruskin discusses his need for room that will give his mind a stage on which to perform. And Ruskin's stage, before all others, is paper: "Mary declined writing to you for a reason which gave me peculiar

---

[5] Robert Fludd, *Mosaicall Philosophy*, p. 52, as quoted in Lovejoy, *Great Chain of Being*, p. 95.

and particular offense, namely, that I wrote nonsense enough. . . . However, I did not quarrel with her, as she surrendered her half sheet to me, which space I was very glad to fill up with my nonsense, as this additional space gave me much greater freedom and play of cogitation. . . . I like elbow room for everything" (xxxvi, 4). Liking "elbow room for everything," though at the same time happily enclosed within the "walls of Eden," he likes it first in miniature, on that stage of paper where the performance is as remote as the epistolary friends of the Camera Lucida. Predictably, the need for "additional space" results not merely in raids on what has been allotted to Mary Richardson, his cousin. He displays the avariciousness of his later parenthetical self, who would assimilate the "outside": "And now having concluded mine epistle, I intend to leave poor mamma a small space of plain paper . . . she is forced to find fragments of room, writing cross, and topsy-turvy. . . . Therefore, in order to obviate the necessity of so much invention on her part, and patience on yours, I am content, without further circumlocution, to leave her this little bit of paper at bottom . . ." (ii, 456).

As long as the typographical borders are flexible, which is to say as long as he can co-opt either the friendly space of Mary or his mother, he can, extending "elbow room," give expression to a special kind of self-indulgence that is not immediately reflexive. For Ruskin, writing is like looking into a mirror that does not reflect his image. It is as if he can be a writer instead of a reader only as long as paginal space holds out. But once he runs out of writing paper, there will be nothing to do but read what has been written, to confront it. Writing prepares for the later mirrored reflection of reading. It would appear that, interested in advertising the first person, Ruskin would like to write autobiography without reading it. Yet feeling that he is running out of space, the model space of the page, even as he will later run out of both distance and future, he begins to understand that he is running out of room for play, for the self-indulgence of infinite extension. Once, he smothered his father with frictionless language. But now, his own words begin to close in on him, like the distance that later fails: "I have not space left for detailed notice of the other exhibitions . . ." (xiv, 83); "I have not space enough here to explain or apply it" (xiv, 128); "I have not space to follow out this most interesting and extensive subject" (xi, 78); "I have not space to follow out this thought,—it is of infinite extent and application" (xi, 24). The subject matter, composed of "infinite extent and application," and luring an encyclopedic Ruskin towards digressions that have no end, requires, if it is to be pursued, infinite typographical space.

Still, if the digressions are potentially endless, the landscape space, upon which the equally limited paginal space is modelled, is walled. Without economy, it is a space that can be used up as quickly as the short life Ruskin feared. Given limitations, digressive ambitions are defined and the mirror becomes inevitable. Ruskin, beginning to understand the practice of economy, begins to become aware of the double aspects of a self that as reader, if not writer, he would banish to the vanishing perspective of recessional space. But it is the writer, who, running out of empty pages, prepares for the reader's eventual narcissism of consciousness. Both "excavatory fancy," which is the work of the writer, and the attempt, impossible in execution, to fill the page with a subject of "infinite extent and application" work without reflexive confrontation only as long as space holds out. When the space is gone, the act of either filling or writing becomes history—something to read about. Both digging and indulgent writing are activities that work only in the present tense. They are without mnemonic joy. When the container has been filled, which is either the space within the four walls of Eden or the "magnificent blank" of the page, Ruskin, having nowhere to turn and nothing to dig or explore, feels the full claustrophobic burden of reflexive space. It is a burden that is the reverse of his agoraphobic response to Nothingness.

Because the enclosed world can be filled too easily, Ruskin begins to practice a conservation of space that is most easily observed in his typographical models. Print, which is the furious multiplication of language, seems to inspire the conservation of page space more readily than longhand: "I must pass, disjointedly, to matters which, in a written letter, would have been put in a postscript; but I don't care, in a printed one, to leave a useless gap in the type" (xxvii, 194); "I have no mind to waste the space of *Fors* in giving variety of instances" (xxviii, 671). Yet if Ruskin attempts, in *Fors Clavigera,* to maintain some kind of limitation on the space used, the "Notes & Correspondence" that is tacked on to the end of each *Fors,* seems to grow as an addenda for refuse that cannot be discarded: "This bit of letter must find room—bearing as it does on the last *Fors* subject" (xxviii, 339). The urge for conservation is also apparent away from public print, in that most private of typographical space, the diaries: "I must spare space or my book will be gone in no time" (*Diaries,* p. 1070). Conserving available room and reluctant to desecrate the "magnificent blank," he begins to finish entries on the left-hand page: "Continued from other side, not to disturb new page" (*Diaries,* p. 811).

All the same, no matter how diligent Ruskin's conservation of paginal space is, he begins to feel the pressures of limitation, of not having enough "elbow room." He tries to combat the movement towards diffusion: ". . . when I wrote the *Seven Lamps of Architecture*, it required all the ingenuity I was master of to prevent them from becoming Eight, or even Nine, on my hands" (xxvii, 82). Sensing the pressures of limitation, he attempts to condense, and, attempting, fails. He cannot consolidate: "I find it wholly impossible to crush into one *Fors* what I have been gathering of Bible lesson, natural history lesson, and writing lesson, and to leave room enough for what I have to give of immediate explanation to the Companions, now daily increasing in number" (xxviii, 538). The result is a feeling of paginal claustrophobia. There is no "additional space" in which to operate. Ruskin's explorations are forced back on themselves. He cannot follow the variety of pursuits in which he is engaged: "I was crowded for room at the end of last chapter, and could not give account . . ." (xxxv, 497).

The need for "additional space" becomes more than a preoccupation. It is the staple of Ruskin's life: "I do not care where the land is, nor of what quality. I would rather it should be poor, for I want space more than food" (xxviii, 19). But switching back and forth between the modelled-after and the model, between topography and typography, exterior space and the space of a page, he can occasionally lament his obsessions as false economy: ". . . how much life have I not wasted, to save paper" (*Diaries*, p. 760). Yet more often, paginal space that is unused, like topographical space that is either unfelt or unexplored, is potential life. It is unused time, a future tense: ". . . I have had more to do than I could do without cramming and ramming, and wishing days were longer and sheets of paper broader . . ." (ii, xxxii). Typographical "elbow room," which is either broader or longer paper, has a temporal equivalent, a kind of "elbow time" that translates to simply longer days. Designs established in space are often recapitulated in time, but space and time are dimensions that are often at odds: spatial autobiography is not temporal autobiography, and frozen language, language as sculpture, is not the coiling, serial language of the later Third Style. But in a demand made great by limited supply, space and time become dimensions that, at least for a while, come close to being interchangeable: ". . . for though I had a month to speak to you, instead of an hour, time would fail me if I tried to trace . . ." (xvi, 182). And again: "I might expatiate all night—if you would sit and hear me—on the treatment of such required subject, or introduction of pleasant caprice by the old workmen; but we have no time to spare, and I must quit this part of our subject . . ." (xvi, 394).

Ruskin has traveled a long way from his agoraphobic response to blankness, negatives, and minus numbers. Finally, when he says, "How I spoil these pretty pages by writing on them" (*Diaries*, p. 765), it is as if he were lamenting the contamination of the earth by the working out of his "excavatory fancy," and, ultimately, the contamination of the "pretty" future tense, the tense of potential life by living it into the present. Too soon, everything will have been touched, everything will have been used up or filled. There will be no more "elbow room," and no more time.

Still, there is mild consolation. Breeding indulgence that is either like writing an interminable autobiography or watching one's reflection for too long, excessive room can cause problems. In a letter to Charles Eliot

Norton, Ruskin, long after his agoraphobia has become history, suggests that too much space can be infernal: "I hope you are well, in that walled paradise of yours—don't try to get out. There's a great deal too much room in Hades". . . (xxxvi, 456). But if Norton is advised not "to get out," Ruskin is rarely content to stay "inside," with the notable exceptions of Ruskin's parenthetical self, who takes space as food, and the later Ruskin who takes interior structures as a defense against the failing, reflexive distance of an inverted perspective. Walls become something other than "Edenic." Home is a problem, vistas a necessity.

INTERIORITY AND THE EFFICACIOUS REFLEXIVE

If we turn from the reciprocal movement between Ruskin's typographical models of his topographical world, to the enlarged and more general subject of his history of landscape and the attitudes, both private and public, that shape those landscapes more than the landscapes shape the attitudes, we can begin to understand Ruskin's own position in that history, as well as his topographical expectations and requirements. We can begin to understand the way, given certain conditions, he chooses to situate himself in relation to a world that is both true to nature and very much his own.

Ruskin's point of departure for his landscape history is the realization of the historical eccentricity of his preoccupations. As a man representative of an age in which "some extraordinary change in human nature" (v, 196) has occurred, Ruskin recognizes the peculiarity of the modern landscape inhabitant's "passionate admiration of inanimate objects," which closely resembles "in its elevation and tenderness, the affection which he bears to those living souls with which he is brought into the nearest fellowship" (v, 199). This "passionate admiration" for the objects that make up the exterior world, the structures and accessories of Ruskin's landscape, can be contrasted with the ancestor of the modern man, who "took . . . very little interest in anything but what belonged to humanity; caring in no wise for the external world, except as it influenced his own destiny . . . thus spending only on the lowest creatures and inanimate things his waste energy, his dullest thoughts, his most languid emotions, and reserving all his acuter intellect for researches into his own nature and that of his gods" (v, 197). Yet the modern man, turning from self to the topography that had previously received only the attention of "waste energy," is engaged in a characteristic act of filling vacant containers:

> Exactly in the degree that the architect withdrew from his buildings the sources
> of delight which in early days they had so richly possessed, demanding, in ac-

cordance with the new principles of taste, the banishment of all happy colour and healthy invention, in that degree the minds of men began to turn to landscape as their only resource. The picturesque school of art rose up to address those capacities for which, in sculpture, architecture, or the higher walks of painting, there was employment no more; and the shadows of Rembrandt, and savageness of Salvator, arrested the admiration which was no longer permitted to be rendered to the gloom or the grotesqueness of the Gothic aisle. And thus the English school of landscape, culminating in Turner, is in reality nothing else than a healthy effort to fill the void which the destruction of Gothic architecture has left. (xi, 225–26).

But landscape art is not an arbitrary substitute for the Nothingness left behind by the destruction of Gothic architecture: the "passionate admiration" of the "inanimate objects" of the landscape represents an attempt to substitute, for the age's general "want of faith" (v, 322), a presence—complexly connected with the self's involvement with landscape—that was, before, manifested by Gothic architecture. The substitution, which is also an act of filling, is not entirely satisfactory: ". . . the void cannot thus be filled; no, nor filled in any considerable degree" (xi, 226). Ruskin's public attitude towards landscape affiliation—the working out of the problems of faith by the relations between self and landscape—vacillates considerably, as his private, obsessive affection and attention do not. His divided, public attitude is everywhere apparent. He can say, before beginning his history of landscape, "I shall merely endeavour to note some of the leading and more interesting circumstances bearing on the subject, and to show sufficient practical ground for the conclusion, that landscape-painting is indeed a noble and useful art, though one not long known by man" (v, 200). And, at the same time, he remains sceptical about the assumptions that the "extraordinary change in human nature," which results in topographical attention at the expense of attention to the self, is a good one: "The simple fact that we are, in some strange way, different from all the great races that have existed before us, cannot at once be received as the proof of our own greatness; nor can it be granted, without any question, that we have a legitimate subject of complacency in being under the influence of feelings with which neither Miltiades nor the Black Prince, neither Homer nor Dante, neither Socrates nor St. Francis, could for an instant have sympathized" (v, 196). If "landscape-painting is indeed a noble and useful art," the landscape obsessions responsible for that art—and presumably, finally, the art itself—can also be something other than "noble":

> . . . respecting the grounds and component *elements* of the pleasure which the
> moderns take in landscape, we have here to consider what are the probable or
> usual *effects* of this pleasure. Is it a safe or a seductive one? May we wisely
> boast of it, and unhesitatingly indulge it? or is it rather a sentiment to be

despised when it is slight, and condemned when it is intense; a feeling which disinclines us to labour, and confuses us in thought; a joy only to the inactive and the visionary, incompatible with the duties of life, and the accuracies of reflection?

It seems to me that, as matters stand at present, there is considerable ground for the latter opinion. We saw . . . that our love of nature had been partly forced upon us by mistakes in our social economy, and led to no distinct issues of action or thought. And when we look to Scott—the man who feels it most deeply—for some explanation of its effect upon him, we find a curious tone of apology (as if for an involuntary folly) running through his confessions. (v, 354)

His public landscape attitudes shifting, Ruskin introduces, in the chapter "Of Classical Landscape" in *Modern Painters* III, an enclosed landscape incapable of being extended infinitely. It is as closed and limited as the garden at Herne Hill or the "magnificent blanks" of Ruskin's empty pages.

The idiosyncrasies of the classical landscape can best be described by a series of negatives. This is so because the classical landscape is self-sufficient. Nothing is done to it. The inhabitant inflicts no performance on an environment that does everything for itself. Unlike Ruskin's models and his adult landscape—a present-tense, essentially modern landscape—the inhabitability of the past-tense, classical landscape does not depend on the process of filling, of creating a plenitude that inevitably leads to both the reflexive space that follows a failing distance, and, given the interchangeability of Ruskin's spatial and temporal designs, a set of tenses without a future. Instead, the classical, Homeric landscape—enclosed but uninvolved in a linear process that would move towards a dead end—operates with a population requiring neither frontiers nor exits. The inhabitant of the classical landscape negotiates his topography without using it up, without creating a waste, without contaminating it with the familiarity of a despised self in search of either pseudonymity or invisibility. Because he does not respond to the aesthetics of plenitude, the classical man, leaving the containers empty, does not have to concern himself with the problems of topographical claustrophobia and an accompanying intensification of self-consciousness caused by reflexive movement. Uninvolved in process, the classical landscape is without beginnings and endings: it is not divided into conflicting areas, into foregrounds that become, later, in the modern landscape, starting points for the penetration of space, and backgrounds that become, later, endings.

Without beginnings and endings, the classical landscape, ungradated, is also without distances. The desire for a containment that denies distances can be seen in Ulysses' "taste for trim hedges and upright trunks" (v, 236).

But the trimness that exercises its "unusual influence" over Ulysses is, when translated into modern English landscape, something a little unworthy: "Then that spirit of trimness. The smooth paving stones, the scraped, hard, even rutless roads; the neat gates and plates, and essence of border, and spikiness and spruceness" (vi, 14). The "spirit of trimness" becomes unworthy because it is connected with the "swept proprieties and neatness of English modernism" (vi, 15). Instead of taking into account "the consciousness of pathos in the confessed ruin, which may or may not be beautiful, according to the kind of it," the "spirit of trimness" is involved in the "entire denial of all human calamity and care" (vi, 15). Furthermore, this "spirit of trimness," connected with "neat gates" and the "essence of border," suggests not only spatial containment but temporal closure as well—the refusal to consider the "pathos in the confessed ruin." The classical landscape that later, as it becomes a past-tense topography, will provide ruins for artists interested in asserting their visions of "human calamity," is itself, like the "swept proprieties of English modernism," without historical distances, without a past to allow the self a time corresponding to "elbow room"—a way out of the present tense. But the psychic disposition of the classical man does not require this temporal room.

Nor does he require the perpetual surprise of a contorted topography— what Arthur Lovejoy calls the doctrine of the "primacy of irregularity."[6] Talking about "Chinese sharawadgi"—first applied to a gardening style and later to an architectural style and linked, by Lovejoy, to the irregularity of the Gothic modes of the first Gothic revival[7]—Lovejoy points out that, according to William Chambers, Chinese designers attempted to appeal to the "pleasure of surprise" rather than the "pleasure of recognition,"[8] to the unfamiliar rather than the familiar. The concern with the "surprise" of the irregular is connected with the idea of "perpetual self-transcendence" that Lovejoy, discriminating versions of romanticism, finds in the "preference for diversity and complexity."[9] Lovejoy's stroller through the landscapes of the eighteenth century, either facing a vista or the objectifying complexity of a Chinese garden, has as little notion of himself as does Ruskin, faced with a vacant space or a blank page, both of which are all potential: only as space is either explored or filled (and the process is similar) does it become familiar—and familiar, it is contaminated by a self who has run out of ploys for transcendence, perpetual or occasional. Then the exits, used, will

[6] Arthur O. Lovejoy, "The First Gothic Revival," Essays in the History of Ideas (New York, 1960), p. 158.

[7] Ibid., p. 159.

[8] Lovejoy, "The Chinese Origin of a Romanticism," Essays, p. 129.

[9] Lovejoy, "On the Discrimination of Romanticisms," Essays, p. 244.

be closed. The rooms will have no views. And there will be only autobiography or self-portraiture left for someone who, at least publically, outside the world of diaries, pretends to despise all that is reflexive and egocentric.

But in the classical landscape, with no "discrimination of romanticisms," the inhabitant has no psychic need for the "perpetual self-transcedence" of topographical contortion or surprise that requires an open-ended world of vistas, frontiers, new space, and complex designs. In the classical landscape, as opposed to the Chinese or Gothic revival landscapes, there is a "delight in regular ploughed land and meadows, and a neat garden" of vines (v, 246). The informing virtues of the ideal landscape of the garden of Alcinous are "order, symmetry, and fruitfulness," and, if the Homeric "god's admiration is excited by the free fountains, wild violets, and wandering vine," the mortal responds to "vines in rows, the leeks in beds, and the fountains in pipes" (v, 235–36). Antipathetic to a topography of surprise and shrinking "with fear or hatred from all the ruggedness of lower nature,—from the wrinkled forest bark, the jagged hill-crest, and irregular, inorganic storm of sky," the classical man observes the "disorderly, unbalanced, and rugged," with "proportionate fear" (v, 234). Furthermore, altitude, or rather the lack of it, answers the same needs as furrowed regularity. Flatness is an ingredient of a landscape that does not require surprise. Although the actual classical landscape may be mountainous, the imaginative landscape constructed by Homer is not only closed, as if walled, but flat. There are few altitudinal surprises: "It is sufficiently notable that Homer, living in mountainous and rocky countries, dwells thus delightedly on all the *flat* bits . . ." (v, 238).

The aesthetic behind the organization and design of the classical landscape, in which "perpetual self-transcendence" serves no function, is an aesthetic of imitation, rather than compensation. But what is imitated, in the case of altitude, is not the actual landscape, but an imaginative topography given shape by the inhabitant's sense of self, his sense of his own symmetry. The rules of organization and design emanate from the inhabitant's idea of himself: "human beauty . . . whether in its bodily being or in imagined divinity, had become . . . the principal object of culture and sympathy to these Greeks . . ." (v, 233). The rules that determined the "principal object of culture and sympathy," which is the inhabitant, the self, are the familiar topographical rules that consist of "orderly, symmetrical, and tender" design (v, 233).

Still, the case for the determination of the design of the classical landscape by an aesthetic of imitation that emanates from a symmetrical self, in a condition of equilibrium, should not be overstated. The essential movement between the inhabitant and the classical landscape is not outward bound, initiated from an informing and designing self, but instead a reflexive movement from topography back to self:

> Now the notable things in this description of the Homeric landscape are, first, the evident subservience of the whole landscape to human comfort, to the foot, the taste, or the smell. . . . (v, 235)

> . . . we shall always be struck by this quiet subjection of their every feature to human service. . . . (v, 235)

The "human service" that the reflexive landscape is geared to perform is not, finally, an aesthetic service, but a utilitarian one: ". . . every expression of the pleasure which Ulysses has in this landing and resting, contains uninterruptedly the reference to the utility and sensible pleasantness of all things, not to their beauty" (v, 240).

The relation between the classical man and his landscape is most characteristically described by a syntax of possession. The landscape is "his own." Attention is devoted to "him." The self operates in the objective case. And that self, attended to by a reflexive landscape, is not concerned with the laws lying behind phenomenal perception, as is the more active, modern self who, impelled by the need for "perpetual self-transcendence," sees reflexive movement as part of a claustral design that will eliminate the distance of "elbow room," a distance necessary for an unself-conscious extension and indulgence that becomes unwitting preparation for autobiography. Instead, the classical man's lack of concern over the distance in which the modern man will both find and lose himself allows the classical man, from his position of equapoise, to ignore abstracting and transcending laws, those laws that are used by the modern man to remove himself from his situation of profound disequilibrium. Needing to go nowhere, the classical man, whose self-importance is taken for granted, is satisfied with phenomena rather than laws:

> When the eyes of men were fixed upon themselves, and upon nature solely and secondarily as bearing upon their interests, it was of less consequence to them what the ultimate laws of nature were, than what the immediate effects were upon human beings. Hence they could rest satisfied with phenomena instead of principles, and accepted without scrutiny every fable which seemed sufficiently or gracefully to account for those phenomena. But so far as the eyes of men are now withdrawn from themselves, and turned upon the inanimate things about them, the results cease to be of importance, and the laws become essential. (v, 199)

But the inhabitant as object, who is satisfied with the perception of phenomena rather than an understanding of principles, does not organize an enclosed world about himself without having available a means of refracting and dispersing his cultivated and intensified sense of self. The classical man, located egocentrically in a reflexive landscape, engages in various acts of self-denial. Attempting "to obtain some persuasion of the immediate presence or approval of the Divinity," he makes "enormous and self-denying efforts" (v, 196). And if the classical man finds his world turned in upon himself as if he were the focal point of that world, he is able, while still maintaining his egocentric position, to get outside himself: "So that, on the whole, the best things he did were done in the presence, or for the honour of his gods; and, whether in statues, to help him to imagine them, or temples raised to their honour, or acts of self-sacrifice done in the hope of their love, he brought whatever was best and skilfullest in him into their service, and lived in a perpetual subjection to their unseen power" (v, 196). Finally, though, transcending nothing and engaging in acts of perpetual self-confrontation, the classical man gets outside himself by subjecting himself not to an "unseen power," but, predictably, to himself. To attend to the self in the right way, which is itself a form of virtuous denial, is to get a sense of something outside that self: ". . . there was another kind of beauty which they found it required effort to obtain, and which, when thoroughly obtained, seemed more glorious than any of this wild loveliness—the beauty of the human countenance and form. This, they perceived, could only be reached by continual exercise of virtue; and it was in Heaven's sight and theirs, all the more beautiful because it needed this self-denial to obtain it" (v, 232).

The reason for the classical man's ability to engage in acts of perpetual self-confrontation is the equilibrium he feels between himself and his world. At ease with his landscape, he is at ease with himself. More precisely, his equilibrium is the result of his disinterest in the distance between vantage and focal points, a disinterest which makes landscape reflexively and egocentrically constructed about the self an attractive and functional design, instead of one that is claustrophobic. Disinterested in distance, he is interested in himself. Equilibrium eliminates the need for distance. It also makes possible efficacious autobiography.

The classical man avoids the self-consciousness of enclosed space by awareness of a dimension that is his equivalent of the modern man's distance. The classical man knows that even though his landscape is enclosed, without either the distances of depth or altitude, there is another form of extension, another dimension, which is the most important component of the classical landscape, and that is the dimension of interiority. His awareness of the inside creates disinterest in the outside, the world of vistas. It is a dimension that permits the landscape to be described by negatives. It is what makes "perpetual self-transcendence" an unnecessary requirement and the ability of the self to exist in proximity with itself, even to confront and admire itself, a possibility. Finally, it is what makes for a homogeneous landscape, a landscape undivided into sectors of near and far, "here" and "there."

Ruskin, describing Vulcan fighting the river Scamander, describes this interior dimension as a "nerve," a "vital part": "At last even the 'nerve of the river,' or 'strength of the river' (note the expression), feels the fire, and this 'strength of the river' addresses Vulcan in supplication of respite. There is in this precisely the idea of a vital part of the river-body, which acted and felt, to which, if the fire reached, it was death, just as would be the case if it touched a vital part of the human body." Unsurprisingly, the operative word in this reflexive landscape that treats its inhabitants as focal points (inhabitants who are, we recall, obsessed with the vocabulary of possession) is the preposition of the interior. The reasoning Greek is concerned with what is "in":

> I can light the fire, and put it out; I can dry this water up, or drink it. It cannot be the fire or the water that rages, or that is wayward. But it must be something *in* this fire and *in* the water, which I cannot destroy by extinguishing the one, or evaporating the other, any more than I destroy myself by cutting off my finger; I was *in* my finger—something of me at least was; I had a power over it and felt pain in it, though I am still as much myself when it is gone. So there may be a power in the water which is not water, but to which the water is as a body;—which can strike with it, move in it, suffer in it. . . . (v, 224)

The animated interior of the objects of the classical landscape permits the topography to take care of itself. There is no need for help from the self-regarding but unself-conscious classical man. Activated from within, the topography does not require the aid of external agencies. The inside, which is the classical analogue of the modern distance, makes the movement or surprise of "perpetual self-transcendence" unnecessary. It is a dimension of immanence that is unknown to either Ruskin's staring self, who cannot be inside without a window, or the later traveler through the modern landscape, a landscape of vistas, in which continual topographical and temporal discriminations must be made—the "here" distinguished from the "there," the "now" from the "then." Travel in a homogeneous landscape is senseless. The classical man stays home, without a thought of either background or transgressing the "essence of border." His vantage and focal points, in this immanent landscape that is unseparated by discrimination, coalesce with an efficacy impossible later. The intervening distance, which is a space of anonymity, has not yet been introduced. Surrounded by Vestal gods, he may write an untroubled autobiography.

TOPOGRAPHICAL AUTOBIOGRAPHY, EFFICACIOUS AND INEFFICACIOUS

Writing a history of the relation between landscape and the inhabitant who constructs, by selective modes of perception, a topography answering his psychic requirements, Ruskin is engaged in simultaneous activities: if there is something like an optical autobiography written only for the self as reader, an autobiography to be culled from the private experience of the diaries, there is also a public, though submerged, autobiography to be found in the landscape history of the third volume of *Modern Painters.* This is not the place to make a case for an aesthetics of "distanced intimacy," or better, an aesthetics of reluctant autobiography that would depend, for its vitality, upon the conflict created by the need of the potential autobiographer to advertise himself, or at least acknowledge his own existence, and the impulse towards pseudonymity, which is a movement that would make the self as difficult to see as a voyeur. But what is important to note, in any case, is that the optical autobiography, written for a voyeuristic audience of one who has turned, or will turn, into a reader, and the landscape material, written for the general public—its autobiography camouflaged by what we shall see is an impulse towards nonexistence— both deal with the relation between self and world: the private, optical autobiography with a reticent self and the nature of the affiliation with the observed world, and the landscape sections with, first, the world, and then reflexively the self. Landscape, shaped by a self who is a gardener, becomes a mirror of that self.

Ruskin's landscape history is an early version of *Praeterita.* In the same way that there is a reciprocal movement between consciousness and language, so there is interdependency between Ruskin's sense of himself and a verbally constructed landscape that is involved in the development of both consciousness and landscape. Constructing his world, bringing it into language, Ruskin, by describing "there " or what he has observed, reenforces that sense of self which is "here." His consciousness of the landscape is the consciousness of himself.

As if turning the overlapping designs of the phylogenic recapitulation of ontogeny to his own advantage, Ruskin makes correlations between history and autobiography. The performance of an individual is a model of the race's performance:

> . . . and in the enchanted light which races, like individuals, must perceive in looking back. . . . (v, 329)

> In the progress of national as well as of individual mind. . . . (viii, 170)

> There is a resemblance between the work of a great nation, in this phase, and the work of childhood. . . . (VIII, 170)

This design of superimposition between the public and the private suggests the key to the relations between the history of landscape and landscape as autobiography. Ruskin's history of the relations between landscape and its inhabitants from the classical to the modern period is a public version of his own shifting relations and attitudes towards landscape, from childhood to maturity.

Despite the fact that Ruskin would be a gardener within the walls of Herne Hill, while the self-sufficient classical landscape is neither tended nor arranged, a comparison between Ruskin's descriptions in *Praeterita* of his own childhood preoccupations and his descriptions in the third volume of *Modern Painters* of the relations of classical man to the landscape demonstrates the overlay of historical and autobiographical designs: the child's proximate focus, his insistence that "I was only interested by things near me, or at least clearly visible and present" (xxxv, 104), which is underscored by his assertion that, "confined to a little garden," he does not "imagine himself somewhere else" (xx, 249), is matched by the inclinations of the classical man who took "no interest in anything but what immediately concerned himself" (v, 198). The emphasis on spatial proximity shared by both the past-tense self, the child, and the classical man, corresponds to the temporal immediacy of the child, who lives "always in the tangible present, having little pleasure in memory, and being utterly impatient and tormented by anticipation" (xx, 249), and the classical man's concerns that, focusing on what is "available, pleasant, or useful" (v, 244), do not leave the present tense.

Moreover, the central location of Ruskin's autobiographical child, who, "perky, contented, conceited," occupies the "central point . . . in the universe" (xxxv, 37), is an equivalent of the egocentric inhabitant as focal point in the reflexive, classical landscape of *Modern Painters* iii. Worringer, describing the origins of the psychic relations between self and classical landscape, might be talking about the Edenic life of Ruskin's enclosed childhood: "Man was at home in the world and felt himself its centre. Man and world were not antitheses and, sustained by this faith in the reality of appearances, a comprehensive sensory-intellectual mastery of the world-picture was arrived at."[10] The central location, the condition of being at home in the world, is used by Worringer to describe "that rare and fortunate state of equipoise 'in the great process of disputation between man and the outer world,' that had arisen in which man and world were fused

[10] Wilhelm Worringer, *Abstraction and Empathy: A Contribution to the Psychology of Style* (New York, 1953) p. 102.

into one. In the field of the history of religions, this state is marked by religions which start from the principle of immanence which, wearing the various colours of polytheism, pantheism or monism, regard the divine as being contained in the world. . . ."[11]

This principle of an animated interior—a concept of immanence fundamental not only to the possibility of efficacious autobiography, of existence in a situation of spatial and temporal proximity, but also to the landscape inhabitant's central location, which is the home as foreground—structures the essential design that, finally, binds collective and individual pasts. It is what binds the past tense of both history and autobiography. Yet it is perhaps more important to read Ruskin's landscape histories, public and private, not for their accuracy, or lack of it, but rather for what they say about his psychic needs: constructed, or recalled, from a present tense, in which the inhabitant is faced by the disconfirmation of an actuality that cannot be manipulated, Ruskin's overlapping landscape histories refer outside that restrictive present tense in order to fulfill the need of the consciousness for periods of equipoise, for points of rest. And that pastoral, both historical and autobiographical, is most removed from fiction in the reality of the needs that it answers. A deciphering of the needs must necessarily be more accurate than the accounts.

Yet there is a second form of autobiography, the autobiography of the pathetic fallacy, that does not so much answer needs as create problems. No areas of pastoral are established. The autobiography of the pathetic fallacy is a peculiarly modern form of autobiography reflecting the anatomy of the landscape inhabitant's mind more directly than the recollected topographies that become styles of pastoral. The working-out of the pathetic fallacy, despite the fact that it occurs in an apparently open-ended landscape—a world of space constructed about the aesthetics of the infinite—ends finally in a condition of autobiographical enclosure as confined as either the Edenic space of the Herne Hill garden or the later, infernal "coal-cellar" of Rembrandt. But while enclosure is no less satisfactory to the classical man than is his egocentric location, Ruskin's modern man, no longer a child and operating in the present tense of landscape history, finds the mirror of the pathetic fallacy—its autobiographical qualities—unpleasant because of a resultant intensification of self-consciousness.

But too much self comes from having too little self. The pathetic fallacy is the result of a condition of disequilibrium between the inhabitant, who is somehow inadequate to the descriptive demands of his landscape, and that demanding landscape. There is no equipoise, no sense of balance between self and world: "The temperament which admits the pathetic fallacy, is, as

[11] Worringer, *Abstraction and Empathy*, p. 128.

I said above, that of a mind and body in some sort too weak to deal fully with what is before them or upon them; borne away, or over-clouded, or over-dazzled by emotion . . ." (v, 208). The ability to feel great emotion, to be subject to potential disequilibrium, is an ingredient of the significant artist's disposition. But the great artist resists that disequilibrium, mastering the emotions that would, in a weaker mind, become dominant ("over-clouded, or over-dazzled"): "A poet is great, first in proportion to the strength of his passion, and then, that strength being granted, in proportion to his government of it . . ." (v, 215). It is a point upon which Ruskin is insistent: "Even in the most inspired prophet it is a sign of the incapacity of his human sight or thought to bear what has been revealed" (v, 218). Yet at the same time, the incapacity to confront with equilibrium and mastery is, occasionally, a necessity: ". . . there being . . . always a point beyond which it would be inhuman and monstrous if he pushed this government, and, therefore, a point at which all feverish and wild fancy becomes just and true. Thus the destruction of the kingdom of Assyria cannot be contemplated firmly by a prophet of Israel. The fact is too great . . ." (v, 215).

In a modern world constructed around intervening distances that would prevent the coalescence of vantage and focal points, the distinctions between self and world begin to blur. Like the encyclopedic Ruskin, the modern man must play all the roles. He faces a world of empty interiors. That open-ended and apparently unreflexive landscape, in which the inhabitant does not receive the services of an obliging landscape, is dependent for its life upon the animation of a modern man, who would substitute his emotions for the "nerves" of the river Scamader, like the persona of Charles Kingsley, who observes "cruel, crawling foam" (v, 205).[12] The modern landscape has the same problem as the room that the young Ruskin notes is a "withdrawing room" because his father is absent. The space of "withdrawing," which is a space of transcendence, is filled by an overblown self, who, animating vacuums, tending to the world as if it were a garden, would create, at least for a moment, a variety of autobiographical immanence. Playing all roles, he would play the part of what is no longer inside. Yet Ruskin knows that this must be heretical. Christ may fill all things, but not Ruskin's modern man. Further, representative of his age, Ruskin has always felt uneasy inside. He has always needed his windows.

But Ruskin's modern man, at once inadequate and overblown, is not a potentially happy autobiographer. The animation of vacant interiors, the shifting of focus, vitality, and emotion between self and world, can only be accomplished with a diminution of the self. Involved in a perverse autobiography of immanence, he is also involved in what Worringer, talking not about the relations between inhabitant and landscape but observer and art

---

[12] Kingsley's phrase appears in chapter 26 of *Alton Locke*.

object, calls "self-alienation"—an impulse that would at first appear to be contradictory to the autobiographical movement towards empathetic affiliation and domination of the landscape by the impulses of the pathetic fallacy. Worringer's "self-alienation" is the result of an "urge to alienate oneself from the individual being," or, put slightly differently, it is an "urge to seek deliverance from the fortuitousness of humanity as a whole":

> In empathising this will to activity into another object, however, we *are* in the other object. We are delivered from our individual being as long as we are absorbed into an external object, an external form, with our inner urge to experience. We feel, as it were, our individuality flow into fixed boundaries in contrast to the boundless differentiation of the individual consciousness. In this self-objectification lies a self-alienation.[13]

Yet, after the initial process of self-alienation, which is a process prompted by feelings of inadequacy, that would lead towards invisibility or nonexistence, the self confronts its own objectified emotions in the landscape of the pathetic fallacy, the landscape of recently filled interiors. For if in the beginning, the externalization and affiliation of self with landscape produces the desired loss of self-consciousness in the form of self-alienation, the final result is the world as mirror. The pathetic fallacy's self-alienation is, in the end, a version of autobiography that, creating a sense of reflexive closure, should never have been written by Ruskin's modern man in search of either pseudonymity or invisibility. Simply, there is no "deliverance from the fortuitousness of humanity as a whole" in the reflexive space of autobiography.

Still, the question of the desirability of the autobiographical impulse remains. It is no problem for the self-regarding classical man, who exists in a condition of equipoise. But for the modern man, and Ruskin in particular, disequilibrium resulting from a sense of "withdrawal" and vacuity makes the mirror or self-portrait something to be regarded only in private. The escape from self-consciousness that may be good for Ruskin's modern man may, at the same time, be bad for his art. With Ruskin, it is

---

[13] Worringer, *Abstraction and Empathy,* p. 24. Or, as Theodore Lipps, multiplying selves, explains: "In empathy . . . I am not the real I, but am inwardly liberated from the latter, i.e. I am liberated from everything which I am apart from contemplation of the form. I am only this ideal, this contemplating I." Theodor Lipps, quoted *ibid.* Yet the animation of the pathetic fallacy, which affiliates with topography in the form of Lipps' "ideal . . . contemplating I," does not finally provide the psychic relief of alienation or liberation from the stationary, "real I": the multiplication of selves is a means of dividing the burden of selfhood. But division works only as long as those multiplied selves do not get in each other's way. Facing each other, selves who would be pseudonymous write each other's biography. The externalized disequilibrium of the "real I" not only animates the landscape with the affiliation of the alienated "ideal . . . contemplating I," but it also subjectifies it.

probably accurate to say that the pressures of autobiographical closure caused by self-activation in a condition of transcendence result in structural and syntactic complexities that form the basis of much of his best art. Coupled with the inability to be at ease with the autobiographical impulse, reflexive space, forcing self-consciousness, can compel eccentric and often brilliant verbal solutions to problems that have spatial origins.

CHAPTER III **The Penetration of Space: Journey to the Background**

ME-OLOGY: THE DUNGEON OF CORRUPTION

From an interior that is activated by autobiography, Ruskin's landscape focus moves outwards, impelled by the farsightedness of Desiring Eyes, towards a frontier or background of anonymity. As the modern man attempts to avoid the reflexive design of closure, which is a design that intensifies the problems of self-consciousness, he travels away from the egocentric location of the pathetic fallacy—a central, foreground location turned into a prison of autobiographical confrontation by the reciprocal movement between self and landscape. It is as if, activating an interior with the false sympathy of the pathetic fallacy, he is afraid he will not be able to get out of the vacuum he has filled.[1]

What sends the inhabitant of the modern landscape to the background, where both knowledge and recognition are designed to fail, is the fear of the dissatisfied solipsist who, unhappy with the prospect of being thrown back on his own devices, his own autobiographical preoccupations, sees walls as

---

[1] John Rosenberg, in "Style and Sensibility in Ruskin's Prose," *The Art of Victorian Prose,* edited by George Levine and William Madden (New York, 1968), p. 197, has carefully examined Ruskin's meter and found, on occasions, a "cadence of enclosure."

neither cloistering structures for prayer nor fortifications for defense, but as a potential prison of pride. Walls threaten to contain more than they defend: ". . . only the walls with which they enclose themselves are those of pride, not of prayer" (xi, 223). Breeding self-consciousness without self-awareness, walls keep the inside from getting out, not the outside from getting in. And since this is the case, what lies inside must be refurbished as best as possible. If one is inside without prospect of finding an exit, then the inside must be made better than it was: "To cleanse ourselves of these 'cast clouts and rotten rags' is the first thing to be done in the court of our prison" (xi, 227).

Yet London, which is a foreground prison, a starting point far from the background or frontier, is beyond mere redecoration. Condensed space prevents movement. Simply, there is no room to operate. Inertia, dreaded in a transcendental landscape, prevails: "Give up all thoughts of work in London. You might as well work in mines or prisons" (xxxvii, 203). At the nation's center or foreground, thousands are "imprisoned by the English Minotaur of lust for wealth, and condemned to live, if it is to be called life, in the labyrinth of black walls, and loathsome passages between them, which now fills the valley of the Thames, and is called London . . ." (xxi, 104).

Occasionally, the inside is turned out, dimensions are inverted, and imprisonment is on the outside looking in: ". . . the precious moments were all thrown away in quarrelling across her, with him, about Neopolitan prisons. He couldn't see, as I did, that the real prisoners were the people outside" (xxxv, 428). But the inversion is play. Except as a later defense against the reflexive space of a failing distance or when he plays the role of a devouring parenthetical self, who, turning the "outside in," would take space for food, to be enclosed is to be trapped. Still, we know that to be enclosed with an exit, even if that exit is only a view, is desirable. A prison that is a vantage point is not a prison. But enclosed space, without a view, is. Death is an eye without desire—a disinterested eye with no prospect but the self-consciousness of autobiography: "I could not live any more in Park Street, with a dead brick wall opposite my windows" (xi, xxviii).

Another kind of death, which is the blindness of the Desiring Eyes, comes from that flatness considered desirable in the classical landscape. Now, flatness is a prison that is not Neapolitan: ". . . if the scenery be resolutely level, insisting upon the declaration of its own flatness in all the detail of it, it appears to me like a prison, and I cannot long endure it" (vi, 418). And that inability to "endure" is deadly: "I turned quite sick with longing this afternoon when I looked round and round the horizon and found not one rising ground to refresh the eye, or to relieve the dead flatness of country and emotion" (Diaries, p. 212). In the early entries of the *Diaries,* in which sight informs what amounts to a topographical morality play, the villain is precisely this flatness that is close to death. The "nasty flat kitchen-garden-ground" (*Diaries,* p. 141), attractive enough when the landscape possesses an animated interior that precludes either vertical or background interest, simply does not permit movement for the eye: "like a dead thing, flat in the sun" (*Diaries,* p. 134); "a dead green flat" (*Diaries,* p. 137); "Hence a dead flat" (*Diaries,* p. 139). And presumably, the artists best equipped to paint the topography of imprisonment are those of the "pure Dutch schools, or schools of the dead flats" (vi, 435).

Without even an option of movement, the "dead flats" become monotonous. Predictably, the landscape breeds claustrophobic recognition: "How every thing loses its delight with its novelty! that was a sensible dialogue with Lucian speaking of somebody's disgust with the eternal monotony of night and day" (*Diaries,* p. 119). As an ingredient of reflexive movement, the inability to make discriminations brings a homogeneity that is death in a transcendental landscape: "An uncommonly monotonous life I lead here. I hardly know one day from another" (*Diaries,* p. 214). And the familiarity that comes from monotony is responsible for an aspiration after what is not "here," but "there." As opposed to Ruskin as a child, who, sharing characteristics with the classical man, finds riches in proximity, the later Ruskin contaminates what is near by his very presence: "I am getting tired of Rome as I thought I should, and long for Venice and the Alps. When I get there I shall long for home; and when I get home, for Rome" (*Diaries,* p. 127). Longing for "there" is an act, not entirely effectual, directed against both monotony and recognition—the death of the Desiring Eyes. It is the beginning of a movement away from the space of autobiography, and the rekindling of optical desire.

If "monotony" is similar to "recognition," "novelty" is close to "surprise." And, as is the case with "surprise," the need for "novelty" swiftly impels the inhabitant through the transcendent landscape—a landscape in which what was once inside is now, having "withdrawn," outside. Essentially, standing still in a hollow landscape is as senseless as confronting the monotonous. Neither homogeneity nor inertia is a tolerable characteristic in a landscape that receives its only animation, its only "nerve," from an inadequate observer, an overblown first person: ". . . my pleasure was chiefly when I first got into beautiful scenery out of London. The enormous influence of novelty—the way in which it quickens observation, sharpens sensation, and exalts sentiment. . . . I find that by keeping long away from hills, I can in great part still restore the old childish feeling about them; and the more I live and work among them, the more it vanishes" (v, 369). Both "surprise" and "novelty," connected with the "infantine sight" of the "innocent eye," are also connected with "ignorance." Ruskin considers writing "an essay on the uses of ignorance, being much struck by the diminution which my knowledge of the Alps had made in my sublime impression of them . . ." (*Diaries*, p. 416).

But Ruskin's attitude towards the recognition of the familiar is subject to variation. Even while cultivating "ignorance" and "surprise," he can announce: "I am sick of strange places. I shall be so glad to get to Padua, and see something to remind me of old times" (*Diaries*, p. 176). With no apparent sense of inconsistency, he can say: "I never can enjoy a place till I come to it the second time" (*Diaries*, p. 165), and, at the same time, state: "Sketching all day at Itri. Disappointed with it—always am with second sights" (*Diaries*, p. 166). Ruskin, like Turner, would generally like to avoid "second sights" in favor of a "passive obedience to . . . first vision" (vi, 41). Yet, the ability to endure "second sights" that become monotonous is an indication of mental strength:

> . . . monotony is, and ought to be, in itself painful to us, just as darkness is . . . but the endurance of monotony has about the same place in a healthy mind that the endurance of darkness has: that is to say, as a strong intellect will have pleasure in the solemnities of storm and twilight, and in the broken and mysterious lights that gleam among them, rather than in mere brilliancy and glare, while a frivolous mind will dread the shadow and the storm . . . exactly in like manner a great mind will accept, or even delight in monotony which would be wearisome to an inferior intellect, because it has more patience and power of expectation, and is ready to pay the full price for the great future pleasure of change. (xi, 210–11)

Unless "monotony" is occasionally endured, change, or "novelty" becomes a worse "monotony." The "monotony" of "novelty" becomes the modern landscape inhabitant's final prison. Without even a view, it is a prison from which there is no escape: ". . . those who will not submit to temporary sameness, but rush from one change to another, gradually dull the edge of change itself, and bring a shadow and weariness over the whole world from which there is no more escape" (xi, 211).

In a world in which something of value, either above or outside, is beyond the frontier of perception, imprisonment becomes an agonizing parody of immanence. To be inside, without either an exit or the option of escape, is to be trapped with a self separated from what, like Ruskin's father, has "withdrawn" from the drawing room. The inside is a territory of the reflexive and the monotonous. It is a territory of autobiography at a time when either pseudonymity or invisibility is all that is desired.

The architecture and topography of containment, throwing the inhabitant back upon his own devices, are models of the enclosing mind. It is a mind that only accommodates the reflexive space leading to that self-consciousness which becomes autobiography. And thrown back upon the images of the self, Ruskin is disconcerted by portraiture:

> . . . when I got a sudden glimpse of myself, in the true shape of me, it was extremely startling and discouraging: . . . I had always been content enough with my front face in the glass, and had never thought of contriving vision of the profile. The cameo finished, I saw at a glance to be well cut; but the image it gave of me was not to my mind. . . . (xxxv, 280)

Finally, no image Ruskin gets of himself, except for the censored and distanced image in *Praeterita,* will be "to my mind." But the casual discomfiture that Ruskin feels about his portrait, unfiltered by the familiarity of "second sights," has implications that, going beyond individual response, involve the more general, modern landscape inhabitant: ". . . there cannot be anything more contrary than that principle of portraiture which prevails with us in these days, whose end seems to be the expression of vanity throughout . . . whence has arisen such a school of portraiture as must make the people of the nineteenth century the shame of their descendants, and the butt of all time" (iv, 193).

The potential self-portraitist in the Evangelical Ruskin rejects his subject matter—the distorted self in a condition of disequilibrium, a condition caused by transcendence in a world that is hollow except for its prisons and trapped emotions:

> . . . we come at last to set ourselves face to face with ourselves; expecting that in creatures made after the image of God, we are to find comeliness and completion more exquisite than in the fowls of the air and the things that pass through the paths of the sea.
>
> But behold now a sudden change from all former experience. No longer among the individuals of the race is there equality or likeness, a distributed fairness and fixed type visible in each; but evil diversity, and terrible stamp of various degradation: features seamed by sickness, dimmed by sensuality, convulsed by passion . . . well for us only, if, after beholding this our natural face in a glass, we desire not straighway to forget what manner of men we be. (iv, 176–77)

The same Ruskin who later uses his mnemonic powers of retrieval to construct autobiography in *Praeterita* now considers the advantages of forgetting the self-portraiture of the "natural face." Avoiding mirrors and portraiture, he would also avoid a philosophy that, as if situating the self at the focal point, he considers reflexive. He writes Frederic Harrison: "I can't think why you don't go on steadily in social reform, instead of writing Theology—or neology—or *me*-ology, for after all what is Positivism but the Everlasting Me?" (xxxvii, 480)

Imprisoned by designs of reflexivity that make portraiture as uncomfortable as autobiography, Ruskin, in characteristic fashion, links "*me*-ology" with topography, self with landscape. But in this case the linkage becomes a form of separation. Self excludes landscape. As focal point, "*me*-ology," returning more than it gives, excludes the possibility of the accurate perception of natural objects—a kind of perception that, as an act of self-objectification, can be a way out of the mind's prison. The obsession with the autobiographical variation of "*me*-ology"

> indicates that the people who practice it are cut off from all possible sources of healthy knowledge or natural delight; that they have wilfully sealed up and put aside the entire volume of the world, and have got nothing to dwell upon, but that imagination of the thoughts of their heart. . . . Over the whole spectacle of creation they have thrown a veil in which there is no rent. For them no star peeps through the blanket of the dark—for them neither their heaven shines nor their mountains rise—for them the flowers do not blossom—for them the creatures of field and forest do not live. They lie bound in the dungeon of their own corruption, encompassed only by doleful phantoms, or by spectral vacancy. (xvi, 265–66)

The imprisoning architecture of the mind, the "dungeon of . . . corruption," has a past extending back to a landscape history that is also topographical autobiography. To arrive at an intelligible examination of both the problems and resultant strategies of the imprisoned self, Ruskin's brief history of fences—structures indicating attitudes between self and world—must be examined.

At first, the medieval world is even more confining than that classical world constructed about its "essence of border." The remarkable feature of the central fifteenth-century castle or garden is the characteristic of "trimness," which is expressed by "the artist always dwelling especially on the fences; wreathing the espaliers indeed prettily with sweetbriar, and putting pots of orange-trees on the tops of the walls . . ." (v, 260). The medieval landscape is no longer an homogenized landscape of perpetual recognition, without the discriminations of continual surprise. Distinctions begin to emerge in the history of fences: "The four rivers are trenched and enclosed on the four sides, to mark that the waters which now wander in waste, and destroy in fury, had then for their principal office to 'water the garden' of God. The description is . . . sufficiently apposite and interesting as bearing upon what I have noted respecting the eminent *fence*-loving spirit of the medievals" (v, 261).

The organization and function of the medieval landscape recalls Ruskin's notion that the real prisoners are not inside, but outside

Neapolitan prisons. The purpose of the design of the medieval landscape is defensive, to keep the "outside" from getting "inside." What lies within is a sanctuary to be protected: ". . . the trouble and ceaseless warfare of the times having rendered security one of the first elements of the pleasantness, and making it impossible for an artist to conceive Paradise but as surrounded by a moat, or to distinguish the road to it better than by its narrow wicket gate . . ." (v, 260).

Still, the enclosure is not as final as it seems: the seeds for release are present. If the medieval man, rejecting all that is "rugged, rough, dark, wild, unterminated . . . as the domain of 'salvage men' and monstrous giants," admires all that is "tender, bright, balanced, enclosed, symmetrical," he admires the symmetrical design in a "free sense" (v, 257). The distinctions between "outside" and "inside" are not as rigid as they at first appear: "A Greek, wishing really to enjoy himself, shut himself into a beautiful atrium. . . . But a medieval knight went into his pleasance, to gather roses and hear the birds sing; or rode out hunting or hawking" (v, 250).

The medieval "essence of border," as opposed to the classical, is constructed to be overstepped. And not only is the borderline between "outside" and "inside" transgressed, but so, as the frontier is invaded and pushed back, is the borderline between "known" space and "unknown" space: ". . . their journeyings and pilgrimages became more frequent than those of the Greek, and the extent of ground traversed in the course of them larger . . ." (v, 253). The vertical equivalent of the frontier, altitude, is also explored, as the landscapes of Dante show: ". . . the second point which seems noteworthy is, that the flat ground and embanked trenches are reserved for the Inferno; and that the entire territory of the Purgatory is a mountain, thus marking the sense of that purifying and perfecting influence in mountains which we saw the medieval mind was so ready to suggest" (v, 272).

Yet what Ruskin calls "the crisis of change in the spirit of medieval art," which divides "the art of Christian times into two great masses— Symbolic and Imitative" (v, 262), is the result of the opening-up of landscape beyond the confining topography of fences. The act of transgression, which becomes the essential, late medieval movement, is offensive, one-way only—away from that architecture of fences, moats, and a "narrow wicket gate" supervised by a "watchful porter." Ruskin's medieval world is opened up by the introduction of space, by the "change from the golden background (characteristic of the finest thirteenth century work) and the coloured chequer (which in like matter belongs to the finest fourteenth) to the blue sky, gradated to the horizon . . ." (v, 262).

This "crisis of change," which occurs "*at once,* many manuscripts presenting in alternative pages, chequered background, and deep blue skies exquisitely gradated to the horizon" (v, 263), culminates in Turnerian topography, and a shift in the location of the inhabitant. As long as the emphasis is not on space and distance, but foreground, the landscape, performing services, is subservient to the self: ". . . in the distance are blue mountains, very far away, if the landscape is to be simply delightful; but brought near, and divided into quaint overhanging rocks, if it is intended to be meditative, or a place of saintly seclusion. But the whole of it always,— flowers, castles, brooks, clouds, and rocks,—subordinate to the human figures in the foreground, and painted for no other end than that of explaining their adventures and occupations" (v, 262). But the shift from "chequered background to sky background" (v, 262), with the introduction of space, signals a rearrangement of subordination between self and topography.

This is a shift that is not at first apparent. For along with the opening up of the world, the medieval man is permitted to conceive of a "perfect liberty" (v, 275), in a "terrestrial paradise where there had ceased to be fence or division" (v, 293)—a "perfect liberty" in which "the fencelessness and thicket of free virtue lead to the loving and constellated order of eternal happiness" (v, 275). But "perfect liberty" is not self-indulgence, or the subordination of everything to the central location of the self. Instead, the inhabitant of the Ruskinian, medieval landscape—a landscape of increasing dimensions and potential for an indulgence unfettered by fences or division—moves into a position of diminishing prominence: "Whatever virtue the pagan possessed was rooted in pride, and fruited with sorrow. It began in the elevation of his own nature; it ended but in the 'verde smalto'—the helpless green—of the Elysian fields. But the Christian virtue is rooted in self-debasement . . ." (v, 290). Ruskin takes Dante's example of Matilda, as contrasted to the activities of Rachel and Leah, in Canto xxvii of the *Purgatorio,* as the perfect model of medieval faith: "Observe: Leah gathers the flowers to decorate *herself,* and delights in *Her Own* Labour. Rachel sits silent, contemplating herself, and delights in her own image. These are the types of the Unglorified Active and Contemplative powers of Man. But Beatrice and Matilda are the same powers, Glorified. And how are they Glorified? Leah took delight in her own labour; but Matilda—'in operibus manuum Tuarum'—in *God's labour.* Rachel in the sight of her own face; Beatrice in the sight of *God's face"* (v, 278).

The passage of Dante that Ruskin calls "the most important, for our present purposes [the examination of medieval landscape] in the whole circle of poetry" (v, 280), substitutes for self-interest a concern for what lies outside a self whose mind can be a prison. This substitution is an equivalent to the opening up of the medieval world by the introduction of space, or the creation of a space that is not reflexive:

> . . . it [Dante's passage] contains the first great confession of the discovery by
> the human race (I mean as a matter of experience, not of revelation), that their
> happiness was not in themselves, and that their labour was not to have their
> own service as its chief end. It embodies in a few syllables the *sealing* difference
> between the Greek and the medieval, in that the former sought the flower and
> herb for his own uses, the latter for God's honour; the former, primarily and
> on principle contemplated Christ's beauty and the workings of the mind of
> Christ. (v, 280)

Both reflexive spaces and self-referring interests are replaced by spaces
without ends and interests not trapped "in themselves," in the "dungeon of
their own corruption." Instead, the interests are points of distant concern,
undefined by the classical man's arsenal of possessive pronouns. The
movement through the medieval landscape is outward bound, from the defensive architecture of the center, which is the habitation of the self and self-
interests, to the extensive, frontier spaces beyond.

CONVERGING ORTHOGONALS: EPISODES IN THE TRANSPARENT

Ruskin's history of fences places in perspective the position of the modern
man within his foreground "dungeon of corruption." In the modern landscape, the architecture of confinement is not a fortress, keeping the "outside" from getting "inside," but a prison, which keeps the "inside" within.
For a self who, although perhaps a writer of diaries, would prefer to have
any autobiographical impulses camouflaged, prison, which is a building of
self-consciousness, is the wrong place to be. If the movement through the
medieval landscape is outward bound, that movement is continued and
finished by the modern man, for whom close quarters, even what lies within
Edenic walls, constitute a prison. As opposed to the tactile apprehension
within the closed world by the classical man who, dealing with time as if it
were, in a recapitulation of Ruskin's own early autobiography, "tangible,"
the spatial penetration of an open-ended world is especially suited to the
qualifications of Ruskin's Desiring Eyes.

The act of penetrating space is a journey of perspective and focus. The
point of departure is the egocentric and potentially imprisoning foreground,
which, earlier, in Ruskin's historical and autobiographical past, was a
landscape of immanence—a landscape in which interiors did not function as
prisons. The point of disembarkation for the penetration of space is the ho-

rizon, the transcendental background of perception where the vanishing perspective eliminates autobiographical impulse.

Penetrating space depends upon a space that Wylie Sypher calls "perforated," a space of "shadow holes" or "funnels,"[2] like the space of Tintoretto, who was a favorite of Ruskin. The interior vacancy of the once animated objects is compensated for and matched by an exterior vacancy, by holes of perception. The topography of depth that emerges with the introduction of space is, first of all, one of transparency and vacancy. The *horror vacui* that culminated in an aesthetics of plenitude is transformed into a cult of Nothingness, as the self's mode of apprehension shifts from a proximate, foreground focus that is close to touching, to a distant focus, in which objects lose their bulk and plenitude.[3]

Ruskin approaches the movement towards frontier vacancy, which is the creation of recessional space, with disclaimers of its importance. Stereoscopic vision, creating depth, doubles more things than vision: "As for the loss of the one ray in the double focus, it is nothing. My mother had only one seeing eye for thirty years, and my two eyes see only double grief" (xxxvii, 602). And Leonardo, despite protestations, needs no more than single sight: "You will find Leonardo again and again insisting on the stereoscopic power of the double sight: but do not let that trouble you; you can only paint what you can see from one point of sight, but that is quite enough" (xx, 122). Unsurprisingly, the business of the painter, whose optical equipment is necessarily accurate, is to paint, if not see, with one eye. Ruskin, making no contribution to the study of optics, explains that the double vantage point of the stereoscopic effect cannot be accounted for by a double focal point within the painted picture:

> I am sorry to find a notion current among artists, that they can, in some degree, imitate in a picture the effect of the stereoscope, by confusion of lines. There are indeed one or two artifices by which, as stated in the text, an appearance of retirement or projection may be obtained, so that they partly supply the place of the stereoscopic effect, but they do not imitate that effect. The principle of human sight is simply this:—by means of our two eyes we literally see everything from two places at once: and, by calculated combination in the brain, of the facts of form so seen, we arrive at conclusions respecting the distance and shape of the object, which we could not otherwise have reached. But it is just as vain to hope to paint at once the two views of the object as seen

[2] Wylie Sypher, *Four Stages of Renaissance Style* (New York, 1955), p. 29.

[3] Ortega y Gasset, in his "Point of View in the Arts," is explicit: ". . . the object seen at close range acquires the indefinable corporeality and solidity of filled volume. . . . But this same object placed farther away, for distant vision, loses this corporeality, this solidity and plenitude." *The Dehumanization of Art and Other Writings on Art and Culture* (New York, 1956), pp. 102–103.

from these two places, though only an inch and a half distant from each other. With the right eye you see one view of a given object, relieved against one part of the distance; with the left eye you see another view of it, relieved against another part of the distance. You may paint whichever of those views you please; you cannot paint both. . . . You might just as well try to paint St. Paul's at once from both ends of London Bridge, as to realise any stereographical effect in a picture. (xv, 215)

Even perspective study, the two-dimensional translation of stereoscopic perception that creates a version of depth without breaking the rules of the single vantage and focal point, is approached with reluctance by Ruskin. For "when perspective was first invented, the world thought it a mighty discovery, and the greatest men it had in it were as proud of knowing that retiring lines converge, as if all the wisdom of Solomon had been compressed into a vanishing point . . . but now that perspective can be taught to any schoolboy in a week, we can smile at this vanity" (xi, 71). Turner, who extends Ruskin's own perceptions visually as well as mnemonically, "though he was professor of perspective to the Royal Academy, did not know what he professed, and never, as far as I remember, drew a single building in true perspective in his life; he drew them only with as much perspective as suited him . . ." (xv, 17). Turner's negligence is not something that Ruskin recommends. But while perspective should be treated with "common civility," the student, according to Ruskin, should "pay it no court" (xv, 17).

Yet Ruskin's reluctant approach to stereoscopics and perspective studies belies the obsessive organization of self and objects along, if not "converging perpendiculars,"[4] at least converging orthogonals—the location of the self on the edge of recessional space. Ruskin begins to promote a mathematical form of stereoscopic depth-perception that he calls "metric vision": ". . . besides this faculty of clear vision, you have to consider the faculty of metric vision. . . . You will find that it takes you months of labour before you can acquire accurate power, even of deliberate estimate of distances with the eye; it is one of the points to which, most of all, I have to direct your work" (xxii, 201–202). Furthermore, if Ruskin's mother requires

---

[4] The young Ruskin, as Kata Phusin, enters into a dispute with one "Candidus," in "The Architectural Magazine." Kata Phusin concludes: "Therefore, perpendiculars which are below the horizon converge to a point beneath his [the spectator's] feet; and perpendiculars about the horizon, to a point above his head. These two points, therefore, are points of sight on a vertical horizon, to which horizontal lines converge; and the distance between the spectator and the base of the perpendicular corresponds to the perpendicular distance between his eye and the commencement of the horizontal line. From all this, it appears that perpendiculars only appear to converge under peculiar circumstances, which can never be represented in a drawing" (i, 219).

only a single focus that does not perceive "double grief," Turner himself has been imprisoned in the "dungeon" of someone else's "corruption"—a dungeon without the option of stereoscopic escape into recessional space: ". . . shut up by one-eyed people, in a cave 'darkened with laurels' (getting no good but only evil, from all the fame of the great long ago)—he had seen his companions eaten in the cave by the one-eyed people . . ." (XIII, 136). The cannibalistic "one-eyed people" must either be avoided or, better, educated towards "double focus." Ruskin's Bible of Perception becomes his *Elements of Perspective.* The vantage point recommended for the reader of *Elements*—"When you begin to read this book, sit down very near the window. I hope the view out of it is pretty; but, whatever the view may be, we shall find enough in it for an illustration of the first principles of perspective" (xv, 241)—becomes the essential vantage point of the optical self, the Desiring Eyes seeking release from the blind or at best "one-eyed" dungeon of overbearing selfhood, the foreground dungeon of corrupt autobiography.

The perspective studies are a model of recessional space. The creation of a model is a selection of the organizing structures to be emphasized, and indicates the particular way the world is seen. Ruskin's worlds, both his model world and his actual world, are organized in three dimensions. He would compound recessional space in any way possible. But before he begins his escape into the recessional space beyond his window, an escape impelled by the intricate perspective diagrams of the *Elements,* Ruskin examines another method of creating penetrable space. He considers "aerial perspective":

> It is a favourite dogma among modern writers on colour that "warm colours" (reds and yellows) "approach," or express nearness, and "cold colours" (blue and grey) "retire," or express distance. So far is this from being the case, that no expression of distance in the world is so great as that of the gold and orange in twilight sky. Colours, as such are ABSOLUTELY inexpressive respecting distance. It is their quality (as depth, delicacy, etc.) which expresses distance, not their tint. . . . So that, on the whole, it is quite hopeless and absurd to expect any help from laws of "aerial perspective." (xv, 157, 158, 159)

But aerial perspective does not appeal to the Desiring Eyes. Tint will not create the third dimension. Another method must be explored. To prevent what Ruskin calls the "severe and painful intersection of near and distant lines" on canvas—an intersection that is impossible in nature—a selection of focus must be made:

> If all objects in a landscape were on the same plane, they should be represented on the plane of the canvas with equal distinctness because the eye has no

greater lateral range on the canvas than in the landscape, and can only command a point in each. But this point in the landscape may present an intersection of lines belonging to different distances,—as when a branch of a tree, or tuft of grass, cuts against the horizon: and yet these different distances cannot be discerned together: we lose one if we look at the other.

On the canvas the selection of focus, which is the selection of landscape, must be made deliberately, by the painter's brush:

> But on the canvas, as the lines of foreground and of distance are on the *same* plane, they *will* be seen together whenever they intersect, painfully and distinctly; and, therefore, unless we make one series, whether near or distant, obscure and indefinite, we shall always represent as visible at once that which the eye can only perceive by two separate acts of seeing . . . . Whenever, therefore, in a landscape, we look from the foreground to the distance, the foreground is subjected to two degrees of indistinctness: the *first*, that of an object laterally out of the focus of the eye; the second, that of an object *directly* out of the focus of the eye; being too near to be seen with the focus adapted to the distance. In the picture, when we look from the foreground to the distance, the foreground is subjected only to one degree of indistinctness, that of being out of the lateral range; for as both the painting of the distance and of the foreground are on the same plane, they are seen together with the same focus. Hence we must supply the second degree of indistinctness by slurring with the brush, or we shall have a severe and painful intersection of near and distant lines, impossible in nature. (III, 642–43)

The selection of a focus is the selection of foreground or background. The architect of topographical models cannot have both proximate landscape and distant and penetrable space. To prevent "painful intersection" between near and far, a choice must be made. This choice avoids the sense of repletion that comes from simultaneity of perception. Simply, if the artist cannot paint stereoscopically, with both eyes—"you might just as well paint St. Paul's at once from both ends of London Bridge"—neither can he paint both foreground and background in focus simultaneously:

> . . . if in a painting our foreground is anything, our distance must be nothing, and *vice versa*; for if we represent our near and distant objects as giving both at once that distinct image to the eye, which we receive in nature from each when we look at them separately; and if we distinguish them from each other only by the air tone and indistinctness dependent on positive distance, we violate one of the most essential principles of nature; we present that as seen at once which can only be seen by two separate acts of seeing, and tell a falsehood as gross as if we had represented four sides of a cubic object visible together. (III, 321)

But another kind of approach towards simultaneity is at work. The foreground is focally more exclusive than the background: to see with distant focus is to see more than with proximate focus. It is to see fewer distinctions, to make fewer retinal adjustments. Coloring optics with a political shade that Ruskin would not have considered, Ortega y Gasset instructively examines differences between proximate and distant focus in a way that would have nevertheless met with Ruskin's approval:

> Compare this [proximate vision] with distant vision. Instead of fixing a proximate object, let the eye, passive but free, prolong its line of vision to the limit of the visual field. What do we find then? The structure of our hierarchized elements disappears. The ocular field is homogeneous; we do not see one thing clearly and the rest confusedly, for all are submerged in optical democracy. Nothing possesses a sharp profile; everything is background, confused, almost formless. On the other hand, the duality of proximate vision is succeeded by a perfect unity of the whole visual field.[5]

The exploration of the proximate focus is a process of division and serialization. The movement towards the background, towards the options and vacancy of the frontier, is a movement that approaches a single unified vision—the vision of a single focus that, nevertheless, sees simultaneously. The movement of the Desiring Eyes towards the background is a movement towards a topography that is as homogeneous as the enclosed classical landscapes of history and autobiography. The background, which is the result of the opening up of a transcendental landscape, takes on characteristics of the immanent landscape, in which no discriminations are made. The immanent foreground has become the transcendent background. But now the landscape unity is always in the distance. It is only attainable through the distant vision of the Desiring Eyes:

> But, be it observed (and I have only to request that whatever I say may be tested by immediate experiment), the difference of focus necessary is greatest within the first five hundred yards; and therefore, though it is totally impossible to see an object ten yards from the eye, and one a quarter of a mile beyond it, at the same moment, it is perfectly possible to see one a quarter of a mile off, and one five miles beyond it, at the same moment. The consequence of this is, practically, that in a real landscape, we can see the whole of what would be called the middle distance and distance together, with facility and clearness; but while we do so, we can see nothing in the foreground beyond a vague and indistinct arrangement of lines and colours; and that if, on the contrary, we look at any foreground object, so as to receive a distinct impression of it, the distance and middle distance become all disorder and mystery. (III, 320–21)

---

[5] Ortega, p. 102.

More often than not, the topography to be sacrificed by Ruskin's ambitious optical traveler is the foreground that requires serial focus, the focus of division and perhaps hedges, for exploration. An artist like Copley Fielding, employing focal methods of propulsion perfected by Turner, can lure the potential traveler away from his initial vantage point into recessional space: "The spectator was compelled to go forwards into the waste of hills; there, where the sun broke wide upon the moor, he must walk and wander; he could not stumble and hesitate over the near rocks, nor stop to botanize on the first inches of his path" (III, 324). Still, Ruskin is neither Turner nor Turner as interpreted by Copley Fielding. There is always the problem of the antithetical ("their complete balance . . . [being] on opposite fulcra"). Between expeditions into recessional space, Ruskin, if not his optical traveler, stops both to "botanize" and "geologize."

Nevertheless, more characteristic than proximate examination, the examination of a divided foreground, is the creation and exploration of recessional space. The outward-bound impulse—which, unifying by distant focus a landscape structured upon discrimination, goes counter to the botanist's analytic process—is Ruskin's shaping impulse. Various topographical areas have various values. And what is further from the divided vantage point of a corrupt self—a vantage point requiring the greatest focal adjustment within the first five hundred yards—is necessarily better: ". . . to sink the distance for the foreground was comparatively easy; but it implied the partial destruction of exactly that part of the landscape which is most interesting, most dignified, and most varied; of all, in fact, except the mere leafage and stone under the spectator's feet" (III, 323). The "mere leafage and stone"—the materials of botany and geology that compose the near landscape which is neither "most interesting" nor "most dignified"—are sacrificed by Turner in order to do what the old landscape masters, who "*never* succeeded in truly representing space" (III, 323), could not:

> Turner introduced a new era in landscape art, by showing that the foreground might be sunk for the distance, and that it was possible to express immediate proximity to the spectator, without giving anything like completeness to the forms of the near objects. This, observe, is not done by slurred or soft lines (always the sign of vice in art,) but by a decisive imperfection, a firm, but partial assertion of form, which the eye feels indeed to be close home to it, and yet cannot rest upon, nor cling to, nor entirely understand, and from which it is driven away of necessity to those parts of distance on which it is intended to repose. (III, 323)

The exact medium through which the penetration of space occurs is significant. Contrary to the spaces of Gaspar Poussin, which are "laid on with a dead coat of flat paint" (III, 349), the model spaces of Ruskin are not made of pigment that is as "flat dead" as the claustrophobic landscape which, without altitude, confines the potential traveler to a flatness that is also a version of death: ". . . I remember Dickens notices the same truth, describing himself as lying drowsily on the barge deck, looking not at, but *through* the sky. And if you look intensely at the pure blue of a serene sky, you will see that there is a variety and fulness in its very repose. It is not flat dead colour, but a deep, quivering, transparent body of penetrable air . . ." (III, 347). The difference between Ruskinian space, as exemplified by Turner, and the space of the old masters, lies precisely in this point of penetrability: "It [Turner's painting] is a painting of the air, something into which you can see, through the parts which are near you, into those which are far off; something which has no surface and through which we can plunge far and farther, and without stay or end, into the profundity of space;—whereas, with all the old landscape painters except Claude, you may indeed go a long way before you come to the sky, but you will strike hard against it at last" (III, 348).

Claude's impenetrability is even more pronounced than the old masters', who at least conduct the optical traveler as far as the unyielding sky. Ruskin, reviving momentarily the competition that Turner established with Claude in Turner's *Liber Studiorum*, contrasts Turner's space with Claude's: ". . . observe how the eye is kept throughout on solid and retiring surfaces, instead of being thrown, as by Claude, on flat and equal edges. You cannot find a single edge in Turner's work; you are everywhere kept upon round surfaces, and you go back on these you cannot tell how, never taking a leap, but progressing imperceptibly along the unbroken back, till you find yourself a quarter of a mile into the picture . . ." (III, 491). And again, with Turner, as opposed to Claude,

> we are permitted to climb up the hill from town, and pass far into the mist along its top, and so descend mile after mile along the ridge to seaward, until without one break in the magnificent unity of progress, we are carried down to the utmost horizon. And contrast the brown paint of Claude, which you can only guess to be meant for rock or soil because it *is* brown, with Turner's profuse, pauseless richness of feature, carried through all the enormous space; the unmeasured wealth of exquisite detail, over which the mind can dwell, walk, and wander, and feast for ever, without finding one break in its vast simplicity, or one vacuity in its exhaustless splendour. (III, 467)

Turner and Claude operate in Ruskin's mind like allegorized figures, representing opposing ways of apprehending spaces.

The vacancy at the frontier becomes something other than nothing, as the optical traveler, penetrating space, moves into the background. Ruskinian space, which had been the diagrammatic, perspective space of the *Elements,* becomes as much an object as a conducting medium. But even as an object, space is still penetrable. The space "through which we can plunge far and farther, and without stay or end," becomes, when intensified, cloud, which contains a much overlooked quality—"the enormous retiring spaces of solid clouds" (III, 376). This condensed space is a kind of "absolute air" that relies upon a sense of going "through" to describe its function: "Observe above everything the varying indication of space and depth in the whole, so that you may look through and through from one cloud to another, feeling not merely how they retire to the horizon but how they melt back into the recesses of the sky; every interval being filled with absolute air, and all its spaces so melting and fluctuating . . ." (III, 365).

The intensified space of cloud, an object, is not yet a constricting object; it is not yet an object that causes the reflexive and claustrophobic movement of the later "Storm-Cloud." Turner's clouds, viscous, are composed of "absolute air" that, performing the same function as the earlier and more diffuse space of Turner, beckons the Desiring Eyes of the self in search of recessional space to "pass from cloud to cloud, from region to region, from first to second and third heaven . . . to walk through the passages of mist as they melt on the one hand into those stormy fragments of fiery cloud"— passages in which the traveler cannot find "an inch without air and transparency" (III, 383), without what amounts to a transparent and plenteous vacancy.

The process of penetration, which is an act of anonymity, not only takes the desiring optical traveler far into either model space or actual space, without map or guide, but loses him in the deep recesses of that space: ". . . and when we see that from his measureless distance up to the zenith, the whole sky is one ocean of alternate waves of cloud and light, so blended together that the eye cannot rest on one without being guided to the next, and so to a hundred more, till it is lost over and over again in every wreath" (III, 388). And just as the eye loses itself in a distance that is "measureless," so another aspect of the ambitious traveler, the imagination, is also happily lost as that traveler is invited to "plunge into the long vistas of immeasurable perspective, that guide back to the blue sky; and when he finds his imagination lost in their immensity . . . let him go to Claude, to Salvator, or to Poussin, and ask them for a like space, or like infinity" (III, 379).

Having left his divided foreground for either the unity of distant focus or the sense of anonymity in recessional space, the traveler occasionally comes back. The Desiring Eyes may be mastered by recessional space, almost defeated. Still, that mastery is close to a cleansing process. It is as if the burden of autobiography had been suitably diminished by a bath taken in the depths of space. Presumably, to return is to find not only a new vantage point, undivided by transcendental discrimination, but also a new self, perhaps the potential subject for autobiography. In any case, a return trip is always possible: "When, on the other hand, we take up such a sky as that of Turner's Rouen seen from St. Catherine's Hill, in the Rivers of France, and find, in the first place, that he has given us a distance over the hills in the horizon, into which when we are tired of penetrating, we must turn and come back again, there being not the remotest chance of getting to the end of it . . ." (III, 388).

THE ANNULLED SELF: LESS THAN NOTHING

After the penetration of transparent space by the Desiring Eyes, another strategy is developed to aid the escape from "*me*-ology." The model for this strategy might be the inversion of an optical image for the penetration of space: if, instead of allowing the traveler to penetrate space by looking through a "telescope glass, darkly . . . that reveals nebula beyond nebula, far and farther, and to no conceivable farthest" (xx, 171), one were to look through the other end of that telescope at the traveler, his magnitude and importance would be, at least optically, greatly diminished. Portraiture would be an impossibility. And, at least from another's point of view, the sense of overweening selfhood, which supplies the architectural energy for the dungeon of corruption, would be tamed. Ruskin's ploy, similar in effect to this optical inversion, is to situate the self before an object that, dwarfing the self in size or significance, establishes a relation of deliberate disequilibrium between self and observed object. The spectator, seeing much, becomes next to nothing in the process.

Ruskin's calculated humiliation is not far from what Amiel calls "cosmography." Georges Poulet, Amiel's interpreter, describes "cosmography" as a process of objectification: "What is it, to forget oneself in things? It is to turn one's curiosity towards the outside. The consciousness becomes pure consciousness of the eternal reality, the consciousness of objects without the intervention of the subject." Poulet continues his discussion of Amiel by describing a situation that is an exaggeration of Ruskin's own autobiographical vacillation: "It is surprising to discover that the human being who was later to manifest so much interest toward himself, he who was to consecrate all his thought to the elucidation of himself, begins by turning his back upon himself, by being entirely uninterested in himself."[6] Similarly, late in his career, but before the auto-

[6] Poulet, *The Metamorphoses of the Circle,* translated by Carley Dawson and Elliot Coleman (Baltimore, 1966), pp. 204–205.

biographical impulse is permitted full expression, Ruskin can say: ". . . from my youth up, I have been seeking the fame, and honouring the work, of others;—never my own. I first was driven into literature that I might defend the fame of Turner; since that day I have been explaining the power, or proclaiming the praise, of Tintoret,—of Luini,—of Carpaccio,—of Botticelli,—of Carlyle;—never thinking for an instant of myself . . ." (xxviii, 648).

Ruskin's concern with the self-opposing Other is connected with categories of "humility" and "pride." They represent the choice between the extensive and the reflexive. The choice between the two must be made, as Ruskin says,

> boldly and consciously, for one way or other it *must* be made. On the dark and dangerous side are set the pride which delights in self-contemplation—the indolence which rests in unquestioned forms—the ignorance that despises what is fairest among God's creatures. . . . And on the other side, is open to your choice the life of the crowned spirit, moving as a light in creation—discovering always—illuminating always, gaining every hour in strength, yet bowed down every hour into deeper humility. . . . (xvi, 292)

The choice must be made "boldly and consciously" because it is not an easy one, and "self-contemplation," that activity of the dungeon of corruption, is not readily banished. Attempting briefly to discriminate between varieties of self-annulment, Ruskin, in the "preface" to the rearranged second volume of *Modern Painters,* discards one form of self-annulment that had doubtless shaped his early attitudes: ". . . note well, that the terror of Eliphaz, the self-abhorrence of Job, the awe of Linnaeus, are all entirely distinct from the spurious and prurient self-condemnation which is the watchword of modern Protestantism" (iv, 5). That Ruskin would avoid "self-condemnation" does not mean he engages in congratulatory "self-contemplation." But, after the camouflaged and diary excursions into autobiography, Ruskin's own vacillations, which are variations of that optical shift between the objectifying Camera Lucida and the sympathetic, subjectifying Moral Retina, end, after all, in one sort of "self-contemplation"—that of an autobiography which is neither camouflaged nor private.

The subversive will towards "self-contemplation," a will that must be restrained before it creates a prison of the self, leads Ruskin to possess and dominate perceived objects in the same way he does that topography which is a version of autobiography: ". . . I feel in this walk, being somewhat tired, very forcibly again how much the power of nature depended upon the quantity of mind which one could give to her" (v, xix). And again: ". . . by throwing my mind full into the fence and field, as if I had nothing else but them to deal with, I found light and power and loveliness. . . . I felt the human soul was all—the subject nothing" (v, xix). But the way outside and beyond "self-contemplation"—a way that is apart from the penetration of space—is the establishment of the already mentioned relation of disequilibrium between self and object, in which the subject is "everything" and the human soul "nothing."

At times, "self-contemplation" is impossible because Ruskin ceases to exist—or, at least, ceases to act, control or animate, while confronting exterior objects: "Languidly, but not idly, I began to draw it [a "small aspen tree against the blue sky"]; and as I drew, the languor passed away: the beautiful lines insisted on being traced,—with weariness. More and more beautiful they became, as each rose out of the rest, and took its place in the air. With wonder increasing every instant, I saw that they 'composed' themselves, by finer laws than any known of men" (xxxv, 314). The artist as annulled self is a Ruskinian ideal that would permit the objects of nature to be seen without the self-contemplative bias that creates the landscape of the pathetic fallacy.

As an analogue for the ideal, annulled self, for whom self-referral is fortunately difficult, Scott, according to Ruskin, comes closer than Wordsworth, who, despite a passiveness that is "wise," has a "vague notion that nature would not be able to get on well without Wordsworth; and finds a considerable part of his pleasure in looking at himself as well as at her" (v, 343). Scott, who has some of the modesty of the optical self as Camera Lucida, combined with an affection that is beyond the emotive requirements of the lens, observes the objects of nature with a love that is "entirely humble and unselfish." Reducing the self to zero and beyond, he can say, " 'I, Scott, am nothing, and less than nothing; but these crags, and heaths, and clouds, how great they are, how lovely, how for ever to be beloved, only for their own silent, thoughtless sake!' " (v, 343) Like the self-abnegating tracer of aspens, Scott shrinks to "less than nothing." The dungeon of corruption does not exist for Scott's negative man.

Annulled, or at least with a portion of himself reduced to microscopic size, Scott cannot intrude into his own field of vision. If Scott does not entirely shrink out of the imprisoning structures of the self, he nonetheless establishes a relation between self and perceived object that results in the disequilibrium necessary to objectification: ". . . instead of making Nature anywise subordinate to himself, he makes himself subordinate to her— follows her lead simply—does not venture to bring his cares and thoughts into her pure and quiet presence . . ." (v, 341–42). The secondary magnitude and position of the artist, as well as the extensive design that must be the artist's concern, become part of a transition that moves with smooth, if submerged, coherence from the exhortation against reflexive space to the discovery and praise of space that is recessional. To be able to think of something other than the self is to be farsighted:

> He has only to ask himself whether he cares for anything except himself; so far
> as he does he will make a good picture; so far as he thinks of himself, a vile one.
> This is the root of the viciousness of the whole French school. Industry they have,
> learning they have, power they have, feeling they have, yet not so much feeling as
> ever to force them to forget themselves even for a moment; the ruling motive is
> invariably vanity, and the picture therefore an abortion.
>
> Returning to the pictures of the religious schools, we find that their open
> skies are also the highest value. . . . (III, 178)

Like space, nature, substituting complexity for recession, should provoke the self to look beyond the immediate, beyond the divided foreground of autobiography. To go to nature is to leave the egocentric baggage of the self behind. It is something the old landscape painters failed to do: "There is no evidence of their ever having gone to nature with any thirst, or received from her such emotion as could make them, even for an instant, lose sight of themselves . . ." (III, 169). It is precisely this, the ability to lose sight of oneself, that Ruskin never tires of praising. To lose sight of oneself is to become an invisible man. And only the invisible man is worthy of self-portraiture: ". . . the moment he [the artist] can make us think that *he* has done nothing, that nature has done all, that moment he becomes ennobled, he proves himself great. As long as we remember him, we cannot respect him. We honour him most when we most forget him. He becomes great when he becomes invisible" (III, 470). Lost with objectifying affection, which is a form of "unselfish sympathy" (IV, 152), the invisible self is found.

That "unselfish sympathy" permits an affiliation with the Other, the perceived object, which is not an intrusion. If the invisible self, reduced to "less than nothing," does not shrink out of both sight and the dungeon of corruption, that self can, by assuming a role of allegorized Nothing—a role in which there can be no pathetic fallacy, no false sympathy—exit by a selfless affiliation. Possession occurs without either animation or distortion: ". . . all egotism, and selfish care, or regard are, in proportion to their constancy, destructive of imagination; whose play and power depend altogether on our being able to forget ourselves and enter, like possessing spirits, into the bodies of things about us" (IV, 287).

The forgetful self, at once active and passive, enters the perceived object only as a negative factor:

> So, in the higher or expressive part of the work, the whole virtue of it depends
> on his being able to quit his own personality, and enter successively into the

hearts and thoughts of each person; and in all this he is still passive: in gathering the truth he is passive, not determining what the truth to be shall be, and in the after vision he is passive . . . .

It follows from all this, evidently, that a great idealist never can be egotistic. The whole of his power depends upon his losing sight and feeling of his own existence, and becoming a mere witness and mirror of truth, and a scribe of visions,—always passive in sight, passive in utterance. . . . (v, 125)

In the act of reading the great word-masters, whose power is also their "self-annihilation," annulled identities are telescoped together into multiplied Nothingness. The reader forgets himself, as he becomes part of a writer, who is himself invisible: "We see as he sees, but we see not him. We become part of him, feel with him, judge, behold with him: but we think *of* him as little as of ourselves." The great writer, involved in this "self-annihilation" that is, in fact, an annihilation of selves, transports the negative identities of the reader, as well as himself, away from anything that would call attention to his idiosyncrasies, "guiding the mind far from himself, to the beauty that is not of his creation, and the knowledge which is past his finding out" (iii, 23).

The self-annulment that is achieved through disequilibrium between the observer and his focal point is the result of the observer's advertised inadequacies: "I have never succeeded . . ."; "Nor can I explain . . ."; "I am for the present utterly unable to speak respecting this matter, and must pass it by, in all humility"; "I have learned during the sixteen years to say little where I said much, and to see difficulties where I saw none" (vii, 162–64). One of the effects that contributes to Ruskin's required inadequacy is "the Sensation of Power," which is "in proportion to the apparent inadequacy of the means to the end; so that the impression is much greater from a partial success attained with slight effort, than from a perfect success attained with greater proportional effort" (iii, 118). Size, a dimension of power, also defies Ruskin's comprehension. Instead of enjoying the hubris of the animating observer, as he throws his "mind full into the fence and field, as if I had nothing else but them to deal with," the inadequate observer is humiliated before mountains: "I have got rather beaten again by those big Alps—it is very ungenerous of them to take such advantage of their size. But I will take the conceit out of them yet, some day" (xxxvi, 176).

Size made transparent and extended is the recessional space that permits a way out of the enclosed structures that intensify selfhood. Finally, the most characteristic lens for Ruskin's Desiring Eyes is neither the Camera Lucida nor the Moral Retina but the telescope that is involved in the penetration of space: "The artist is a telescope—very marvellous in himself." But if the artist is a telescope, he is a telescope who would best be forgotten:

> But I think, on the whole, the stars are the principal part of the affair. The artist, however, is, when good, a telescope not only of extra-ordinary power, but one which can pick out the best stars for you to look at—display them to you in the most instructive order—and give you a mute but, somehow or other, intelligible lecture on them. We thus become of considerable importance, but may always be dwarfed in a moment by the question—Suppose there were no stars? The best artist is he who has the clearest lens, and so makes you forget every now and then that you are looking thro' him. (xxxvi, 213)

The telescopic artist, seeing far, sees through vacancy instead of seeing vacancy itself. There is "numerical superiority" in the background. Turner's background distances, beyond comprehension, are the distances of plenitude. Like the Alps, Turner's abundant distances miniaturize the self: "And now, take up one of Turner's distances. . . . Abundant beyond the power of the eye to embrace or follow, vast and various beyond the power of the mind to comprehend . . ." (iii, 335). Still, the plenitude that cannot be embraced is not always in the actual distance. Ruskin discovers a focus that perceives a model distance, creating an immediate mystery that annuls the self as effectively as anything the telescopic artist might discern:

> Nor is this mode of representation true only with respect to distances. Every object, however near the eye, has something about it which you cannot see, and which brings the mystery of the distance even into every part and portion of what we suppose ourselves to see most distinctly. Stand in the Piazza di San Marco, at Venice, as close to the church as you can, without losing sight of the top of it. Look at the capitals of the column on the second story. You see that they are exquisitely rich, carved all over. Tell me their patterns: you cannot. Tell me the direction of a single line in them: you cannot. (iii, 337)

Annulled in firm negatives—"you cannot"—the self is defined by what it cannot do. But with no "*me*-ology," the self is no longer held prisoner in the dungeon of corruption.

THE MODERN BACKGROUND: ADJACENT SPACES, ADJACENT TIMES

With the idea, whether finally fallacious or not, that the "divinity is . . . separated from the life of nature; and imagining our God upon a cloudy throne, far above the earth, and not in the flowers or waters" (v, 231), the focus of attention has turned from that centrally located and ultimately imprisoning foreground, to the frontier or background. The inhabitant of the modern landscape, which is both open and empty, has been left with a sense of spatial and temporal immediacy that fails to serve his need for options and annulment. The creation and penetration of recessional space is in response to this need, which is, essentially, a need to imitate the "withdrawal" of Ruskin's father from the enclosed space of that early "withdrawing room." The dissatisfaction with a vantage point that has become a starting point is an analogue for the modern man's response to the most available tense, which, immediately surrounding the self, is the tense of the unannulled self. If the modern man observes himself in magnifying mirrors—"we, the living occupy a space of too large importance and interest in our own eyes"—those mirrors are fixtures in a building that is only for transients: ". . . we look upon the world too much as our own, too much as if we had possessed it and should possess it for ever, and forget that it is a mere hostelry, of which we occupy the apartments for a time, which others better than we have sojourned in before . . ." (III, 203).

Ruskin, whose complex and contradictory attitudes towards the present tense can only be touched upon here, is reluctant to jump into that Heraclitian flux which fascinates Pater, who, from multiple vantage points of extreme proximity, discriminates sensations at microscopic intervals. The already magnified present tense of Pater is expanded even further by the very number of his discriminations:

> Every moment some form grows perfect in hand or face; some tone on the hills or the sea is choicer than the rest; some mood or passion or insight or intellectual excitement is irresistibly real and attractive to us,—for that moment only. Not the fruit of experience, but experience itself, is the end. A counted number of pulses only is given to us of a variegated dramatic life. How may we see in them all that is to be seen in them by the finest senses? How shall we pass most swiftly from point to point, and be present always at the focus where the greatest number of vital forces unite in their purest energy?[7]

With psychic requirements different from Pater's, Ruskin agrees that the magnified present, in which we "occupy a space of too great importance and interest," is, as the tense of unannulled selves, the prevalent tense: "And we find that whereas all the pleasure of the medieval was in *stability, definiteness,* and *luminousness,* we are expected to rejoice in darkness and triumph in mutability; to lay the foundation of happiness in things which momentarily change or fade; and to expect the utmost satisfaction and

---

[7] Walter Pater, "Conclusion," in *The Renaissance* (Library Edition, 1910), p. 236.

instruction from what it is impossible to arrest, and difficult to comprehend" (v, 317). But Ruskin, given the option of a different landscape, which is to say a landscape that is distinctly old-fashioned, would prefer the stability of a single vantage point, a vantage point as homogeneous as the background perceived by the distant focus of the Desiring Eyes (past the "first five hundred yards")—a vantage point, finally, that would yield stable perception, instead of the perpetual adjustment of an unannulled self requiring perpetual relativistic accommodation. Thus Ruskin complains about what comes too easily:

> . . . the easily encouraged doubt, easily excited curiosity, habitual agitation, and delight in the changing and marvellous, as opposed to the old quiet serenity of social custom and religious faith,—is again defined in those few words, the "dethroning of Jupiter," the "coronation of the whirlwind."

> Nor of whirlwind merely, but also of darkness or ignorance respecting all stable facts. (v, 318)

Yet Ruskin's apparent fear that the Herclitian stream might overflow its banks, or that the magnified present—the time that Ruskin describes as occupying the hostelry of history—might expand until it excludes both past and future, does not prove to be well-founded. For like the false bottom of a trunk, or a secret cellar under time's hostelry, a past lurks beneath that swollen present. But unlike both false bottom and secret cellar, the past tense is public—the product of a specious and collective daydream: "Again: as another notable weakness of the age is its habit of looking back, in a romantic and passionate idleness, to the past ages, not understanding them all the while, nor really desiring to understand them, so Scott gives up nearly the half of his intellectual power to a fond, yet purposeless, dreaming over the past, and spends half his literary labours in endeavours to revive it, not in reality, but on the stage of fiction . . ." (v, 336–37). The conjuring up of a fictional history is the result of an attempt to compensate for a present tense that, although overblown, larger than life, is inadequate to the self's emotional requirements.

Those needs are for a tense and landscape outside the boundaries of immediacy. Ruskin advertises the failures that lie close at hand. Like the "useful truths" that are "biped," antithetical structures are required. If the modern man is unable, for one reason or another, to penetrate space, to get to adjacent locations, he can at least import the antithetical. In the same way that he steals his cousin's letter space, Ruskin can raid the hostelry of history. But even if the furnishings are authentic, there are problems that the modern man, who is by nature an optical traveler, plunging along converging orthogonals, exporting himself rather than importing fittings of the past, does not face:

> . . . while we yield to the present fashions, or act in accordance with the dullest modern principles of economy and utility, we look fondly back to the manners of the ages of chivalry, and delight in painting to the fancy, the fashions we pretend to despise, and the splendours we think it wise to abandon. The furniture and personages of our romance are sought, when the writer desires to please most easily, in the centuries which we profess to have surpassed in everything. . . . (v, 325–26)

Bad faith is in operation—a refusal to recognize that the hostelry's historical furnishings cannot be integrated with the inhabitant's foreground. Followed by deceit, it is a split between aspects of the self. The fradulence reduces at once to the inability of the modern man to face his own reflection, to engage in the right kind of portraiture—"well for us only, if, after beholding this our natural face in a glass, we desire not straightway to forget what manner of men we be" (IV, 177)—while, at the same time, maintaining the certainty of his own superiority over those who have preceded him. His superiority is borne out of a multiple and relativistic perspective that is without a vantage point of elevation sufficient to include past and future tenses in relation to both the present and the self. The proximate and multiple perspectives—Pater's passing "swiftly from point to point . . . present always at the focus where the greatest number of vital forces unite"—permit a parcelling of unintegrated perception that allows the modern man to function simultaneously with dual values: "All other nations have regarded their ancestors with reverence as saints or heroes; but have nevertheless thought their own deeds and ways of life the fitting subjects for their arts of painting or of verse. We, on the contrary, regard our ancestors as foolish and wicked, but yet find our chief artistic pleasure in descriptions of their ways of life" (v, 326).

One who is guilty of this split into parts, or better, halves, is the Scott who "gives up nearly the half of his intellectual power to a fond, yet purposeless, dreaming over the past," attempting to revive that past "not in reality, but on the stage of fiction." Because of this, Ruskin is compelled to point out: "The excellence of Scott's work is precisely in proportion to the degree in which it is sketched from the present nature" (v, 337). But, large and inclusive, Scott's "present nature" is not the swollen, overblown present of the reflexive self. Rather, "present nature" is both a mnemonic and prefigurative structure: for, "dear to Scott," Nature contains "those remains or memories of the past, which he cannot find in the cities," and permits Scott to consider the future, as a tense for possible revelation of the past, by giving "hope of Praetorian mound or knight's grave, in every green slope and shade of its desolate places" (v, 345). Involvement with "present nature" neither leaves the modern man trapped within a claustrophobic present between the extensive tenses of the past and future, nor forces him to summon, as an antithetical *mise en scène,* the furnishings of the past.[8] "Here," Scott's "present nature" offers a way out—a way "there."

Shifting from tense to topography, it is apparent that the problems of proximity have been worked out more clearly spatially then temporally. But then Ruskin's instincts are to spatialize even his language. And the problems, the original models for the problems, are spatial. At Herne Hill, time is "tangible" only because objects in space are not. But while spatial designs are clearer than the temporal counterparts (and we recall that the two sets of designs are rarely synchronized), they are not without intricacy. If Ruskin's optical traveler, impelled by the desire of his farsighted eyes, is involved in the telescopic penetration of space, he is also involved in a microscopic attention to foreground: "With this romantic love of beauty, forced to seek in history, and in external nature, the satisfaction it cannot find in ordinary life, we mingle a more rational passion, the due and just result of newly awakened powers of attention. Whatever may first lead us to the scrutiny of natural objects, that scrutiny never fails of its reward" (v, 326).

Still, riding converging orthogonals, Ruskin would just as soon sacrifice the foreground, as "botanize" over it: ". . . the sky is considered of so much importance, that a principal mass of foliage, or a whole foreground, is unhesitatingly thrown into shade merely to bring out the form of a white cloud" (v, 317). And if he sees this sacrifice as "a type of subjection of all plain and positive fact, to what is uncertain and unintelligible" (v, 319), he can nevertheless admire the Venetians, who threw more than a "principal mass of foliage" into shade for the sake of recessional space: overcome by the "splendour of the sky itself," they annihilated the ostensible focal point, "sacrificing . . . their subject to the passion of its distance" (iv, 85).

Ruskin's critics, unable to accommodate apparent contradiction, attacked him for what they considered to be his inconsistency in admiring both the foregrounds of Millais and the distances of Turner (v, liii). But, in fact, Turner's distances are executed in the same way as his foregrounds: ". . . these modulations are countless; heaving here, now breaking; giving, in fact to the foreground of this universal master precisely the same qualities which we have before seen in his hills . . ." (iii, 486). And depth

---

[8] An early, simplified declaration, perhaps too much to the point, cannot be called entirely characteristic: ". . . it is evident that the chief feeling induced by woody country is one of reverence for its antiquity. There is a quiet melancholy about the decay of the patriarchal trunks . . . and the whole character of the scene is calculated to excite conservative feeling. The man who could remain a radical in a wood country is a disgrace to his species" (i, 69).

can be created by attending to foreground, not sacrificing it: "The introduction of the two boats in front is interesting, as an example of the way in which depth may be given to a picture by the perspective lines of its foreground objects. Remove these two boats, and the town at once loses all its distance . . ." (xiii, 199). Ruskin's attitude towards foregrounds and the backgrounds of recessional space cannot be reduced to formula. Still, the prevalent bias is undisguised.[9] Those who do not feel this passion for recessional space are artists who, having "less exalted feeling than the others," may either, like Titian, overpower their "silvery distances with a foreground splendour," or, like Veronese, sacrifice those distances "to a luscious fulness of colour . . ." (iv, 86).

The translation from the world of the canvas, with its manipulated foregrounds and backgrounds, to an actual geography, is the work of someone who travels by other locomotion than that provided by following plunging orthogonals. But translation, suggesting that the canvas world comes before what it imitates or distorts, is perhaps not the right word: like the relation between sight and memory, Ruskin's movement between canvas and actual topography is reciprocal, each landscape supporting and informing its counterpart.

In any case, here is Ruskin's continental traveler describing a foreground that is actual. And without extensive space, it is a landscape that, like the classical landscape, can be defined mainly in negatives:

> England is a country whose every scene is in miniature. Its green valleys are not wide; its dewy hills are not high; its forests are of no extent. . . . Its champaigns are minutely chequered into fields: we can never see far at a time; and there is a sense of something inexpressible, except by the truly English word "snug," in every quiet nook and sheltered land. The English cottage, therefore, is equally small, equally sheltered, equally invisible at a distance. (i, 13–14)

The traveler's foreground is a biedermeier landscape of cozy miniatures. It is a home space—a divided vantage point—in which the inhabitants "can never see far at a time," and the cottages are "equally invisible at a distance." On the other hand, the continental traveler's distant landscape, or more accurately, middle-distant landscape, "comfortless" and "of a higher order," is a landscape of retiring spaces, in which vistas can be ob-

---

[9] The bias is, in fact, everywhere apparent. If the selfhood of the optical traveler is purged by the penetration of space, the colors of the painter of recessional space are also purged of impurities: "There is, however, I think, one law about distance, which has some claims to be considered a constant one: namely, that dulness and heaviness of colour are more or less indicative of nearness. All distant colour is *pure* colour: it may not be bright, but it is clear and lovely, not opaque nor soiled; for the air and light coming between us and any earthy or imperfect colour, purify or harmonise it . . ." (xv, 158).

served from any vantage point:

> But France is a country on a large scale. Low but long, hills sweep away for miles into vast uninterrupted champaigns: immense forests shadow the country for hundreds of square miles, without once letting through the light of day . . . there are no fences; we can hardly place ourselves in any spot where we shall not see for leagues around; and there is a kind of comfortless sublimity in the size of every scene . . . but we shall see, presently, that it can arouse feelings which, though they cannot be said to give it sublimity, yet are of a higher order than any which can be awakened at the sight of the English cottage. (i, 14)

The French middle distance, as opposed to the "chequered" English foreground, is a landscape of liberty, without fences, like the late medieval landscape that, breaking with the early, enclosed landscape of "chequered background," anticipates the modern, open topography: "The next thing that will strike us . . . ," Ruskin announces in "Of Modern Landscape," "is the love of liberty. Whereas the medieval was always shutting himself into castles, and behind fosses, and drawing brickwork neatly, and beds of flowers primly, our painters delight in getting to the open field and moor, abhor all hedges and moats" (v, 319). The love of liberty that is evident in the modern landscape, which is a landscape with a distance (not the chequered foreground of an England without vistas), manifests itself in other kinds of escape from enclosure or domination: ". . . and carrying the love of liberty even to license, and the love of wildness even to ruin, [the inhabitants of the modern landscape] take pleasure at last in every aspect of age and desolation which emancipates the objects of nature from the governments of men" (v, 319–20).

For Ruskin, the love of liberty can easily be carried to excess. Yet the continental traveler's foreground does not possess that temporal liberation from the "governments of men" even in moderation. England, the traveler's starting point, as he moves towards adjacent spaces, is the landscape of the present tense:

> England is a country of perpetually increasing prosperity and active enterprise; but, for that very reason, nothing is allowed to remain till it gets old. Large old trees are cut down for timber; old houses are pulled down for the materials; and old furniture is laughed at and neglected. Everything is perpetually altered and renewed by the activity of invention and improvement. The cottage, consequently, has no dilapidated look about it; it is never suffered to get old; it is used as long as it is comfortable, and then taken down and rebuilt; for it was orginally raised in a style incapable of resisting the ravages of time. (i, 15)

On the other hand, the middle distance of France offers alternative landscape tenses:

> that of the old pedigreed population, which preserves unlimitedly; and that of
> the modern revolutionists, which destroys unmercifully . . . little is renewed:
> there is little spirit of improvement. . . . The French cottage, therefore, is just
> such as we should have expected from the disposition of its inhabitants . . . all
> tell the same tale of venerable age, respected and preserved, till at last its di-
> lapidation wears an appearance of neglect. (i, 15)

It is the French cottage, preserved, telling a "tale of venerable age," rather than the destroyed fragments, beyond ruins, of the revolutionists, that is characteristic of the middle distance. As the continental traveler leaves the foreground, journeying towards what is the painter's background, he is also leaving the present tense and moving backwards in time. The penetration of space, which will be completed in the future, is the penetration of past tenses. Going forwards, the traveler, aware of history, is going backwards.

The spaces next to the middle distance, even further removed from the initial vantage point, is the landscape of the background or frontier. As opposed to the "serene fields and skies of medieval art," from which Ruskin's reader is roughly manipulated in the sentence that begins the "Of Modern Landscape" chapter—"We turn our eyes, therefore, as boldly and as quickly as may be"—the background is a landscape of magnitude and exaggeration. If, as we have seen, the classical man "dwells thus delightedly on all the *flat* bits" (v, 238), he is not alone. For not only are the Dutch painters "perfectly contented with the flat fields and pollards" (v, 238), but also Shakespeare "never speaks of mountains with the slightest joy, but only of lowland flowers, flat fields" (v, 238). Yet the modern man prefers vertical to horizontal lines: "Some few of them [modern painters] remain content with pollards and flat land; but these are always men of third-rate order; and the leading masters, while they do not reject the beauty of the low lands, reserve their highest powers to paint Alpine peaks . . ." (v, 320).

Essentially, what Ruskin calls "the rectitude of the verticals" (i, 238) is in operation, shaping distant design. In the background, there is no place for the transcendental impulse to be satisfied, no place to follow the perspective of "withdrawal" but upwards: "Throughout the extent of mountain, not one horizontal line, nor an approach to it, is discernible" (iii, 433). In an age in which "the admiration of mankind is found . . . to have in great part passed from men to mountains" (v, 329), Ruskin, even as a child requesting that "two rounded hills, as blue as my shoes," be included in the background of an early venture into portraiture, "had already generally connected the idea of distant hills with approach to the extreme felicities of life" (xxviii, 273). Facing the painted image of himself, the child, anticipating the requirements of the man, places potential "felicities" on a vertical axis.[10]

The most satisfactory landscape, for the requirements of the modern man who has become a continental traveler, is a landscape constructed about recessional space in which distance is combined with memory, space that will be explored in the future with the past tense: ". . . putting Lincolnshire, Leicestershire, and one or two such other perfectly flat districts aside, there is not an English county which I should not find entertainment in exploring the crossroads of, foot by foot; yet all my best enjoyment would be owing to the imagination of the hills, colouring, with their far-away memories, every lowland stone and herb . . ." (vi, 419). Ruskin, executing a fancy step that is like Scott's, with his "present nature" containing "hope of Praetorian mound," compounds "felicities" by going forwards, impelled by the "imagination of the hills," in order to go backwards, sent by "faraway memories."

In the forward movement from foreground and the backward release from the present tense, a future tense, reluctantly faced at times, is greeted with eagerness because of potential:

> There is not a wave of the Seine but is associated in my mind with the first rise of the sandstones and forest pines of Fontainebleau; and with the hope of the Alps, as one leaves Paris with the horses' heads to the southwest, the morning sun flashing on the bright waves at Charenton. If there be *no* hope or association of this kind, and if I cannot deceive myself into fancying that perhaps at the next rise of the road there may be seen the film of a blue hill in the gleam of sky at the horizon, the landscape, however beautiful, produces in me even a kind of sickness or pain. . . . (vi, 419)

Without the future tense that has the potential for either vertical or mnemonic "felicities," the traveling man is trapped without "hope" or "association," on a horizontal plane that forces him back, in "sickness and pain," into the dungeon of corruption that has been expanded to include both topography and tense as extensions of the self, of "*me*-ology."

But in a period of transcendence, the potential of rising ground, to be approached in a future tense, can carry a desiring observer, activated by the "rectitude of the verticals," away from the contamination of "*me*-ology." The experience of rising ground hurries Ruskin and his observer towards

[10] This discussion of Ruskin's "rectitude of the verticals" does not pretend to exhaust the subject of altitude in a transcendent topography. The subject may not require an enormous amount of elucidation. For a general discussion of altitudinal obsession and the aesthetics of the infinite see Marjorie Hope Nicolson's *Mountain Gloom and Mountain Glory* (Ithaca, 1959).

"felicities" that are heavenly by carrying them "unawares higher and higher . . . until, when we are all but exhausted with endless distance, the mountains make their last spring, and bear us, in that instant of exertion, halfway to heaven" (III, 468). As the traveler is catapulted towards heaven, his hope is prospective—the hope of a prolonged future that will be, finally, beyond tense. Still, it is in the retrospective act of autobiography that Ruskin describes the almost religious reactions of the young continental traveler to his first trip to the frontier, where the dimensions of "withdrawal" are compounded as background meets verticality:

> It is not possible to imagine, in any time of the world, a more blessed entrance into life, for a child of such a temperament as mine. True, the temperament belonged to the age: a very few years—within the hundred—before that, no child could have been born to care for mountains, or for the men that lived among them. . . . But for me, the Alps and their people were alike beautiful in their snow, and humanity; and I wanted, neither for them nor myself, sight of any thrones in heaven but the rocks. . . . (XXXV, 115–16)

Carrying the continental traveler "halfway to heaven," those mountains, once either despised or considered unremarkable, have now become substitutes for "thrones in heaven." The background landscape, exaggerated even as the divided foreground is miniaturized, either permits an approach to heaven, or, if that is not enough, if the intervening space is impenetrable, becomes a replacement for what was once inside but what has now withdrawn—a principle of divine animation that, apparently "separated from life of nature," is imagined by the modern man to be on a precarious seat, a "cloudy throne, far above the earth, and not in the flowers or waters" (V, 231).

POTENTIAL TRAVEL AND OPTIONAL SPACES

But, finally, the traveler, no matter how desirous his eyes are, may not be a traveler after all. The traveler may find that at heart, if not in his eyes, he is a homebody. He may come to feel, despite his high esteem for the background, that there is no reason to go anywhere. In the same way that stereoscopic focus creates a recessional space that the traveler can penetrate, so another kind of double focus answers the needs of the potential traveler who stays home. It is a double focus of options, of alternative and complementary spaces that is serviceable only as long as a choice is not made, only as long as the option of the background remains available. Simply, what this means is that the foreground is not felt to be claustrophobic if there is a way out: "Neither will any amount of beauty in nearer form make us content to stay with it, so long as we are shut down to that alone; nor is any form so cold or so hurtful but that we may look upon it with kindness, so only that it rise against the infinite hope of light beyond . . . " (IV, 83).

In this double focus that accommodates optional spaces, both the foreground and the background are highlighted. And the highlighting of either territory elicits a pleasurable response. Still, the focus is characteristically undemocratic. The highlighting of the foreground emphasizes that "tangible present" which, when the divinity has withdrawn to his "cloudy throne," fails to appeal to instincts that are spiritual. But the background, removed from "animal and present life," suggests a future that will be both spiritual and memorable:

> Whatever beauty there may result from the effects of light on foreground objects . . . there is yet a light which the eye invariably seeks with a deeper feeling, I say, not perhaps more acute, but having a spiritual hope and longing less for animal and present life. . . . I am willing to let it rest on the determination of every reader, whether the pleasure which he has received from these effects of calm and luminous distance be not the most singular and memorable of which he has been conscious. . . . (IV, 79–80)

Nevertheless, all distances are not "calm and luminous." And there are landscape painters, capable of imposing preference, painting what they want to see, who do not illuminate their backgrounds. Separating painters into those who employ light backgrounds and those who employ dark backgrounds, Ruskin is separating the sacred from the profane, and—with the single exception of Rembrandt, whom Ruskin, as we shall see, is compelled to attack because of a failure of distance that arrives with the inversion of perspective—the intelligent from the ignorant:

> . . . I know not any truly great painter of any time, who manifests not the most intense pleasure in the luminous space of his background, or who ever sacrifices this pleasure where the nature of his subjects admits of its attainment; as, on the other hand, I know not that the habitual use of dark background can be shown as having ever been coexistent with pure or high feeling, and, except in the case of Rembrandt (and then under peculiar circumstances only), with any high power of intellect. (IV, 81–82)

In order to go nowhere, the traveler who would keep his travel potential and conditional must have the option of an exit, a way out. Reflexive space is a burden that cannot be tolerated. But claustrophobia can be tamed by alternatives. The mere thought or glimpse of a distance suggesting both "elbow room" and an elevating future, which will become memorable, is enough: ". . . the painter of interiors feels like a caged bird, unless he can throw a window open, or set the door ajar; the landscapist dares not lose himself in forest without a gleam of light under its farthest branches, nor venture out in rain unless he may cling to some closing gap of variable blue above" (IV, 82). Room enough in which to operate is the antiautobiographical room of anonymity.

The transcendental impulse, which is a desire for anonymity, must be taken into account in a canvas space that Ruskin considers an ideal model for spatial arrangements. And that impulse, which cannot be satisfied in the immediacy of either a foreground or a present tense, is activated by a need to escape from what lies close to the self:

> The absolute necessity, for such I indeed consider it, is of no more than such a mere luminous distant point as may give to the feelings a species of escape from all the finite objects about them. . . . I cannot tell whether I am at present allowing too much weight to my own fancies and predilections, but without so much escape into the outer air and open heaven as this, I can take permanent pleasure in no picture. (IV, 82)

Outside canvas space, where manipulation and control of distance are impossible, the night sky, with an ominously dark background, threatens the delicate equilibrium of an observer who requires the option of the transcendental escape into anonymity. The night sky is not the recessional space that permits release. Instead, reflexive, it is, as we shall later see, similar to the inverted space of Rembrandt. The night sky becomes an enlarged Dungeon of *Me*-ology, in which there is nothing to do but play the part of a self-conscious but reluctant autobiographer: "For the night sky, though we may know it boundless, is dark; it is a studded vault, a roof that seems to shut us in and down . . ." (IV, 81).

The "studded vault," eliminating the possibility of the transcendental movement towards what is either outside or above, forces us back towards the "animal and present life" of the "tangible present." Distance, necessary to Ruskin's equilibrium, fails. The situation is designed for a condition of immanence, but there is no animated interior—nothing to prevent the vault from becoming claustrophobic. With a dark background that has stars in front of that background—stars which might later be transformed into either fireflies or a falling rocket painted by Whistler—distance is reduced to a dimension of enclosure. The space between the "studded vault" and the observer of the night sky is the space of a prison:

> It is not then by nobler form . . . that this strange distance space possesses its attractive power. But there is one thing that it has, or suggests . . . and that is—Infinity. It is of all visible things the least material, the least finite, the farthest

withdrawn from the earth prison-house, the most typical of the nature of God, the most suggestive of the glory of His dwelling-place. (IV, 81)

Repetition, like "recognition," leads to confrontation rather than "perpetual self-transcendence"—to autobiography rather than invisibility or anonymity. But with a focal point which is Infinite, a focal point which is everything, there is no repetition, nothing is recognizable and recessional space never becomes reflexive. The Desiring Eyes of the traveler who would remain home have the potential to move forwards without fear of a return trip:

> Escape, Hope, Infinity, by whatever conventionalism sought, the desire is the same in all, the instinct constant: it is no mere point of light that is wanted in the etching of Rembrandt above instanced, a gleam of armour or fold of temple curtain would have been utterly valueless; neither is it liberty, for though we cut down hedges and level hills, and give what waste and plain we choose, on the right hand and the left, it is all comfortless and undesired, so long as we cleave not a way of escape forward. . . . (IV, 83)

Essentially, the "earth prison-house," of which the Dungeon of *Meology* is simply a smaller version, can become at night, despite the post-medieval attempts to open up the sky, as closed as that "studded vault." Yet the awareness of a different kind of sky, which does not threaten to organize the distance along an inverted perspective, can make even a prison livable—at least in the manipulative model space of canvas. Predictably, this is accomplished by Ruskin's "biped" instincts, his instincts towards doubleness that shaped the requirements of discrimination and separation of the Camera Lucida, whose small room of controllable space needed, above all things, a view—a sense of the "there," of "Escape, Hope, Infinity." For Ruskin's traveler who, choosing not to be a "caged bird," would remain home in body if not in the desire of his eyes, the dimensions of the "here" and "now" are unliveable without the perception of the "there" and "then." Finally, the activity of the penetration of space, which is the transcendental movement along a vanishing perspective, performs most satisfactorily as merely potential energy, energy that is locked in a tense of conditional aspiration. And if the traveler leaves his journeying in that tense, he may become something other than a traveler who will eventually, during a return trip, have to write his autobiography. A distance, available but never used, never fails. The eyes remain desirous of something other than the self. The reward of inactivity may be a page that is "magnificently blank."

CHAPTER IV The Syntax of
Consciousness:
Broken Sentences

VITAL PRESENT: PUBLIC AND PRIVATE

The penetration of space, which is the activity of a solitary traveler in
search of a focal point that is so exclusive it becomes a vanishing point, is
organized about a private depth perspective. After the private depth
perspective has yielded what it has to offer, there is a public perspective
that encompasses areas that had been previously excluded. Knowing more,
Ruskin begins to include horizontal lines. His optics become panoramic.
These areas, peripheral to the solitary traveler of converging orthogonals,
include architecture, economics, and a highly idiosyncratic sociology—areas
that can be no more than mentioned here. It must be enough to say that
there is a shift from depth perspective, which is concerned with the position
of the self in recessional space, to an inclusive horizontal perspective that is
as public as the depth perspective, ending in a vanishing point, is private.

The temporal equivalent to the horizontal perspective is a present tense
that includes public experience. It is a tense of social responsibility in the
same way that the horizontal, surface perspective is a spatial scheme organized for an enlarging social conscience. At its broadest, the public

present considers that a history not constructed from the original artifacts of the past is a forgery. As an advocate of that public present, Ruskin reasons that the first half of the nineteenth century has made a "double blunder": "It has, under the name of improvement, done all it could to EFFACE THE RECORDS which departed ages have left of themselves, while it has declared the FORGERY OF FALSE RECORDS of these same ages to be the great work of its historical painters!" (v, 129)

Ruskin's desire for a public present does not indicate antagonism towards the collective, historical past: rather, it suggests a reverence for a past that is constructed without intervening and falsifying distances between vantage and focal points—without the intervening distances that Turner needs between composition and "first vision," or that Ruskin requires in his own private, mnemonic tenses. Ruskin's ideal, historical past is the result of recording in absolute proximity—of recording as close as possible to the historical subject's point of origin, in a public tense that accommodates social responsibility. For the public present and Ruskin's valid, historical past—not the specious and collective daydream that is part of Scott's "stage of fiction"—are the same tense, viewed from different vantage points: the public present becomes, in the future, Ruskin's historically valid past. And without that public tense, the historical past yields no more than decor, the *mise en scène* of history's hostelry:

> Of all the wastes of time and sense which Modernism has invented—and they are many—none are so ridiculous as this endeavour to represent past history. What do you suppose our descendants will care for our imaginations of the events of former days. Suppose the Greeks, instead of representing their own warriors as they fought at Marathon, had left us nothing but their imaginations of Egyptian battles. . . . What fools we should have thought them! how bitterly we should have been provoked with their folly! And that is precisely what our descendants will feel towards us, so far as our grand historical and classical schools are concerned. What do we care, they will say, what those nineteenth-century people fancied about Greek and Roman history! If they had left us a few plain and rational sculptures and pictures of their own battles, and their own men. . . . (xii, 151–52)

The possessive pronouns and intensifiers, banished by Ruskin as part of a private, reflexive vocabulary that moves the modern man uncomfortably towards the center of autobiography and self-consciousness, become a necessity in the public lexicon. In the same way, portraiture, presenting private problems, is an art of the public present that will move into the historical past as something other than forgery: ". . . the only historical painting deserving the name is portraiture of our own living men and our own passing times . . ." (v, 128). And the public present that is transformed into the historical past is a tense charged with vitality:

> Finally, as far as I can observe, it is a constant law that the greatest men, whether poets or historians, live entirely in their own age, and that the greatest fruits of their work are gathered out of their own age. Dante paints Italy in the thirteenth century; Chaucer, England in the fourteenth; Masoccio, Florence in the fifteenth; Tintoret, Venice in the sixteenth; all of them utterly regardless of anachronism and minor error of every kind, but getting always vital truth out of the vital present. (v, 127)

A present that is both public and "vital" becomes, with the help of Longfellow's "Psalm of Life," a "LIVING PRESENT."[1] The title of one of Ruskin's letters, in *Arrows of the Chace,* exhorts the reader to involve himself with problems of immediacy: "'ACT, ACT IN THE LIVING PRESENT'" (XXXIV, 508). Visions of the future, also outside the public present, appeal no more than visions of the specious, collective daydream of the past. Simply, what is outside immediate perception is rejected by a Ruskin whose perspective has shifted from a private, depth perspective—the perspective of vanishing points, with a foreground and a present tense that must be sacrificed for distant and future considerations—to a horizontal, surface perspective, in which the public and lateral aspects of foreground are to be examined. The suburbs of time—tenses beyond close inspection—compose an outlaw time of historical or eschatological irresponsibility: "Our Earth is now encumbered with ruin, our Heaven is clouded by Death. May we not wisely judge ourselves in some things now, instead of amusing ourselves with the painting of judgments to come?" (XXII, 108).

If the general "judgments to come" of a public trial are outside and ahead of the scope of the Living Present, Ruskin asks that private judgments, which do not bear the responsibility of public opinion, also be made within the bounds of a Living Present that may become, at times, a personal present: "But remember, all that you did for me . . . you were working for the feelings of others after I am dead—not for me. I do not care two straws what people think of me after I am dead. . . . But I do care, and very much, for what is said of me while I live. It makes an immense difference to me *now,* whether Joan and Dora find a flattering review of me in the morning papers, or one which stings and torments them, and me through them" (XXXVI, 586). Yet precisely what Ruskin would have done for himself, in a personal present that is no longer as claustrophobic as the foreground had been, he has not done enough for others: "It may perhaps

---

[1] For a general discussion of the "LIVING PRESENT," see Jerome Buckley's chapter, "The Living Present," in *The Triumph of Time: A Study of the Victorian Concepts of Time, History, Progress, and Decadence* (Cambridge, 1966).

surprise, but I think it will please you to hear me, or . . . to hear the author of *Modern Painters* say, that his chief error in earlier days was not in over estimating, but in too slightly acknowledging the merit of living men" (xx, 25).

The recognition of "living men" in a Living Present suggests that this "vital" tense is the temporal analogue to the enclosed classical landscape. That landscape, as animated as Ruskin's public tense, is organized about lines that can be endured despite their reflexive curves. A self-referring design that is efficacious because of interior animation avoids both autobiography and claustrophobia. The first person is not reenforced by self-consciousness. And this animated present tense—a tense of "nerves"—recapitulates the earlier, spatial movements that become the informing designs of the landscape of immanence. Approximating a condition of immanence that suggests felicitous existence within close temporal bounds, this tense is pinpointed as it is narrowed from a public to a private tense. Specifically, Ruskin's new motto signals precise definition: ". . . beginning to study heraldry with attention, I apprehended, that, whether a knight's war-cry, or a peaceful yeoman's saying, the words on the scroll of a crest could not be a piece of advice to the other people, but must be always a declaration of the bearer's own mind. Whereupon I changed, on my own seal, the 'Age quod agis,' into 'To-day,' tacitly underlined to myself with the warning, 'The night cometh, when no man can work'" (xxxv, 390–91).

Like many of Ruskin's titles, "To-day" either concentrates meaning, or explodes, as if Ruskin were unable to control multiplying significance, into interpretations that range from Psalms xcv. 7, to Hebrews iii. 13: "The motto means—as you say—a great many things. *You* may read it—'To-day if ye will hear his voice'—or 'To-day, while it is called to-day'" (xxxvi, 451). Uncertified by Biblical authority, Ruskin's own interpretation suggests that the present, both public and private, is the only certain tense, the only tense for performance: "To me it ['To-day'] has another meaning, which is of no special consequence to anybody else. But practically, and especially, to help cure myself a little of procrastination, if it may be" (xxxvi, 451).

But "To-day," the motto of Ruskin's maturity, is not precise enough. His diaries, as days shorten, become elaborate records of light or time left:

August 29th, Saturday.	Alas, the short days
[sunrise] 5.9	[sunset] 6.52
instead of 3.44	8.15

as they were when I began this book. A year's nothing! (*Diaries*, p. 807)

Running out of potential time, Ruskin finds that "To-day" is not a fine enough calibration to measure a vital present that is becoming increasingly rare. His later diaries, constructed from entries of "To-day," are further divided like the relativistic discriminations of Pater's moments, into entries of hours and minutes. The staccato syntax matches the quick division of a present that is now a private tense of vital moments: "At 1/2 past one, morning of 22nd (rose at 12) on Calais Pier—Turner's—*met* by a ghastly railroad train! Passengers shivering for full quarter of an hour—English boat not ready! [Word illegible], late up! Off at 1/2 past two. Into train at 1/4 past 4; at Cannon St. at 6, morning" (*Diaries*, p. 818).

Forced back upon himself, Ruskin, attending microscopically to a tense that becomes increasingly vital as it becomes rare, adjusts language to tense:

> Illustration of the meaning of the temptations of St. Anthony, at nine in the morning. . . . Puts me in mind of appointment with gondoliers at nine, to pay them for waiting with me last night in the mist, under San Giorgio Maggiore. . . . Mercy on me, the postman brings me in Mr. Oliver's second letter from Kew; just after I've withdrawn a provoking letter I had written in pride, nine o'clock. Wrote another and dated 1/4 past nine instead—had to withdraw another to Kew! The Kew new one dated 1/4 past nine.
>
> 1/2 past nine.
> (*Diaries*, p. 921)

Instead of being written from the stability of a daily vantage point—a point that is of necessity much less firm than either the novelist's or the essayist's—the entry of moments, like Pater's passing "swiftly from point to point," as if counting "pulses," is written in a private present of discontinuous time that is close to the diarist's consciousness. This personal present is part of a syntax of consciousness that is translated into a style of immanence, which is the "nothing but process" of the next section—a style that is the result of the writer learning to manipulate himself within the "interior distance" of his own thoughts. It is a finely calibrated tense permitting the felicitous release of interior pressures that are largely the result of the public information obtained from the horizontal, surface perspective.

TOWARD THE INTERIOR: NOTHING BUT PROCESS

As Ruskin's horizontal perspective takes in more removed peripheral areas, control over that material becomes increasingly difficult. Indexing, for example, is a problem. The possibility of avoiding the burden of that perspective, which seems to require a system to organize and master disparate material, becomes increasingly appealing. As early as the third volume of *Modern Painters*, Ruskin begins his attack on those products of systems and system-mongering:

> I do not intend, however, now to pursue the inquiry in a method so laboriously
> systematic; for the subject may, it seems to me, be more usefully treated by
> pursuing the different questions which arise out of it just as they occur to us,
> without too great scrupulousness in marking connections, or insisting on se-
> quences. Much time is wasted by human beings, in general, on establishment
> of systems; and it often takes more labour to master the intricacies of an arti-
> ficial connection, than to remember the separate facts which are so carefully
> connected. . . . (v, 18)

At this point, one portion of Ruskin, no longer mechanically "marking connections, or insisting on sequences," begins a variation of the penetration of space: from the point of departure, where, if control were to be exercised, system-mongering would seem to be required, he starts to move towards a new kind of frontier. But with this movement, the vanishing points of transcendence do not beckon. Instead, it is an interior position towards which he moves, a position that records the maneuverings of consciousness in a tense that avoids the panoramic responsibilities of the vital present. Yet this is done not by employing historical or utopian vision, but by getting so close to the present—magnifying intervals—that a sense of peripheral context is lost. It is an interior position where there exists neither the demands of mastery nor the need for self-annulment, a position, which is an interior frontier, where the present tense is, if not public, at least "vital" enough to support the existence of an active consciousness that, not focusing on the transcendent exits of the infinite, is instead, proximate and intimate—a consciousness of immanence. Ruskin's travel plans, as he moves towards this interior position, carry him off the main track: "I purpose, therefore, henceforward to trouble myself little with sticks or twine, but to arrange my chapters with a view to convenient reference, rather than to any careful division of subjects, and to follow out in any by-ways that may open, on right or left, whatever question it seems useful at any moment to settle" (v, 18).

Yet relinquishing the locus of system-mongering is not merely the abandonment of a demanding landscape, the exchange of straight, fast highways that cannot treat secondary, digressive problems in favor of felicitous and leisurely "by-ways"; it is also an exchange of method that allows an indirect, meandering approach to a problem's solution—an approach that is ultimately more significant than the unaccommodating system-mongering of the central highway. Simply: ". . . the writing of a systematic treatise was incompatible with the more serious work" (xxvi, 273).

The exploration of the peripheral areas of the "by-ways," which is governed by inspiration that occurs in the vital present, "at any moment," is an organic process that Ruskin likes to compare with the growth of a tree or plant: "So that, as the work changed like a tree, it was also rooted like a tree—not where it would, but where the need was . . ." vii, 10). The growth is the result of a "need" that cannot be predicted from the undigressive highway of systematization. The arrival at a truth or solution becomes the arrival at an end, that, in horticultural imagery, is the root of the matter. But the process of arrival at the root, which is a working backwards to an end that is also a point of origin (a regressive movement that follows the pattern of Ruskin's later focal point) begins far from that root— theoretically, among subdivided branches: "The reader must pardon me for making in the outset one or two statements which may appear to him somewhat wide of the matter, but which, (if he admits their truth,) he will, I think, presently perceive to reach to the root of it" (v, 70).

Continually exploring branches or "by-ways," Ruskin begins far from where he will end, almost as if he does not want to arrive: "I must ask permission, as I have sometimes done before, to begin apparently a long way from the point" (v, 176). The involvement in branches and "by-ways," despite the incantation about roots, suggests that the "point," if it exists at all, is merely a target to launch Ruskin's exercise in discursiveness—that the end exists only for the beginning, or, more accurately, for the process of the middle, a process between the point of origin and a conclusion that is not to be arrived at as swiftly as Ruskin's optical traveler would arrive at self-annulment. For Ruskin, digression is life. It is the sly beginning of autobiographical immanence. The middle, delaying the end, delays the progress towards the interior frontier. Extend the middle enough, by the exploration of branches and "by-ways," and the end is not reached. The delaying middle, which charts obscure "by-ways," is, curiously, not central. It is a middle that is as peripheral as the farthest reaches of the horizontal, surface perspective.

At first, Ruskin attempts to withstand the impulse to wander from his highway of consecutive and systematic thought: "I must not, however, weary the reader with this subject, which has always been a favourite one with me, and is apt to lead me too far . . ." (x, 155). Professing concern for the stamina of the reader, he attempts to establish boundaries that he will not transgress: "It would, however, too much weary the general reader if, without illustrations, I were to endeavour to lead him step by step through the aisles of St. John and Paul; and I shall therefore confine myself . . ." (xi, 83). The final geography of the Ruskinian page, which is the product of both Ruskin and his later editors, is marked by an increasing number of parenthetical signs, above and below the page's last line of text, which announce that Ruskin has resisted digressive temptation:

(I will return to this point afterwards[1])

---

[1](This, however, was not done.)

(xxxv, 619)

Still, the mere announcement of a potential digression, to be undertaken in an unspecified future tense, allows Ruskin to have it both ways: to resist the digression and, at the same time, by suggesting it, to relieve, imaginatively, the confining pressures of the highway.

Resisting, on occasions, the temptations of a digressive middle, Ruskin admits, without worrying about the weary reader, that the "by-ways" have nothing to do with the end, the "point": "I could be led far from the matter in hand, if I were to pursue this interesting subject" (x, 202). Yet the "matter" seems to lie less and less "in hand." Even the act of guarding against discursiveness is, itself, a process of meandering in that peripheral middle. In a fragment from an early poem, "Iteriad"—a fragment that is fittingly called "Ullswater; a Digression"—Ruskin is exercising a verbosity whose purpose is closer to filling the "magnificent blank" of a page than drawing a conclusion, arriving at a point:

> But I am digressive! Oh, pray, do not blame me!
> In description I know it would go on but lamely.
> . . . .
> "I, I"—oh, dear me!—But I'll make a confession
> —I'm digressive when I do but talk of digression.

(II, 310)

But more often, digressions are defended. And if there is an ending, a "point," it should be approached indirectly, in a style antithetical to that employed in the penetration of space, in which the entire concern was with the quick, economical movement along the lines of depth perspective toward a background that is also a vanishing point. Now, before an end that may or may not exist, the concern is with the lateral exploration of "by-ways." Before concluding, Ruskin would fill all peripheral space with verbal tracings. Almost always, as if he were flirting with the indulgent dangers of self-portraiture, Ruskin is concerned about the stamina of the reader. And almost always, it is not the governing factor for the road taken: ". . . the reader may already be somewhat wearied with a statement which has led us apparently so far from our immediate subject. But the digression was necessary" (x, 231). Ruskin anticipates the charges of the weary reader: "You think, perhaps, I am quitting my subject, and proceeding, as it is too often with appearance of justice alledged against me, into irrelevant matter" (xx, 212). Nevertheless, it is apparent that it is precisely the "irrelevant matter" that is significant. The peripheral areas—the extended middle between the origin and the end—have become the areas of a central, if eccentric, concern. The immanent consciousness, as opposed to the transcendent consciousness that is guided through space towards the self-annulling focal point of the infinite, is involved in the extension of this peripheral middle through digression. As with the topography of immanence, the immanent consciousness employs the reflexive design efficaciously: the act of digression, incorporating everything except "irrelevant matter," turns back upon itself. Without syntactic or logical goals, digression becomes its own focal point, existing easily within the confining turns of its meandering "by-ways." And as its own focal point, the digressive mode, whose logic unravels rather than progresses, is the incarnation of the immanent consciousness.

By the fifth and last volume, *Modern Painters* has turned into anything but a work on modern painters: the initial goals, along with point of origin, have disappeared. The peripheral areas of digression, the "by-ways" that are explored in the vital present, have effaced both highway and conclusion. Ruskin points out that the initial concerns of *Modern Painters* have been "continually altered in shape, and even warped and broken, by digressions respecting social questions, which had for me an interest tenfold greater than the work I had been forced into undertaking" (VII, 257). The "social questions" that extended the panorama of the public, horizontal perspective, at the edges of Ruskin's vision, now threaten to overwhelm not only Ruskin, but Ruskin's weary reader, whose stamina is no longer considered. The reader is asked to supplement Ruskin's digressions, with digressions of his own, to be carried out under Ruskin's supervision: "And if now the reader will compare the sentence at the bottom of that page, respecting the more gross violations of such law by Adultery and Usury, with the farther notes on Usury in page 17, and then, read, connectedly, the 14th and 15th Psalms in Sidney's translation . . ." (XXIX, 179). Attempting to control the exploding discursiveness of *Fors Clavigera,* Ruskin trims peripheral areas by increasing those areas in the reader. Ruskin's demands are felt syntactically as his sentences become an unvaried sequence of urgent requests: "I want you to read,—ever so many things. First of all, and nothing else till you have mastered that, the history of Montenegro. . . . After that . . . After that . . . After that . . ." (XXIX, 368).

In a variation of the digressive mode, Ruskin constructs an alternative syntax to that employed by the monger of systems, who, map in hand, perhaps even his own autobiography in hand, speeds along his highway of consecutive thought towards a pre-arranged conclusion—a rhetorical focal point that is born as soon as the first sentence is begun. This alternative syntax, taking place in that animated present tense of "nerves," is a process of interrogation which precludes the paternal, dogmatic assertion that Ruskin, mongering systems himself, enjoys. Exploration, the fact that he is continually at a frontier, subverts announcement. As if he were strolling through a Chinese garden, in search of the "surprise" of "perpetual" self-transcendence, Ruskin begins to wander in the present, without the consideration that would allow him to manipulate his material. That in-

terval which would permit control, the movement toward mastery, is
avoided: "My own books have thus sometimes become little more than
notes of interrogation" (xxvi, 342). Relinquishing the distance of control
for the immediacy of a present tense that seems to provide not only its own
vitality, but its own design, Ruskin replaces statement with a questioning
process that is subject to continual correction, a process that is possible because the tense in which is occurs is always "living":

> For, as my reader must already sufficiently perceive, this book is literally to be
> one of studies—not of statements. Some one said of me once, very shrewdly,
> when he wants to work out a subject, he writes a book on it. That is a very
> true saying in the main,—I work down or up to my mark, and let the reader
> see process and progress, not caring to conceal them, but this book
> [*Proserpina*] will be nothing but process. I don't mean to assert anything posi-
> tively in it from the first page to the last. Whatever I say, is to be understood
> only as a conditional statement—liable to, and inviting, correction. (xxv, 216)

A book that is "nothing but process" is a book that watches its own
unfolding, a book whose "progress" is its "process." It does not so much
proceed towards an ending as peregrinate in the middle. Involved in
"process," Ruskin, as if considering an autobiography of consciousness,
begins to advertise the movements of his mind: "I pause, here, to think over
and put together the little I do know: and consider how it should be told
Agnes. For to my own mind, it occurs in a somewhat grotesque series of
imagery, with which I would not, if possible, infect hers. . . . I wonder why
elephants don't build houses with their noses . . . then I wonder . . . finally,
I think I had better stop thinking, and find out a fact or two, if I can . . ."
(xxviii, 277–78). The more proximate the scrutiny within the present
tense, the closer the perceptions, the less chance to reach the end. Furthermore, the more immediate the present, the more active it appears. Ruskin is
often manipulated by the swift movements of an immanent consciousness
that seems to be at odds not only with his dogmatic, system-mongering self,
but the peripheral self who would delay the middle in hopes that the end
might never come: "And I am the more provoked and plagued by this, because my brains being, as all the rest of me, desultory and ill under control,
I get into another fit of thinking what a bee's lips can be like, and of
wondering why whole meadows-full of flowers are called 'cows' lips' and
none called 'bees' lips'. . . . I go on wondering how soon . . ." (xxviii, 279).
Ruskinian assertion, shaped by a gymnastic consciousness, becomes a
process of exploration, an examination of the "by-ways" of Ruskin's mind
in the act of cognition:

> Assuming my shell to be Helix virgata, I take down my magnificent French—
> (let me see if I can write its title without a mistake)—"Manuel de Con-

chyliologie et de Paleontologie Conchyliologique,"... Eight hundred largest octavo—more like folio—pages of close print, with four thousand and odd (nearly five thousand) exquisite engravings of shells; and among them I look for the creatures elegantly, but inaccurately, called by modern naturalists Gasteropods ... and among these I find, with much pains, one that is rather mine.... On the whole I am not disposed to think my shell is here described, and put my splendid book in its place again ... and then I come, by order of Atropos, on this amazing account of the domestic arrangements of a little French snail, "Helix decollato" (Guillotined snail?) ... Bulimus,—what's a bulimus? Helix is certainly a screw, and bulimus,—in my Riddle's dictionary—is said to be "empty-bellied." Then this French snail, revolutionary in the manner of a screw, appears to be a belly-walker with an empty belly, and no neck,—who literally "breaks up" his establishment every year! Query—breaks? or melts? Contraction or confusion? (xxviii, 552–53)

A language that is "nothing but process," reflecting a mind in the act of interrogating itself, is a language of interruption. Given form by a syntax of discontinuity not unlike the urgent structure of the diary entries of multiple vantage points, Ruskin's present tense is beyond his control. It is a tense manipulated by allegorical agents. Happily, Ruskin is not responsible for the incipient autobiography of discursive indulgence: "And here I'm interrupted again by a delightful letter about the resurrection of snails, Atropos really managing matters, at present, like the daintiest and watchfullest housewife for me,—everything in its place, and under my hand" (xxviii, 551). But before this present tense of interruption becomes private, referring to the activities of the self, it is public. The syntax of this public present, which, at its origin, does not imitate the peregrination of the "byways," is almost architectural in style.

At once modulated and stately, the opening sentence of "The Two Boyhoods" chapter of the last volume of *Modern Painters* is a public embryo of the reflexive, digressive mode that later occurs in Ruskin's private style: "Born half-way between the mountains and the sea—that young George of Castelfranco—of the Brave Castle:—Stout George they called him, George of Georges, so goodly a boy he was—Giorgione" (vii, 374). Going nowhere fast, the sentence is without conventional syntactic conclusion. More accurately, the conclusion, "Giorgione," is the beginning—the subject of a sentence that is organized about a middle of accumulative redefinition, a process that is a variation of digression. Another example of definition as a syntactic progress that is "nothing but process" occurs later in the same chapter:

Full shone now its awful globe, one pallid charnel-house,—a ball strewn bright with human ashes, glaring in poised sway beneath the sun, all blinding-white with death from pole to pole,—death, not of myriads of poor bodies only, but of will, and mercy, and conscience; death, not once inflicted on the flesh, but daily fastening on the spirit; death, not silent or patient, waiting his appointed hour, but voiceful, venomous; death with the taunting word, and burning grasp, and infixed sting. (vii, 388)

Ruskin's description of a particular kind of "death" proceeds from a bloated middle of balanced negative and positive definition that is only a ceremonious anticipation of the end-retarding "by-ways" to come.

Bloated middles are early versions of intrusions that translate to instructions or directions for those peripheral "by-ways." And the intrusions of allegorical fortune, of Atropos, are all the more remarkable because Ruskin's early life is structured about continuity. Like his private uninterrupted penetration of space, Ruskin's childhood is marked by the serene continuity of existence in a vacuum, a vacuum in which interruption is only a potential factor to be described parenthetically, by negation: "After our chapters [of Bible study] (from two to three a day, according to their length, the first thing after breakfast, and no interruptions from the servants allowed—none from the visitors, who either joined in the reading or had to stay upstairs—and none from any visitings or excursions, except real traveling) . . ." (xxviii, 318). But the adult, Atropos aside, does not require external agencies for discontinuity. Attempting to do everything, Ruskin supplies his own intrusions: "My dear friend, I can't bear to interrupt your pretty letter; but . . ." (xxvii, 532). Interruptions flourish. The flow of syntax is broken. Interrogating himself and interrupting others, Ruskin, as if imitating the reflexive space that threatens his world, starts turning on himself: "I interrupt myself, for an instant or two, to take notice of two little things . . ." (xxviii, 208). If discontinuity is a means of getting on the "by-ways" of digression, Ruskin begins to learn how to shift interruption to discursive advantage.

The indulgence of the discursive middle turns interruption not into a way of avoiding ends, but an end, or point, in itself. Interruption becomes a new kind of syntactic orthodoxy. Ruskin frames a two page digression with advertisements of his intentions: "Yes; that is all very well when it's a pig; but if it be—Wait a minute;—I must go back to the Fair-ladies before I finish my sentence" (xxvii, 534). Two pages later, he moves towards a completion that is not the "point": "I will finish my sentence now, paused in above" (xxvii, 536). Sentences of letters addressed to the "Workmen and Labourers of Great Britain" are turned in reflexively towards themselves— a design to be avoided in transcendental space—until the only conclusion possible is the enclosing, self-contained parenthesis without exit:

> I couldn't go on about my cousin Jessie, for I was interrupted by the second post with more birthday compliments, from young ladies now about Jessie's

age—letters which of course required immediate answer,—some also with flowers, which required to be immediately put into water, and greatly worried me by upsetting themselves among my books all day afterwards; but I let myself be worried, for love;—and, from a well-meaning and kindly feeling friend, some very respectful and respectable poetry, beautifully written (and I read part of it, for love, but I had much rather he had sent me a sixpence, for I hate poetry mostly, and love pence, always). . . . (xxvIII, 549)

Also operating in a present that is almost claustrophobic, another kind of interruption, which is a severe departure from sequence, is used to explore an area other than those "by-ways" that extend the middle. Playing with words the way he plays with sentences, Ruskin, or rather his logic, begins to jump backwards and forwards, toying with the solemn progression of serial thought: "And you don't care for the young Buccleugh? Cut away the cleugh, then, and read the Buc backwards. Do you care for your own cub as much as Sir Walter would have cared for his own beast? (see, farther on, how he takes care of his wire-haired terrier, Spice), or as any beast cares for *its* cub" (xxvII, 568). Chopping words in half, spelling them backwards, inserting parenthetical teasers of future events, Ruskin begins to undercut the texture of the vital present in which he operates. Discontinuity ends in an anti-sequential design that circles back on itself. The immanent consciousness, which is the consciousness of the reflexive and confining present, begins to take into account the tenses behind the present: "And now look back to my 25th letter, for I want you *not to forget* Alice of Salisbury" (xxvII, 569). His sentences are constructed about brief retrospectives: "All good judging, and all good preaching, must be given gratis. Look back to what I have incidentally said of lawyers and clergy . . ." (xxvII, 58).

The immanent consciousness' development of an historical tense becomes, in fact, an attempt to charge old material with new significance, to rescue what lies behind, in the past, from obscurity. Ruskin asks his reader to retrieve a past that is five years old: "I must ask you to look back to *Fors* of August, 1872; and to hear why the boy with his basket of figs was so impressive to me" (xxIx, 33). This awareness of the retrospective is a perception that, compounded with the indulgence of digression, of "nothing but process," becomes autobiography. Rather than engage in the annulment of self that occurs at the edge of recessional space, the background of the Desiring Eyes, this digressive, present-tense self, focusing on the interior and the immediate, also looks away from the immediate towards the focal point of an earlier, past-tense self, a self who is neither invisible nor pseudonymous. Kata Phusin, after the fact and protected by an interval that is as necessary as the optical self's intervening space between vantage and focal points, can shed his pseudonymity. "Nothing but process" leads to density instead of transparency, autobiography instead of annulment.

FORS CLAVIGERA: BITTER PLAY

Before the living, vital present, whether public or private, is entirely subverted by anticipatory and retrospective attentions, by a digressive and discontinuous style that, including all tenses, is, essentially, the style of the immanent consciousness, the construction of *Fors Clavigera* should be examined. Composed of letters, *Fors* is not written from a vantage point of consideration. Ruskin's "first vision" is his only vision. There is no mnemonic and imaginative distance between observation and composition. Furthermore, there is no second, editorial composition. As Ruskin says earlier, of a different kind of letter: "You see I write you my letter straightforward, and let you see all my scratchings out and puttings in . . ." (xvii, 354). The epistolary Ruskin, involved in many things, is also involved in a "process" that yields an autobiographical focus, a focus, unlike the reflexive landscape structure of the pathetic fallacy, that requires no self-annulment.

But if the letter writer is not displeased to look occasionally in the mirror, that act of self-referring examination is the only restraint he feels. For the letter, rushing headlong, unlike even the "by-way" digressions involving peripheral exploration, is, at least at first, an entirely prospective form. It is as if the letter writer were riding the converging orthogonals of recessional space. As a thin line of thought moving "straightforward," not bothering to backtrack in order to clean up the "scratchings out and puttings in," the mind shaping Ruskin's letters functions in absolute proximity: "Yet letters never thrive on mature consideration. The same impulse continues, or ought to continue, from the 'My dear' at the top to the 'Your affectionate' at the bottom. The momentum once given and the impetus obtained, the word is forward, and it is enough to guide without restraining the pegasus of thought" (xxxvi, 5). Like Ruskin's proximate focusing, his letters, written in the present, are so close to the scrutinized subject that the subject becomes abstracted, or magnified from context, allowing Ruskin's mind to move, a "pegasus of thought," without the hesitation and qualification of "mature consideration." Unravelling without retardation, the syntax of the letters becomes a syntax of felicity that performs some of the same psychic functions of release that distance serves the transcendent consciousness.

Yet unlike the proximate focusing that occurs as Ruskin engages in his botanical and geological cataloging, which is a labor of love, epistolary classification, the control and manipulation of material in letters, is as undesirable as that masterful vantage point of "mature consideration" which impedes the release of the "pegasus of thought." Writing a series of letters entitled *A Museum or Picture Gallery*, Ruskin will make certain concessions to what he calls "museum-like order," which is the stringing together, each morning, of yesterday's subjects. Still, after that gesture towards enforced sequence, he avoids epistolary systematization, just as he avoided the system-mongering of the "highways":

> The only chance of getting these letters themselves into fairly consistent and Museum-like order is by writing a word or two always the first thing in the morning till I get them done; so, I shall at least remember what I was talking of the day before; but for the rest—I must speak of one thing or another as it may come into my head, for there are too many to classify without pedantry and loss of time. (xxxiv, 249)

The syntax of felicity, instead of being modelled after "Museum-like order," is constructed from thought that is recorded "as it may come into my head."

Ruskin's letters permit the exploration of a different kind of knowledge from that treated in a genre not geared to problems of immediacy. Accommodating the immanent consciousness, letters accommodate "the chances of the day," which present material that "would otherwise never get said at all." Simply, Ruskin is enthusiastic about "this great advantage in the writing of real letters":

> . . . the direct correspondence is a sufficient reason for saying, in or out of order, everything that the chances of the day bring into one's head, in connection with the matter in hand; and as such things very usually go out of one's head again, after they get tired of their lodging, they would otherwise never get said at all. And thus to-day, quite out of order, but in very close connection with another part of our subject. . . . (xvii, 333)

Writing letters, Ruskin can employ a felicitous syntax that is autonomous, having its own rules—a syntax that describes the activities of a mind maneuvering beyond system, "in and out of order."

As a series of letters, employing the advantages of "direct correspondence," *Fors Clavigera* presents problems in response: if reading *Fors* is, as Cardinal Manning says, like listening to "the beating of one's heart in a nightmare" (xxxvi, lxxxvi), the persistent reader becomes an invader of intimacy, similar to the Ruskinian Peeping Tom, who, rather than perform or engage, would watch. But if Manning is correct, the reader is closer to an eavesdropper than a Peeping Tom. For a shift has occurred from optical perception to an apprehension that is almost exclusively aural. No matter how myopic one might be, there is still not enough room to see. The new designs, based on the original spatial patterns, are temporal and interior. Just as the apprehension of the transcendent consciousness was designed for the eye, so the apprehension of the immanent consciousness, beating in a nightmare, is designed for the ear.

Still, the feeling persists that the letters, which are after all directed towards the "Workmen and Labourers of Great Britain," are not directed merely towards the eavesdropper, the aural version of Ruskin's earlier eye-obsessed self. Instead, they appear to be sent towards anyone who will listen with care, which, at times, seems to be no one at all. A sense of disequilibrium results that is similar to the disequilibrium of the inadequate observer, as he confronts the monumental. It is the disequilibrium of a man exhibiting the pirouettes of an agonized consciousness that has become public enough to include the social concerns of the horizontal perspective. But it is almost as if Ruskin were being most private when being most public. The pirouettes, despite the fact that they are prompted by public concerns, seem to take place in an arena of profound vacancy, like those private spaces organized by Ruskin's earlier transcendental depth perspective, which would not only eliminate an audience of "others," of, say, the "Workmen and Labourers of Great Britain," but would even, in its impulse towards privacy, annul the self.

Like Ruskin's letters in general, *Fors*, belonging to a genre of the present tense, is not subject to revision—the editing of "scratchings out and puttings in"—that might achieve the undesired effect of a polished surface, a surface created by the editorial return of a second or third vision. But with the writing of immediacy, which is a product of the immanent consciousness, the only vision is the first vision, which becomes what Ruskin, outside of *Fors*, calls "my third way":

> I have always had three different ways of writing; one, with the single view of making myself understood, in which I necessarily omit a great deal of what comes into my head; another in which I say what I think ought to be said, in what I suppose to be the best words I can find for it; (which is in reality an affected style—be it good or bad;) and my third way of writing is to say all that comes into my head for my own pleasure, in the first words that come, retouching them afterwards into (approximate) grammar. (xix, 408)

Ruskin's Third Style, allowing the immanent consciousness the release of a felicitous syntax that coils back upon itself as if it were modelled upon a labyrinth, is the style of the interior frontier, where digression anticipates autobiography. And as a stylistic metamorphoses of a labyrinth, with a meandering consciousness tracing the intricate, peripheral design of "byways," it becomes a means of deactivating the repletion of a horizontal perspective that includes economics, architecture, and social criticism. As a variation of digression, the Third Style can only be touched upon here. Still, what is important to note is that it is a style that is unravelled for what Ruskin calls "my own pleasure." More specifically, tracing the labyrinth's vertiginous design, following "any thread of thought," it is a style that is "a kind of play":

> . . . none of this work can be done but as a kind of play, irregularly, and as the humour comes upon me. For if I set myself at it gravely, there is too much to be dealt with; my mind gets fatigued in half-an-hour, and no good can be done; the only way in which any advance can be made is by keeping my mornings entirely quiet, and free of care, by opening of letters and newspapers; and then by letting myself follow any thread of thought or point of inquiry that chances to occur first, and writing as the thoughts come,—whatever their disorder; all their connection and cooperation being dependent on the real harmony of my purpose, and the consistency of the ascertainable facts, which are the only ones I teach; and I can no more, now, polish or neatly arrange my work than I can guide it. So this fragment must stand as it was written, and end,—because I have no time to say more. (xxviii, 461)

If writing with the Third Style, in a present tense far removed from either the solemnity or responsibility of the historical past, is "a kind of play," it is, nevertheless a "play" that is often more "bitter" than sweet:

> *Fors is a letter*, and written as a letter should be written, frankly, and as the mood or topic, chances; so far as I finish and retouch it, which of late I have done more and more, it ceases to be what it should be, and becomes a serious treatise, which I never meant to undertake. True, the play of it (and much of it is a kind of bitter play) has always, as I told you before, as stern final purpose as Morgiana's dance; but the gesture of the moment must be as the humour takes me. (xxix, 197)

The "gesture of the moment," when not manipulated by a kind of "humour," is guided by the allegorical Atropos, whose wandering presence is even contained within the title, *Fors Clavigera*. About many things, *Fors* means many things: "'Fors' is the best part of three good English words, Force, Fortitude, and Fortune" (xxvii, 27–28). Playing, Ruskin establishes a complex design of interlocking meaning, complete with variables, as if he were certain that meaning improved with "numerical superiority." Options, like recessional space, permit release. Ruskin will no more be pinned down to a single meaning than he will find himself in enclosed space without a window: "Each of the three possible meanings of Clavigera corresponds to one of the three meanings of Fors" (xxvii, 28). More to the point, it is the "Third Fors," who, governing the Third Style, also governs Ruskin:

> This disappointment I accept thankfully as the ordinance of my careful and prudent mistress, Atropos,—the Third Fors; and am indeed quickly enough apprehensive of her lesson in it. She wishes, I doubt not, to recognize that I was foolish in designing the intrusion of technical advice into my political letters. . . . I must needs do her bidding. . . . (xxviii, 443)

The Third Fors, Atropos, controlling the uncontrolled, charting a land-scape that is mapless, provides directions as needed: "It has chanced, by help of the Third Fors (as again and again in the course of these letters the thing to my purpose has been brought before me just when I needed it) . . ." (xxvii, 360). As the designer of Ruskin's intricate digressions, the Third Fors relieves Ruskin of the public responsibility of peripheral vision. He is guided rather than guiding. The "Master," feeling the pressure of excess, would be mastered: "It chanced by the appointment of the Third Fors, to which, you know, I am bound in these letters uncomplainingly to submit . . ." (xxvii, 270).

Ruskin feels that the extensive use of the Third Style—his syntax of fe-licity that operates in a tense that cannot employ the assertive tone of paternal control—may indicate to eavesdroppers and workmen alike that, led by the Third Fors, he has no idea where he is taking either himself or his problematic audience: "I wonder if Fors will let me say any small pro-portion, this year of what I intend. I wish she would, for my readers have every right to be doubtful of my plan till they see it more defined . . ." (xxviii, 235). Yet announcing his doubts, Ruskin is also formulating an aesthetics of the desultory, of the planless plan. Guided by "principle and tendency," rather than a floor plan authorized by his occasional voice of dogmatism, Ruskin, writing *Fors*, is involved in a calculated process of digressive exploration, a process, occupying peripheral areas, that would at-tempt "to paint St. Paul's at once from both ends of London Bridge":

> . . . yet to define it [Ruskin's plan] would be to falsify it, for all that is best in it depends on my adopting whatever good I can find, in men and things, that will work to my purpose; which of course means action in myriads of ways that I neither wish to define, nor attempt to anticipate. Nay, I am wrong, even in speaking of it as a plan or scheme at all. It is only a method of uniting the force of all good plans and wise schemes; it is a principle and tendency, like the law of form in a crystal; not a plan. If I live, as I said at first, I will endeavour to show some small part of it in action; but it would be a poor design indeed, for the bettering of the world, which any man could see either quite round the out-side, or quite into the inside of. (xxviii, 235)

The defense of the planless plan, of the following of a Third Fors that is bent upon seeing both "outside" and "inside," rather than the dictates of the dogmatic self, whose mastery is occasionally a burden and never "play," becomes increasingly urgent: "It would be difficult to give more distinct evidence than is furnished by these pieces of manuscript, of the in-curably desultory character which has brought on me the curse of Reuben, 'Unstable as water, thou shall not excel.' But I reflect, hereupon, with resolute self-complacency, that water, when good, is a good thing, though it be not stable; and that it may be better sometimes to irrigate than excel" (xxviii, 275). Perhaps watered by Atropos, *Fors* becomes a tree. But it is a tree, virtually autonomous and defying pruning, that is responsible for its own growth, its own rules:

> A friend, in whose judgment I greatly trust, remonstrated sorrowfully with me, the other day, on the desultory character of *Fors*; and pleaded with me for the writing of an arranged book instead.
>
> But he might as well plead with a birch-tree growing out of a crag, to arrange its boughs beforehand. The winds and floods will arrange them according to their wild liking; all that the tree has to do, or can do, is to grow gaily, if it may be; sadly, if gaity be impossible; and let the black jags and scars rend the rosewhite of its trunk where Fors shall choose. (xxviii, 254)

Despite the defense of the planless organic nature of his epistolary form, Ruskin, who would see not only the "outsides" and "insides" of a problem, but St. Paul's simultaneously from both ends of London Bridge, can sympathize with the more orthodox requirements of any readers he might have: "But I can conceive how irritating it must be to any one chancing to take special interest in any one part of my subject—the life of Scott for instance,—to find me, or lose me, wandering away from it for a year or two; and sending roots into new ground in every direction: or (for my friend taxed me with this graver error also) needlessly re-rooting myself in the old" (xxviii, 254). Occasionally, Ruskin announces that he has reformed. The reform will keep him off the digressive "by-ways," which, "unstable as water," have now been transformed into the bad water of "unprogressive inlets":

> Were I to yield as I was wont in the first series of these letters, without scruple, to the eddies of thought which turned the main stream of my discourse into apparently irrelevant and certainly unprogressive inlets, I should in this place proceed to show how true-love is inconsistent with railways, with joint-stock banks, with the landed interest, with parliamentary interest, with grouse shooting, with lawn tennis, with monthly magazines, spring fashions, and Christmas cards. (xxix, 445)

But the reform, which is a road rarely taken, is not to the point. Predictably, it is the "irrelevant" that is significant. The most important territory of Ruskin's mind—landscape or waterway—is "unprogressive." If the optical traveler, penetrating space, requires the recessional space of the third dimension, the discursive and "unprogressive" writer of *Fors*, more interested in water than space, appears to be concerned about distant focal points and future tenses only insofar as they activate present-tense digression. Eddying with thought, Ruskin's mind, which is "unstable" water, creates "inlets," perhaps like "Ullswater; a Digression," that are off the "main stream." Irrigation occurs at the side. And the "bitter play" of that eddying mind is the result of a highly associative consciousness operating in a private and vital present, a tense that summons, without mastering, an echoing past: "I do not know if children generally have strong associative fancy about words; but when I was a child, that word 'Crocodile' always seemed to me very terrific, and I would even hastily, in any book, turn a leaf in which it was printed with a capital C. If anybody had but told me the meaning of it—'a creature that is afraid of crocuses!'" (xxvii, 484) Ruskin's thoughts, in "Letter 26, Crocus and Rose," revolve about his watery and unstable obsession with the dragon-slaying St. George, eddying from "crocodiles" to "crocuses," from "roses" to a curious definition of the devil: "For as the wise German's final definition of the Devil (in the second part of *Faust*) is that he is afraid of Roses, so the earliest and simplest possible definition of him is that in springtime he is afraid of crocuses . . ." (xxvii, 485).

But if the devil is afraid of roses and crocuses that remind the young Ruskin of a crocodile that is also afraid of crocuses, Ruskin's thoughts, bitterly playing in apparently peripheral areas, eddy through internal and "unprogressive inlets" that are like the "muddy waters" at Manchester and Rochedale—waters that, uninhabitable for fish, might contain meat for Ruskin's thought. Slaying dragons of water, St. George, accommodating himself to the present, becomes a butcher in a mercantile England that is appropriately polluted:

> We have surely brickfields enough to keep our clay from ever rising to famine prices, in any fresh accession of prosperity;—and though fish can't live in our rivers, the muddy waters are just of the consistence crocodiles like: and, at Manchester and Rochdale, I have observed the surfaces of the stream smoking, so that we need be under no concern as to temperature. I should think you might produce in them quite "streaky" crocodile,—fat and flesh concordant,— St. George becoming a bacon purveyor, as well as seller, and laying down his dragon in salt (indeed it appears, by an experiment made in Egypt itself, that the oldest of human words is Bacon); potted crocodile will doubtless, also, from the countries unrestrained by religious prejudices, be imported, as the English demand increases, at lower quotations; and for what you are going to receive, the Lord make you truly thankful. (xxvii, 504)

Bringing the historical past into the present tense, where contamination is underscored by claustrophobia, the Third Style brings about the collapse of temporal distance, something that Ruskin is careful not to do, with rare exceptions, in autobiography. But it is not altogether clear whether the Third Style represents a failure of the discrimination of tenses, or an almost homogeneous triumph over that previously gradated temporal distance. At times, the writer or reader, as if angelic and traveling above the sequence of orthodox verbal form, seems to move with extraordinary speed. The result, virtually eliminating the middle, the distance of sequential transition, approaches a spatial form of juxtaposition that permits not only brutal criticism on contemporary economics and religious attitudes but also a sense of freedom, as if one were in fact delivered from Worringer's "fortuitousness of humanity as a whole." It is, at least at first, as if the writer or reader were hovering in an open space above the text, where, with the quick turning of a vast number of pages, time might skillfully be manipulated or treated with angelic simultaneity. But then, with Ruskin, the instincts towards spatialization always come first.

Still, the Third Style, while eliminating an intervening temporal distance, is itself a style of the middle, of the "nothing but process" that lies between beginnings and endings. But rapid movement through collapsed space becomes a style of the transforming middle. The movement embodied in those aspects of the Third Style which transform crocodiles into dragons and St. George into a purveyor of bacon creates an effect of options and metamorphosis, an effect that seems to be self-generating, as if the end, the final mark of punctuation, would not be reached no matter how fast the travel. Like the later diary entry of the Supper Guest, each transformation is a birth. There is no vanishing perspective. And like the multiple definitions of *Fors Clavigera*, nothing can be pinned down. Despite the instincts towards the spatialization of the St. Mark's description, words are like water. And the approach towards the condition of masterful juxtaposition takes place without the attention to conventional rules of time and space. Control, once the area of dogmatic assertion, is tempered by a playful irresponsibility, the irresponsibility of metamorphosis that is also a searing social indictment. In the same way that peripheral digression becomes of central significance, so the playful becomes serious. And as opposed to the public perspective's burden of excessive inclusion—a process, taken soberly and with a full sense of final implication, that can lead to madness, the later vision of "bloody carcasses"—the labyrinthine syntax of felicity, manipulated playfully by Atropos, the Third Fors, offers a way out, a coiling externalization from the pressures of inclusion and closure. Simply, hovering angelically above the text or coiling mortally through it, employing a spatial form with a serial temporal style, Ruskin does not have to seek the straight lines of a vanishing perspective. His style is his existence.

The present tense of an immanent consciousness that has public aspects to what is essentially a private style—often making private allusions to public material, which sends the puzzled, problematical audience nowhere—becomes more complex and less "present" the more it is examined. For not only does it hold an historical awareness, but it also anticipates the future in a way that subverts its apparently autonomous nature. Drawing energy from outside the present, it is a tense, finally, composed of a patchwork of temporal structures that work against the notion of an exclusive present—a present that has expended a good deal of energy turning in on itself, as if to anchor itself at a precise moment of reflexive admiration: "Consider, for instance, what I am doing at this very instant—half-past seven, morning 25th February, 1873. . . . Having written this sentence, I go to the fire, warm my fingers, saunter a little, listlessly, about the room, and grumble because I can't see to the other side of the lake" (xxvii, 514–15).

Opposing this almost narcissistic awareness of the moment, what is close to an autobiographical instant—"Consider . . . what I am doing at this very instant"—Ruskin, talking about "plumes" in the letter "Servant's Wages," suggests the typological structure of both history and *Fors*. It is a structure, existing incomplete in the present, that requires the future to complete a tense that is, after all, incomplete in itself. The vitality of an exclusive present—a present that is entirely self-reliant—is suspect: "Do you see how one thing bears out and fulfills another, in these thoughts and symbols of the despised people of old time?" (xxvii, 513) The typological structure, bearing out and fulfilling, eliminates the middle. Serial connections, important in the transcendental penetration of space, are banished. To read *Fors* is to sit in an echo chamber of almost infinite extent. Hundreds of pages must be skipped before the source of an obscure, muffled echo is uncovered. The result is that *Fors,* with a middle that is often jumped over, becomes a structure, like juxtaposition, that is at odds with words that are as shapeless as water. And like the style of transformation, which is a process of rebirth, the echoes and reverberations have a life of their own, a life that creates the design of a grid. In a letter for July 1872, Ruskin establishes an image of no apparent consequence within the privacy of a parenthesis: ". . . nor hinder this miserable mob (which has not brains enough to know so much as what o'clock it is, nor sense enough so much as to go aboard a boat without being whistled for, like dogs) from choking the sweet sea air with pitch-black smoke . . ." (xxvii, 329). Locked in a parenthesis, the image becomes certified almost a year later, in the April *Fors,* of 1873, as a quotation that puts an almost ludicrous demand on any reader but the writer turned angelic reader: ". . . but I find that clocks are now no more comprehensible in England than in Italy, and you also have to be 'whistled for, like dogs,' all over Yorkshire . . ." (xxvii, 515).

The establishment of outside references, of allusions beyond the present tense, is part of the "principle and tendency" in *Fors* towards patchwork. Predictably, Ruskin writes *Fors* in the same way he learned to read:

I absolutely declined to learn to read by syllables; but would get an entire sentence by heart with great facility, and point with accuracy to every word in the page as I repeated it. As, however, when the words were once displaced, I had no more to say, my mother gave up, for the time, the endeavour to teach me to read, hoping only that I might consent, in process of years, to adopt the popular system of syllabic study. But I went on to amuse myself, in my own way, learnt whole words at a time, as I did patterns. . . .

This effort to learn the words in their collective aspect, was assisted by my real admiration of the look of printed type. . . . (xxxv, 23)

Tending toward the grid, which is always Ruskin's essential impulse, the "collective aspect" of *Fors* begins to subvert the serial or "syllabic" impulse. Ruskin describes this "collective aspect," which is the impulse towards "patterns," as a "mosaic": "And to the few readers whom these letters find, they will become more useful as they go on, for they are a mosaic-work into which I can put a piece here and there as I find glass of the colour I want; what is as yet done being set, indeed, in patches, but not without design" (xxvii, 669). The establishment of designs of "patterns" and "patches" imposes a version of mastery over the digressions of the Third Style, the wanderings of Atropos—a flexible mastery that becomes possible as both writer and reader see where they have been. It is essentially a mastery of rereading in which the past is known and the future can be predicted.

The will towards the mastery of the "mosaic" reflects the potential for an underlying dissatisfaction with the style of the immanent consciousness, a style that results in a sense of intimacy that can become claustrophobic if unrelieved by either release into distance, or reference outside the present. That vast number of pages have to be turned in order to pinpoint the source of echoes is no different from the liberating process of juxtaposition. Both activities are based upon the elimination of a serial middle that does not always offer the relief from pressures afforded by the dexterous weaving of the Third Fors. A style of both immanence and intimacy, the Third Style, coiling towards externalization, requires either a way out, a sense of distance and open space, or that angelic feeling of mastery that puts the reader or writer in an open space above the collapsed space of juxtaposition.

Intimacy, coming with the failure of recessional space, the space of the vanishing perspective, requires its opposite. The letters from *Fors* coming closest to an intimacy verging on the confessional are sent from a geographical point that allows the greatest distance between writer and audience. For example, "Letter 72," which traces Ruskin's unprogressively eddying thoughts, as they search for the release of a shore that is "unencumbered" by orthodox logic, is sent to an audience presumably located in Manchester and Birmingham from Venice. The need is for distance from the pressures of responsibility that, now condensed and transformed into the grotesque, have become not merely burdensome, omnipresent, and claustrophobic, but internalized and hallucinatory. It is as if, unable to eat his dinner because of the assaults of his world, Ruskin has, like the later parenthetical self, who would turn the "outside in," taken that world for his dinner: "For this green tide that eddies by my threshold is full of floating corpses, and I must leave my dinner to bury them, since I cannot save; and put my cockle-shell in cap, and take my staff in hand, to seek an unencumbered shore" (xxviii, 758). In Ruskinian cartography, Venice lies next to Manchester. And the only way to write to and about the agonies of Manchester—and this with the further distance of "bitter play"—is to go to Venice.

But Ruskin would say that Manchester, or at least England, is a version of Venice. As he does continually in *Fors,* Ruskin refers back to previous digressive material in an attempt to make conventional sense out of his antic, devouring "play." Nothing is dead or the product of incipient madness. Everything is potentially useful. And the second time around is merely a time of deciphering. The "first vision," seen twice, creates Ruskin's new map:

> You thought, I suppose, that in writing those numbers of *Fors* last year from Venice and Verona, I was idling, or digressing?
>
> Nothing of the kind, the business of *Fors* is to tell you of Venice and Verona; and many things of them.
>
> You don't care about Venice and Verona? Of course not. Who does? And I beg you to observe that the day is coming when exactly in the same sense, active working men will say to the antiquarian who purposes to tell them something of England, "We don't care about England.". . .
>
> That England deserves little care from any man nowadays, is fatally true; that in a century more she will be—where Venice is—among the dead of the nations, is far more than probable. And yet—that you do not care for dead Venice, is the sign of your own ruin; and that the Americans do not care for dying England, is only the sign of their inferiority. (xxviii, 91–92)

Needing intimacy and distance, Ruskin has it both ways. The distinctions between time and space collapse into a present and a foreground that is "vital" and "living" because it is no different from the past and distant. Still, the collapse is an inclusive process that occurs even as Ruskin depends upon a mailing point that is greatly separated from the readership of his letters. The distance the mail travels is the equivalent of looking at Turner's "first vision" the second time around.

The establishment of an interval, a new distance like an ambitious mail route, begins to make the past, which will be the territory for efficacious autobiography, as attractive as Venice. Ruskin starts a retrospective movement that will carry him out of a present that can be as uncomfortably reflexive as the landscape of pathetic fallacy, despite the playful discursiveness of the immanent consciousness. The movement backwards begins in the same letter that rescues the Venetian digressions of the year before—"Letter 42" of June 1874: "I must construct my letters still, for a while, of swept-up fragments; every day provokes me to write new matter; but I must not lose the fruit of the old days. Here is some worth picking up, though ill-ripened for want of sunshine (the little we had spending itself on the rain), last year" (xxviii, 90). The "swept-up" material is presumably "new matter" on August 1, 1873, the date of the quoted material. But on August 1, 1873, Ruskin is no more able to work than he was at the beginning of his retrospective movement. As a substitute for work, making something of nothing, he describes his reasons for inactivity, ending in a lengthy parenthetical redefinition that is itself an activity close to work:

> Not being able to work steadily this morning, because there was a rainbow half a mile broad, and violet-bright, on the shoulders of the Old Man of Coniston—(by calling it half a mile broad, I mean that half a mile's breadth of mountain was covered by it,—and by calling it violet-bright I mean that the violet zone of it came pure against the grey rocks; and not, by the way, that essentially all the colours of the rainbow are secondary;—yellow exists only as a line—red as a line—blue as a line; but the zone itself is a varied orange, green, and violet). . . . (xxviii, 90)

Unable to work on the first of August, 1873, except by describing why he cannot work, Ruskin again does what he did at the beginning of the July, 1874 letter. He returns to the "swept-up fragments" of a diary from 1849, when, presumably unable to work, he again turned what attention he had to sweepings—this time, having run out of past time, to fragments that are not his, fragments from 1740: " —not being able I say, for steady work, I opened an old diary of 1849, and as the Third Fors would have it, at this extract from the *Letters of Lady Mary Wortley Montagu.*" The problem of the present tense, the inability to work at anything but avoiding work, is telescoped back through a series of temporal Chinese boxes that enclose varieties of more or less private experience. The structure, approaching metaphysical "bitter play," is one of comic intricacy. The problem of enclosure, which is often imprisonment, is turned into a joke: at the center of Ruskin's Chinese boxes is a letter from 1740, within a diary that is, in turn, within a fragment of a letter. All this is surrounded by the enclosing forty-second "Letter" of *Fors,* a letter that, on the circumference of this curiously concentric structure, is written in the present tense, which is the initial tense of all Ruskin's vantage points.

The telescoping of time is another form of digression. But instead of working in the present tense, it works against it, permitting a felicitous release from the obligations of the present that is similar, in effect, to the present-tense release of "bitter play." Both forms of digression combine to make Ruskin an architect without plans. He has no feeling for an ending. He would rather build forever, as if he were constructing a museum, with additions to be built as needed. As the planless architect of *Fors*, Ruskin alludes to Luke: "I have a house to build; but none shall mock me by saying I was not able to finish it, nor be vexed by not finding in it the rooms they expected" (xxviii, 106).

Yet if Ruskin is an architect without plans, he is an architect who is not without calculation. Characteristically, the man who understands that most "useful truths" are "biped" will construct his building out of antithetical styles. The middle is eliminated as Ruskin, hovering above text, shows how things "bear out and fulfill." But a different kind of middle is inserted, almost as a cushion against what might at times be the pain, instead of deliverance, of juxtaposition—a middle that takes the form of the Third Style's coiling, associative digression. Essentially, *Fors* is an example of eclectic architecture, with the patchwork, mosiac design of the spatial grid contending with the temporal and sequential. It is as if Ruskin had learned to write, if not read, in both the "syllabic" and "collective" aspects. Still, without plans, there is no end. *Fors,* feeding upon itself, returning to the "first vision" of past material for sustenance, is as open-ended as the white focal points of infinity that mark the success of distant, recessional space, the space of the vanishing perspective.

DIARY DESIGN: THE GASTRONOMIC REFLEXIVE

One of the differences between the letters of *Fors* and Ruskin's diaries is that the letters, digressing privately, are only partially written to the self, while the diaries, in which the self, often both observer and observed, occupying both vantage and focal points, are written not only by the diarist, but, as Ruskin says, "all to myself": "It has been a great disappointment to see S. again; but the world's made up of morts and disses, and it's no use always saying 'Ay de mi!' like Carlyle. I'm really ashamed of him in those letters to Emerson. My own diaries are indeed full of mewing and moaning, all to myself, but I think my letters to friends have more a tendency to crowing, or, at least, on the whole, try to be pleasant" (xxxvii, 495–96). The world of the diary finishes what the intimate letters, following the tracery of the immanent consciousness, begin. The world that in *Modern Painters* has been as open as the endless *Fors* now appears to be reflexively sealed off by the audience of the self. Like the autobiographer who comes face to face with himself, writer confronts reader and the only interval, the only distance between the two activities, is time.

Nevertheless, if it is true that the intended audience of *Fors,* the workmen of Great Britain, is an audience whose existence is at the least a necessary fiction—the real audience appearing, at times, to be a solitary but attentive eavesdropper, who may be either Manning or Ruskin himself—it is also true that, in his diaries, Ruskin, writing "all to myself," is further writing to both more and less than himself. Recording varieties of private experience, Ruskin writes multiple and simultaneous diaries. In an entry for December, 1880, in *The Diaries of John Ruskin,* edited by Joan Evans and J. H. Whitehouse, Ruskin alludes to a missing diary outside the published ones: "Then 14th December begun at Brantwood in long diary, p. 233" (*Diaries,* p. 996). In an entry from *The Diaries* for March, 1868, Ruskin refers to what may be a simultaneous diary for 1868 that is also missing: "The dream was very distinct, but the memory of it is wholly indistinct, and I had forgotten it, till I came just now by chance on Carlyle's name in my other diary" (*Diaries,* p. 645). Aside from the "long diary" and the "other diary" which may or may not be related, Ruskin, earlier, in an entry for May, 1854, mentions another diary unknown to E. T. Cook and Alexander Wedderburn, editors of the Library Edition: "On Friday the 24th I got the greatest treasure I have yet obtained in all my life: St. Louis's Psalter, see my private diary" (*Dairies,* p. 491). Essentially private, the diaries are as exclusive as the private vanishing perspective of *Modern Painters.* But with the diaries, the exclusion does not have the open recessional space that leads the observer towards transcendental release.

In Ruskin's early diaries, the exclusion yields division. The diaries are not merely private, they are components of a whole. Like "useful truths," the self is split in two. On the thirty-first of March, 1840, the entry records the determination to keep a divided diary. The diary audience, less than Manchester, is also, presumably, less than the self: "I have determined to keep one part of a diary for intellect and another for feeling" (*Diaries,* p. 74). But if Ruskin begins divided and private, he turns, at the same time, a private genre public—or, at least, semipublic, with a private version of what is public. Without developing an aesthetic of the banal, of conversational waste, but with the same sense of retrieval that perpetuates his rescuing the past in *Fors* ("You thought, I suppose, that in writing those numbers in *Fors* last year from Venice and Verona, I was idling, or digressing?"), Ruskin decides that a private slant on a public arena is worthy of preservation: "I shall put down here whatever is worth remembering of the casual knowledge that we gain so much of every day, in conversation, and generally lose every tomorrow. Much is thus lost that can never be recovered from books" (*Diaries,* p. 74).

Still, the shape of the Ruskinian diary moves towards the claustrophobic condition of a diarist writing about himself for himself. But the reader of even unpublished diaries is not entirely the same person as the writer. There is the necessary separating interval between the writer and the reader which makes autobiography feasible. The reader, even if once upon a time he was the writer, stands at a temporal distance from the diarist. Assuming a retrospective posture, the reader is involved in the writer's present tense, which may be the reader's past. Ruskin writes his diary not in order to indulge a whim for the exploration in a vital present, but for the satisfaction that the reader will get from examining himself in a past tense: "It is a great bore to keep a diary but a great delight to have kept one" (*Diaries,* p. 129). And again: "I have kept this stuff for a year; it has taken up quantities of time, and is a heavy thing in one's desk—I don't know much else it is good for, yet it may be amusing, some time or other" (*Diaries,* p. 165). The act of diary reading, then, is like the mnemonic act: it is the dealing with immediate experience from a manipulative distance that permits juxtaposition and comparison. While reflexive in the sense that writer and reader are almost the same person, the diary offers Ruskin a structure that holds enough space not only in the distance of the interval between writing and reading but also in the hovering space above the text (as Ruskin, flipping pages backwards and forwards, works out his preoccupation with the comparison of "anniversary dates"), to permit release from the potentially claustrophobic present tense of a daily diary entry.

The diarist, writing for a self who, in a later tense, becomes the reader, also writes for his immediate self. Yielding a burden of increment that is like "syllabic" reading, the diary with dates piling up behind, still provides the coherence of a serial design, a coherence that the hovering "collective aspect," mastering sequence, necessarily neglects: "These entries are of no use, yet my days get disordered if I don't make them" (*Diaries,* p. 1006). The coherent and consecutive diary entries achieve a temporal organization that is as linear as Ruskin's no less private, spatial vanishing perspective. But Ruskin, as diarist, is less anxious to penetrate the future, to employ serial entries as the equivalents of the gradations of depth perspective, than he is, in another role, to penetrate space. Having used one dimension, he would save the other. The focal point of time, unlike the white focal point of space that is also a vanishing point of self-annulment, is ominously dark, even at the age of twenty-eight: ". . . the 'it is time enough yet' excuse has utterly failed me, and that though I still feel the weakness and confess the ignorance of childhood, I have lost its happiness. Death casts its long shadow towards me, and seems to reach me across the mirage of years" (*Diaries,* p. 354).

Employing a variation of his mathematics of sunset and sunrise, a mathematics with which he determines the hours and minutes left in what appear to be ever-shortening days, Ruskin, who would not penetrate the "mirage of years" any sooner than necessary, calculates the shift of prospective time, as the incremental burden of entry dating continues:

> January 1st. Friday. BRANTWOOD. I am really getting gradually, as I near the end of my days, into setting them down orderly. Supposing I were to live fifteen years more—or Hezekiah's sixteen—and usefully, they might still come to something.

> $$\begin{array}{r} 365 \\ 16 \\ \hline 2190 \\ 365 \\ \hline 5840 \end{array}$$ Five thousand, eight hundred, and forty days. Greatly diminished from the 11000 I used to count in my early diaries, and the thousand I used—impiously—to count once upon a time wishing they might pass. (*Diaries,* p. 833)

Composed of 5840 gradations on the first day of 1875, the coherence of sequence, the temporal depth perspective, begins to fail, in much the same way as Ruskin's recessional space will also fail. The elimination of the serial is considered: "I begin not to care to put dates down more now" (*Diaries,* p. 1037). Or when serial dating occurs, it is often subverted, sometimes only by a day: "Dates all in a mess, and I've been putting in order and missed a day . . ." (*Diaries,* p. 1102). But occasionally, on the gradated perspective that converges at the "long shadow," Ruskin retreats as much as a month. In a short period of June, 1885, Ruskin manipulates, if not time itself, model time—the dates of a series of entries: "June 2nd . . . May—No—June 3rd . . . May 4th—June—I mean . . . May—June—5th" (*Diaries,* p. 1112). Still, the breakdown of sequence is not the movement towards mastery, towards the "collective aspect" of the "mosaic." Simply, it is response to the tyranny of the serial, a serial progression that can only end, after much eddying, on a shore washed by Ruskin's "green tide," a shore that is finally "unencumbered." The vanishing perspective has lost some of its early appeal.

The break-up of the temporal, serial progression is reflected in a diary syntax that, bending back towards the diary writer, is more "broken" than even the "bitter play" of *Fors.* The entries following the September twenty-first, 1881, arrangement of past experience are entries employing a logic and tense of immediacy that are antithetical to the system-mongering of Ruskin's "main stream," a "stream" that is the shortest route to the "unencumbered shore." Opposite the page of the September twenty-second entry, Ruskin describes his movement from distanced judgment and manipulation to a version of the intimate, Atropos-manipulated Third Style: "This 22nd September begins the time of excitement following arrangement of diaries with Alic: and it goes on virtually to 20th October, when I collapse" (*Diaries,* p. 999, note).

During the "time of excitement," Ruskin's diary experience follows a logic of metamorphoses—an associative, Atroposian logic that seems to feed off itself as much as the material it is confronted with. It is as if the consciousness were involved in a curious act of self-cannibalization. The entry for the twenty-third of September shows the "bitter play" of perpetual transformation creating a verbal fabric that indicates at once Ruskin's psychic instability and his attempt to maintain some kind of balance in the face of that instability. Rich in allusions, quotations, and underlinings, the entry conducts a dialogue with various aspects of a self on the verge of either disintegration into fragments, or multiplication into double or triple selves.[2]

The dialogue is structured about a series of "queries," followed by "happy thoughts" numbered in serial progression, a process that parodies the apparent logic organizing the entry. But Ruskin's mind does not have the distance for parody. Instead, it is as if he were transforming or digesting immediate material in order to keep from collapsing before it. It is as if there were a battle between the appetites of self and world. Predictably, the source of transformation comes from the liturgy of the table—food, potential food, both animal and human, the ceremony of eating, the "Feast of the sucking pig," and the process of ingestion or internalization, which is, itself, a process of metamorphoses ending, after Ruskin's kaleidoscopic changes, in "one leg [of] dung":

September 23rd. Friday. Joan home y[esterday], and Lollie. Feast of sucking pig. (Q[uery]: what had Tobit for dinner—the father?)

I, a spot in their feast of charity! But carry my wine best, being the servant of the 'gluttonous man, and winebibber.'

Q[uery]—happy thought!—when and how often *did* Christ enjoy himself and—the company—with any of his apostles who took after him? St. Martin, suppose, or—St. Crumpet—Crumpin! Frenchman not liking me cold—will he like me hot?

I *opened* just now (down to coffee in good time) at the entry for 23rd Oct. last year—page 153, A, B—and must mind what I'm at. This morning, thought of *Sortes Virgilianae,* and the sign of angle-dial of paper, turned accidentally in folio yesterday, to *Infelix sedebit,* but *hiding* the anatomical part to the left.

Q[uery]. Where, and who, sits *infelix*—Unhappy? or unlucky? "Lead me, as he leads his flocks" &c.—Wild *deer*—Chamois—Fawn at Lucerne. Aig[uille] *d'Argentière*—(*Silver* How?). Set Alic to find diary of day when I went up—I and Couttet—alone in early morning, on aiguille *Bouchard* (not Argentière) and saw the three flocks of wild *deer,* not goats.

[2] For a passage to a similar effect, also written during a "time of excitement," see pp. 101–103 of *The Brantwood Diary of John Ruskin* (New Haven and London, 1971), brilliantly edited and annotated by Helen Gill Viljoen.

"The High hills are a refuge for the wild *goats,* and the (Brantwood) rocks for the conies."

Scapegoat—Melville's sermon on the *two* Goats. "*Aha*; the TWO *goats* are now in the hands of their enemies.". . .

His [Mr. Melville] last call upon me when I was at dinner. I came to him in the drawing room, intimated to him I *was* at dinner. "Go to your dinner," he said, benevolent, contemptuous—and left; and I never saw him seriously again, unless perhaps, for some chance form of call, or knock-head-together in street.

"Revenons à nos moutons"—goats, I should say, Moses and *his* horns. Zedekiah the son of Chenaanah, and *his* horns of iron or iron clad—or iron cast.

"With these shalt thou push the *Syrians* till thou have *consumed* them"— i.e. Caffres, New Zealanders, Afghans, & c. and the Gallant Colonel and my lady Clara (*Gallant*—galantes) Coloneless—shall have their pipe, and pot, of Champagne, in peace, and punkah fans of Japanese design, on the hills of the Himalaya.

"I will lift up mine eyes unto the hills from whence cometh my—income and coolies."

"Revenons—Revenons—à nos moutons," and Lambs that are slain, and made Chops of, and cutlets. Human *grillades*.

(N. B.) Happy thought No. 1. "Vous y grillerez Cicéron, et le bon Socrate, le divin Platon." (N. C.) Happy thought No. 2. If Aristophanes had run away with Xantippe, would Socrates have forgiven him? Perhaps—Perhaps! See Socrates' last love message to Xantippe, while "on old Aegina's rock &c.—the God of (matrimonial) gladness, sent his *parting* smile." But—Q[uery]. Happy thought No. 3 (both of these given me last night with a few more). Did Socrates ever forgive him the *Clouds?* and *if* he had written the *Clouds after* having run off with Xantippe! Or instead of *writing* the *Clouds,* gone on Back-biting *behind* the clouds! fog—of the Acheron.

St. Ulpha's Frogs, and Dionysus's—same beasts—virtually, and the *one leg dung* of the first specter—what was the other leg of?

(Part of iron—part of clay. Stone cut out without hands; see Amiens.) . . .

Enough, for this morning, anyhow. But see to left page.

Not quite enough, neither. Remember, yesterday afternoon, invented possible or probable title of next part of "Our Fathers have told us"; "The Font of Cluse" or "Bells of Cluse"—i.e. Springs at Magland and Baptism (see *Fors*). Arve stream at Cluse, and Turner's 'Bains' at foot of Church on Rock in *Splugen.* This may be of course said to be not in *his* mind—but in mind! It would be good for nothing, if it were intended by him to the full. Its power is in being "the word of God" to *me* through—"The Bagpipe singing in the Nose"—(See context of *that*)—Bagpipe—blown by Angels, by Angelico, by Devil in rich man's ear (Holbein). The Two modern Bagpipes! Gladstone and

D'Israeli! blown into by the Devil at Britannia's (Cockney Britannia of the *Market's*) ear; see proposed Statue of *her*—long ago. (*Diaries*, pp. 1000–1002)

Approaching collapse, Ruskin's mind refuses to confront without metamorphoses. It is as if, avoiding recognition, he were involved in the perpetual "self-transcendence" of the Chinese garden. If autobiography or self-portraiture is difficult, so is the condition of being "face to face" with anything. During this "time of excitement," confrontation means transformation. Only the appetite is constant. And even that seems increasingly ambitious. Livestock is transformed from sucking pig to deer, "three flocks of wild *goats*," and from "wild *goats*" to goats that are not goats at all but scapegoats, and from scapegoats, Ruskin urges one portion of his disintegrating or multiplying self to return to the point of *La Farce du Maitre Patelin*, a point of sheep—"Revenons à nos moutons." But, characteristically, the sheep are in goats' clothing, or perhaps, neither sheep nor goats, they are "Lambs," introduced in upper case, which become "Chops" or "Human *grillades*," returning Ruskin to a point he would avoid, the point of himself. Still, earlier in the entry, as neither "Chops" nor "Human *grillades*," but as bread—as St. Crumpet, Rose La Touche's name for Ruskin—he wonders whether he ought to serve himself "hot" to the "Frenchman," who doesn't like him "cold."

At the table, struggling against collapse, Ruskin appears to be not so much digesting as digested. The final metamorphoses is that of the self. It is a gesture against autobiography, a vigorous display of slight of hand in a confined space. The "Feast of the sucking pig" is the celebration of a self-annulment that is gastronomic rather than optical. Appetite, exploding beyond the ambitions of even the largest stomach, has become cosmic, and the hallucinatory "Feast" is finally the feast of Ruskin's transforming consciousness. Attempting to get "outside," to achieve distance in the face of a failing recessional space—the reflexive space of a pathetic fallacy that, later, with the inverted perspective, turns into an aggressive dimension of invasion, bringing the "outside in"—Ruskin, fighting the eddies of a mind on the brink of madness, has become, like either his parenthetical self or his Neapolitan prisoner, Jonah instead. If, multiplying selves, he is seated at the table, he is also regarding a menu or platter that, in large portion, includes himself.

OUTSIDE IN: THE ANTITHETICAL ARCHITECTURE OF THE PARENTHESIS

Describing Turner's topographical double-mindedness, Ruskin, both supper and supper-guest, both writer and reader, is describing an operation of the mind that shapes his own syntax: ". . . Turner's mind was, in two great instincts, at variance with itself. The *affections* of it clung, as we have just seen, to humble scenery, and gentle wildness of pastoral life. But the *admiration* of it was, more than any other artist's whatsoever, fastened on largeness of scale. With all his heart, he was attached to the narrow meadows and rounded knolls of England; by all his imagination he was urged to the reverence of endless vales and measureless hills . . ." (VI, 303). Yet with Ruskin, far from being limited to "two great instincts," which is the condition of a mind "at variance with itself," the taking into account of the "biped," the contrary, is an essential part of his will to form. One end of London Bridge calls forth the other. And St. Paul's, to be observed with the stereoscopic ideal, should be seen antithetically, from both ends of the bridge at once.

Like the young lady of *Les Pourquoi de Mademoiselle Suzanne*, who is *"par parenthese* entertained with the history and picture of the suicide of the cook Vatel" (XXXIII, 354), Ruskin increasingly entertains himself with parenthetical counterpoint. Even early in his career, he can talk about all of *Modern Painters* as an extension and elaboration of a parenthetical seed: "All *Modern Painters* together will be the explanation of a parenthesis in *The Stones of Venice"* (X, xlvii). As opposed to the unannounced digressions of Atropos, which occur on the "outside" of syntax, Ruskin often advertises, both before and after the event, the fact of his tidy, parenthetical digressions. Peripheral thought, brought to the center, is proudly enclosed in interior syntax, as if the process of internalizing and separating were a form of verbal housekeeping:

> Here ends my necessary parenthesis, with its suspicion of preachment, for which I crave pardon, and I return to my proper subject of to-day. . . . (XXXIII, 332)
>
> I may in this place, I think, best introduce—though again parenthetically—the suggestion of a healthy field for the labouring scientific fancy. . . . (XXXIII, 335)
>
> In my last lecture, I noted to you, though only parenthetically. . . . (XXXIII, 338)

The reader, invited to digress, is also invited to entertain himself *"par parenthese"*: "In parenthesis, just read this little bit of Plato . . ." (XXVII, 294). Inflated, the parenthesis can occupy a vast area of Ruskin's syntactic topography. A parenthesis can be the five volumes of *Modern Painters*, or the five lectures of *Val d'Arno*: ". . . I have at last got to the end of the parenthesis which began in my second lecture . . ." (XXIII, 109).

Yet more often the parenthesis, unadvertised, is not inflated, and the digression, condensed, is more accurately an antithetical interruption that occurs in a small, parcelled period of the present tense. The conflict of split selves and double tenses is apparent as Ruskin interrupts his own reading from Antonio Caccianiga's *Vita Campestre*: "'The Venetian Republic founded in Padua'"—(wait a minute; for the pigeons are come to my window-sill and I must give them some breakfast)—"'founded in Padua, 1765, the first chair of rural economy appointed in Italy . . .'" (xxvii, 328–29). The parenthetical self does not participate in up-dating a "first vision." In a relation of absolute intimacy to experience, with no intervening and manipulative distance between self and focal point, the parenthetical self observes "first vision" in such a way that vision becomes "nothing but process." But Ruskin is able to indulge in this intimacy because the parenthetical self is merely an alternative self. The distance provided by options—an "outside" self and an "inside" self—allows the proximity of a syntax that revolves about the simultaneity inherent in "as":

> My boy with his basket of rotten figs *could* only sell them in front of the sculpture of Noah, because all the nobles had perished from Venice, and he was there, poor little costermonger, stooping to cry fighiaie between his legs, where the stateliest lords in Europe were wont to walk, erect enough, and in no disordered haste. (Curiously, as I write this very page, one of the present authorities in progressive Italy, progressive without either legs or arms, has gone whizzing by, up the canal, in a steam propeller, like a large darting water beetle.) He could only sell them in that place, because . . . (xxix, 37)

The "as" syntax—"as I write this very page"—is a structure employed to indicate a double consciousness that is not necessarily "at variance with itself." At the least, it permits the simultaneous exploration—as if from both ends of London Bridge at once—of a multiple series of perceptions that often link up for a dramatic, cubistic effect, an effect that surrounds the problem, or focal point, with a variety of tones from different tenses:

> . . . it may be understood what England also had once to bring forth of blessing in her own vales of peace; and how her gathering iniquity may bring upon her,—(and at this instant, as I write, early on Good Friday, the malignant hail of spring time, slaying blossom and leaf, smites rattling on the ground that should be soft with flowers), such day of ruin as the great hail darkened in the going down to Beth-horon, and the sun, that had bronzed their corn and flushed their grape, prolonged on Ajalon, implacable. (xxviii, 598)

The simultaneous recording of experience in different tenses, which creates a version of the Chinese box effect of *Fors*, in which the telescoping of time becomes historical digression, also creates a design of juxtaposition that is a model of the mosaic-like structure of *Fors*.

The parenthetical topography, containing a variety of voices and tenses that allow Ruskin to play multiple roles, is apparently felicitous enough, in

its simultaneous, cubistic release, to inspire parentheses *ad infinitum.* If un-
checked, the impulse towards parenthesis threatens to force the exterior
text—what lies "outside"—off the page. At one point, it appears that all of
Ruskin will become interior and digressive: "But if I wrote a parenthesis of
that length every now and then, the entire book would overlap into the next
planet or nebula; and if I began putting notes to explain, or confirm, I
should probably write a new book on the trotting of Centaurs and
Lapithae, or the riding of Bellerophon, or the crawling of the Tortoise of
Aegina, or the flying of Harry the Fifth's tennis balls . . ." (*Diaries,* p.
1136).

Predictably, the syntax of parenthesis, animating pages with interior
"nerves" like the landscape of immanence, may also become subterranean,
as it does in *Munera Pulveris,* where asterisks lead into parentheses that
run under the text like a basement necessary to the structure above. And
intensifying the character of this subterranean, parenthetical architecture,
parentheses are found within parentheses, as digression retreats further
from the responsible "outside" of serial thought:

> *(The meaning of that, in plain English, is that we must find out how far
> poverty and riches are good or bad for people, and what is the difference
> between being miserably poor—so as, perhaps, to be driven to crime, or to pass
> life in suffering—and being blessedly poor, in the sense meant in the Sermon
> on the Mount. For I suppose the people who believe that sermon, do not think
> (if they ever honestly ask themselves what they do think), either that Luke vi.
> 24 is a merely poetical exclamation, or that the Beatitude of Poverty has yet
> been attained in St. Martin's Lane and other back streets of London.) (xvii,
> 180–81)

> *(Large plans!—Eight years are gone, and nothing done yet. But I keep my
> purpose of making one day this balance, or want of balance visible, in those so
> seldom used scales of Justice.) (xvii, 181)

In the densely parenthetical space of *Munera,* the subterranean parenthesis, carrying its own embryonic parenthesis, is followed immediately by
still another parenthesis that is written neither in the Third Style that is
close to the workings of consciousness nor with the simultaneity of the "as"
syntax. Rather, it is constructed in a present tense that is merely eight years
closer to the reader's present. In this work that appears about to become a
counterpoint of parentheses with nothing left "outside" to counter, as if
Ruskin's dinner guest has swallowed his world, parentheses are not only
piled on top of each other, as well as placed inside each other, but the
writer can lead his agile reader hopscotching from parenthesis to parenthesis, without ever entering the diminishing exterior body of text that,

being forced off the page, has never been more "outside":

(In the first case the money is as an atmosphere surrounding the wealth, rising from it and raining back upon it; but in the second, it is as a deluge, with the wealth floating, and for the most part perishing in it.†

†(You need not trouble yourself to make out the sentence in parenthesis, unless you like, but do not think it is mere metaphor. It states a fact which I could not have stated so shortly, *but* by metaphor). (xvii, 205)

At this point, it is as if the enclosing space of the parenthesis has become the sacred space of the early medieval castle. Paginal emphasis is on the interior. It is as if what lies "outside"—the text proper, which is no equivalent to the purifying recessional space of the third dimension—is something polluted, something to be avoided. And the parenthetical labyrinth will lead both writer and reader to a place of interior safety. Like Ruskin's Neapolitan prisoners, Ruskin is syntactically free "inside."

Unsurprisingly, the parenthetical landscape performs some of the same functions as the felicitous syntax of Atropos' style. Enclosing the peripheral, parentheses permit the observation of a problem from a variety of vantage points, vantage points that are divided in a way that the homogeneous classical landscape is not. But parenthetical division, creating more than a circle of tones and attitudes with which to surround a problem, allows necessary play, the indulgence of whim—"(Wait a minute; for the pigeons are come . . .)." What lies "outside," the exterior text, if it is not entirely ingested, owes its existence to the parenthesis. Precisely because of the playful release within enclosure—the "inside" having become defensive and privileged rather than imprisoning and infernal—the "outside" is written. Release comes from an interior syntactic space that is not yet felt to be claustrophobic. Instead, it is a playground for digressive indulgence.

Yet the antithetical architecture only functions in counterpoint. With Ruskin, there is always the danger of too much of a good thing. When the parenthetical impulse becomes recognized as primary instead of a response, the parenthesis is no longer a version of pastoral, a space of optional voices and tenses. The loss of parenthetical felicity begins with a parenthetical recording that is neither whimsical nor optional, but required—a parenthetical recording of an aural assault that signals a painfully intense awareness of the present tense:

So also architecture, sculpture, painting—Sheffield ironwork. Natural to Sheffield,—joyful to Sheffield, otherwise an entirely impossible form of poetry there. (Three enormous prolonged trumpetings, or indecent bellowings—audible, I should think, ten miles off—from another steamer entering the

Giudecca, interrupt me again,—and you need not think that I am peculiar in sensitiveness: no decent family worship, no gentle singing, no connectedly thoughtful reading, would be possible to any human being under these conditions, wholly inevitable now by any person of moderate means in Venice. With considerable effort, and loss of nervous energy, I force myself back into course of thought.) (xxix, 85)

An inversion of the position of felicitous space has taken place. The parenthesis, which had been an arena of indulgence, of "play," has now become part of an enclosing architecture, holding a present tense that is more infernal than felicitous. The "inside," which is present tense, is to be held within for the good of what lies "outside."

Still, what lies within the parenthesis cannot be avoided. The "prolonged trumpetings," which are part of a claustrophobic present tense, cannot be censored as they will be in the autobiography of *Praeterita*. But Ruskin attempts to tame those "trumpetings" by a process of calculation that is a kind of mathematical "play":

> (I am interrupted in my work at this moment,—Oxford, Sunday, 13th July, 1876, seven, morning,—first by a long rumble, which,—thinking it for a while to be something going on in the next rooms,—I make out to be a luggage train; and then, just as I begin again, and am considering whether to say "simple" or "general" terms,—by a steady whistle,—which, coming in with the morning air through the open window, worries me as if a cat were in the room, sustaining her mew at a high note. Vainly trying to fix my mind for ten or twelve seconds, as I find the noise going on, getting louder, and at last breaking into startling demi-semiquavers, I give up my business, for the present,—and count fifty-three, slowly, before this musical entertainment and psalm of modern life stops. Actually there's another train coming, just as I have finished this paragraph. I have counted eighty, and it is still not over;—at last things are getting quiet, and I will try to go on.) (xxxi, 124–25)

The separation of the silent and timeless from the aural and temporal is dramatized in a description of a version of Ruskinian pastoral that is in conflict with the attempt to write that description:

> Of "Cluse," the closed valley,—not a ravine, but a winding plain, between very great mountains, rising for the most part in cliffs—but cliffs which retire one behind the other above slopes of pasture and forest. (Now as I am writing this passage in a country parsonage—of Cowley, near Uxbridge,—I am first stopped by a railroad whistle two minutes and half long,* and then by the rumble and grind of a slow train, which prevents me from hearing my own words, or being able to think, so that I must simply wait for ten minutes, till it is past.)
>
> *Counted by watch, for I knew by its manner it would last, and measured it.

This enclosed version of pastoral, the "closed valley," that Ruskin, with his special topographical requirements, would have open—"I am bound to declare to be blameful, and to ask you, with more than an artist's wonder, why this fair Valley of Cluse is now closed indeed" (xxvi, 154)—itself surrounds the parenthetically enclosed, assaulting present that proceeds simultaneous to, but separated from, the pastoral description of "Cluse." The result is a "mosaic" that dramatizes the difference between what is described outside the parenthesis, the world of timeless pastoral, and what is described inside, the world of aural invasion that is measured by an awareness of the present tense that is as intense as the diarist's, who divides his entry of "To-day" until it approaches the fine discriminations of Pater's pulsing moments.

A more elaborate example of "mosaic" can be found in the "Benediction Letter" of *Fors*. An incremental series, which is a design, like his diary design, that Ruskin would avoid, builds from one to seven, as Ruskin, employing dashes inside parentheses, punctuates towards what is infernal, as if by punctuation he could separate an assaulting present tense from a world without the claustrophobic pressures of a diminishing future tense. Unable to eliminate either his obsessive subtraction of days, or the steam-whistles that define a present tense that has become as aggressive as reflexive space, he attempts to contain, with as much punctuation as possible, what he would ignore. As opposed to the "nerves" of the immanent classical landscape, what is enclosed is enclosed to be kept out of the way. Instead of banishing the infernal to borders, the outskirts of vision, it has been placed in a syntactic prison:

Again, with regard to the limbs, or general powers of the body. Do you suppose that when it is promised that "the lame man shall leap as an hart, and the tongue of the dumb sing"—(Steam-whistle interrupts me from the *Capo d'Istria,* which is lying in front of my window with her black nose pointed at the red nose of another steamer at the next pier. There are nine large ones at this instant,—half-past six, morning, 4th July,—lying between the Church of the Redeemer and the Canal of the Arsenal; one of them an ironclad, five smoking fiercely, and the biggest,—English and half a quarter of a mile long,—blowing steam from all manner of pipes in her sides, and with such a roar through her funnel—whistle number two from *Capo d'Istria*—that I could not make any one hear me speak in this room without an effort),—do you suppose, I say, that such a form of benediction is just the same as saying that the lame man shall leap as a lion, and the tongue of the dumb mourn? Not so, but a special manner of action of the members is meant in both cases: (whistle number three from *Capo d'Istria*; I am writing on, steadily, so that you will be able to form an accurate idea, from this page, of the intervals of time in modern music. The roaring from the English boat goes on all the while, for bass to the *Capo d'Istria's* treble, and a tenth steamer comes in sight round the Armenian Monastery)—a particular kind of activity is meant, I repeat, in both cases. The lame man is to leap, (whistle fourth from *Capo d'Istria*, this time at high pressure, going through my head like a knife) as an innocent and joyful creature leaps, and the lips of the dumb to move melodiously: they are to be *blest*, so: may not be unblest even in silence; but are the absolute contrary of blest, in evil utterance. (Fifth whistle, a double one, from *Capo d'Istria*, and it is seven o'clock, nearly; and here's my coffee, and I must stop writing. Sixth whistle—the *Capo d'Istria* is off, with her crew of morning bathers. Seventh,—from I don't know which of the boats outside—and I count no more.) (xxvii, 341–42)

The syntactic structure of what Ruskin calls "these broken sentences," which attempt to explain "life positive, under blessing,—life negative, under curse,—and death, neutral between these" (xxvii, 342), organized about contrasting spaces and tenses, is also organized about the contrast between motion and inertia. Outside, the serial progression from subject to verb to object is recorded in gentle cadences, as if the writer were involved in the felicitous penetration of space—or as if, instead of either writing or penetrating space, he were involved in "connectedly thoughtful reading." But inside, there is the perpetual redefinition of an aggressively intimate present tense that is the parenthetically imprisoned "psalm of modern life," a life which, going noisily nowhere, is "negative, under curse." Essentially, with nowhere to go, with no possibility of organizing space around a vanishing perspective, there is only noise, the friction of objects attempting to move in a space as limited as a tense that has to be expanded by microscopic attention to intervals.

Yet the sameness is not the homogeneity of the classical landscape which, unlike the modern landscape, is not structured about distinction and surprise. Rather, it is a sameness and intertia resulting from a sense that everything has been used up, that there is nowhere to go, that distinctions, now necessary to survival, as they were not before, have broken down. But if what occurs inside the parentheses suggests sameness, the sentences, taken as a whole, are "broken" in two. And, as split sentences for a mind "at variance with itself," they contrast the claustrophobic noise of the assaulting present with the hushed voice of the exterior, a voice that, beyond the oppressive tenses of immediacy which may describe spatial restrictions, "may not be unblest even in silence."[3]

Parenthetical syntax, which may be either protective or imprisoning, is, in either case, dependent upon counterpoint, the options between what is inside and what is outside the "broken" parenthetical sentences. What is required, in fact, is that the syntax be "broken," in order that Ruskin's consciousness, "at variance with itself," achieve a kind of equilibrium and

---

[3] See John Rosenberg's "Style and Sensibility in Ruskin's Prose," pp. 190–91, for a lucid and sensitive analysis of the same passage to similar effect.

balance through split expression. This need for "doubleness" is something that Ruskin, whether establishing that truth is "biped" or stereoscopically penetrating space, has always required. Simply, the possibility of options based upon distinctions, the ability to make discriminations, is essential to the topography of Ruskin's mind—as essential as the modern landscape's element of surprise that permits perpetual "self-transcendence."

But when the parenthetical impulse, which is the impulse for the heterodox, becomes more than counterpoint, it loses its ability to allow either digressive, whimsical release, or contain an aggressive present tense that is more contaminated and claustrophobic than "vital." To enclose all paginal space in parentheses is to have no parentheses at all, no "broken sentences," and no optional performances. To enclose all paginal space in parentheses is to have a breakdown in the function of sentences that are balanced because "broken." It is a movement towards a condition of homogeneity that, permitting no distinction, permits no release.

Increasing, Ruskin's parenthetical appetite begins to devour exterior text, in the same way that his optical traveler uses up recessional space. It is as if the Supper Guest of Ruskin's diary were ingesting not St. Crumpet, which is to say himself, but all that is outside: "They're all [Ruskin's sentences] nothing but parentheses and bad grammar, and when I can't help coming to the end of a parenthesis, I turn it outside in and put the bit of the text nearest, inside" (xxxvi, 476). But turning the "outside in," Ruskin is without even the limited and decreasing space for "variance" that he has as the self-cannibalizing Supper Guest. Ruskin can no longer be the satisfied, potential traveler who goes nowhere because he can go anywhere. With the exchange of a used and failing depth perspective for both peripheral vision and a sense of public inclusion, Ruskin, eliminating the "there" or what is "outside," is without the alternative parenthetical spaces that perform the same function as the distinction between foreground and background, vantage point and focal point, a distinction that Ruskin has always found necessary.

Parenthetically enclosed, without a "broken" sense of the outside, Ruskin is trapped in the syntactic equivalent of his subjective Dungeon of Corruption, which is the cave of Turner's one-eyed people. He is, as the parenthetical self, in a solipsistic and claustrophobic space that is rapidly becoming as uninhabitable as a room without a view, or Rembrandt's later "coal-cellar." But now, with the outside no longer where it belongs, there can be no stereoscopic escape, no escape to the exterior text. Trapped, the parenthetical self approaches inertia. It is as if Ruskin, in this guise, had employed only the spatializing impulse towards "mosaic," and, instead of being angelically delivered from the tyranny of sequence, had been delivered, locked in a spatial grid, from the possibility of movement, the "nothing but process" of the Third Style, which is Ruskin's style of survival.

In any case, before the parenthetical self becomes more than an important and anticipatory aspect of Ruskin, before the complete reduction to inertia, homogeneity, and the simultaneity of the "as" syntax, there is still motion left in Ruskin's world, motion and temporal distinctions. Everything is not yet the same. Everything has not yet reached the condition of "as." St. Paul's cannot be seen, much less painted, from both ends of London Bridge at the same time. And both ends are not necessarily the same. Finally, what is left is the retrospective movement towards autobiography, which has been anticipated by, if not the perpetually transforming diarist, the diarist's Supper Guest, who decides to dine off himself. But the autobiographer, discovering his subject in the past, instead of at the table, will only be able to write as long as there is a distinction between the autobiographer and his past-tense self. And the discriminations will become fewer as the temporal distance, or potential for movement between the two selves, becomes less—as homogeneity and simultaneity displace distinctions. The predicament of the parenthetical self offers a warning: the outside should not be turned in. But the warning is too late.

CHAPTER V

The Inverted
Perspective:
The Regression
of the Focal Point

DOME OF ASHES: THE REVERSE CREATION

The regression of the focal point from the distant light beyond a background that is also a vanishing point, a point of transcendental release, began as Ruskin's vision turned from private to public, in an attempt to incorporate the peripheral areas of surface perspective—the problems of economics and society. Incorporating much, the vision of inclusion crowded the self, putting a premium on antithetical structures, on optional spaces, on versions of the lost recessional space of stereoscopics. By the time Ruskin adopts the syntax of consciousness, the Third Style, he is running out of future, as he has already run out of distance.

Like Ortega's theory of the historical regression of attention from the solid forms of Giotto to the contemporary, intrasubjective analysis of "the contents of consciousness,"[1] Ruskin's individual regression is, first, towards the self, then beyond, into the topography of consciousness. An embryonic version of this inverted perspective, with the self or the self's "contents of consciousness" as the focal point, can be seen as early as the last volume of *Modern Painters*. Instead of looking outwards, away from autobiography and self-portraiture, away from self-consciousness, Ruskin begins to popu-

[1] Ortega y Gasset, "Point of View in the Arts," *The Dehumanization of Art,* pp. 100–20.

late his landscape: "Man is the sun of the world; more than the real sun. The fire of his wonderful heart is the only light and heat worth gauge or measure. Where he is, are the tropics; where he is not, the ice-world" (vii, 262).

This anticipation of the self as focal point, the sense of man as the "sun of the world," is similar to looking in a mirror. But the reflexive image is more than the self: ". . . the soul of man is a mirror of the mind of God. A mirror, dark, distorted, broken, use what blameful words you please of its state; yet in the main, a true mirror, out of which alone, and by which alone, we can know anything of God at all" (vii, 260). Yet the danger is that, looking within, this observing self may not be able to get out. The suitability of the self's prominent position as "the light of the world" is dependent upon a sense of "due relation": "In this best piece not only is he bound to take delight, but cannot, in a right state of thought, take delight in anything else, otherwise than through himself. Through himself, however, as the sun of creation, not as *the* creation. In himself, as the light of the world. Not as being the world. Let him stand in his due relation to other creatures, and to inanimate things—know them all and love them, as made for him, and he for them; and he becomes himself the greatest and holiest of them" (vii, 263). When this "due relation" is disregarded, when the self loses the sense of a surrounding astronomy, the problems of the inverted perspective—the reflexive movement with the self as focal point—are activated: "But let him cast off this relation, despise and forget the less creation round him, and instead of being the light of the world, he is a sun in space—a fiery ball, spotted with storm" (vii, 263). The inverted focal point, without "due relation," becomes a prison where the confinement is solitary: "All the diseases of mind leading to fatalest ruin consist primarily in this isolation. They are the concentration of man upon himself . . ." (vii, 263). Predictably, with no sense of the background, of either proper context or transcendental space, the self becomes its own prison, its own corrupt Dungeon of *Me*-ology.

The background of Ruskin's world is, at least partially, atmospheric, with an atmosphere that is pristine, unsullied—an immaculate atmosphere in touch with its origins: "Let us begin then with the simple open blue of the sky. This is of course the colour of the pure atmospheric air, not the aqueous vapour, but the pure azote and oxygen, and it is the total colour of the whole mass of that air between us and the void of space" (iii, 346). Yet original space, immaculate atmosphere, easily penetrable for the transcendent consciousness, anticipates a mixture both more complicated and less pristine than azote and oxygen:

> It is a strange thing how little in general people know about the sky. It is the part of creation in which nature has done more for the sake of pleasing man,

more for the sole and evident purpose of talking to him and teaching him, than in any other of her works, and it is just the part in which we least attend to her. There are not many of her other works in which some more material or essential purpose than the mere pleasing of man is not answered by every part of their organization; but every essential purpose of the sky might, so far as we know, be answered, if once in three days, or thereabouts, a great, ugly, black rain-cloud were brought up over the blue. . . . (III, 343)

The "great, ugly, black rain-cloud," much later transformed into the subject of *The Storm-Cloud of the Nineteenth Century*, is, then, after the regression of the focal point towards the self, no longer whimsically regarded, or, as Ruskin would have it, "once in three days." The deadly claustrophobia of the horizontal plane, the "dead flat" of the early diaries, has become another kind of death, the death of impenetrability: "Black rain, after utterly black dead afternoon" (*Diaries*, p. 859); "Rain and the usual deadly black sky" (*Diaries*, p. 866); "Deadly black all yesterday" (*Diaries*, p. 869).

If the young Ruskin can announce, "All drawings with black skies, without exception, are fine" (XIII, xxv), an older Ruskin, whose entire future is about to become memory, a subject for censored autobiography, inverts the maxim. The skies of "deadly black" are the result of an uncreation similar to Jeremy's "great reverse of Creation" described in *Fors* (XXVIII, 177–78). Ruskin, in order to write his own "great reverse of Creation," starts with a more orthodox version: "You will, by persevering in the practice, gradually discover that it is a pleasant thing to see stars in the luminous east; to watch them fade as they rise; to hear their Master say, Let there be light—and there is light; to see the world made, that day, at the word; and creation, instant by instant, of divine forms out of darkness" (XXVIII, 463). Against orthodoxy, Ruskin, whose regression of the focal point is the dark side of the penetration of space, describes the dark side of the creation:

At six o'clock, or some approximate hour, you will perceive with precision that the Firm over the way, or round the corner, of the United Grand Steam Percussion and Corrosion Company, Limited (Offices, London, Paris, and New York), issues its counterorder, Let there be darkness; and that the Master of Creation not only at once submits to this order, by fulfilling the constant laws He has ordained concerning smoke,—but farther, supernaturally or miraculously, enforces the order by sending a poisonous black wind, also from the east, of an entirely corrosive, deadly, and horrible quality, with which, from him that hath not, He takes away also that light he hath; and changes the sky during what remains of the day,—on the average now three days out of five,—into a mere dome of ashes, differing only by their enduring frown and slow pestilence from the passing darkness and showering death of Pompeii. (XXVIII, 464)

The ratio of atmospheric oppression is almost reversed: the "great, ugly, black rain-cloud" that Ruskin would summon "once in three days" has become a "dome of ashes" that crushes the inhabitant "three days out of five."

The coherence of Ruskin's mind is in the process of becoming as "broken" as his parenthetic sentences. But whereas his "broken," parenthetic thought, as long as it was balanced, permitted a kind of equilibrium between what was inside and what was outside, this new notion of breakage has more to do with disconnection than options, total separation than the "biped" quality of useful truth. The diction of disconnection, of separation from various versions of recessional space by the "dome of ashes," revolves precisely around this notion of "breakage." Days are either "broken" or "unbroken": "a wistful broken day, wandering about bits of Verona new to me" (*Diaries*, p. 913); "Broken sunshine, and now the old black evil sky—very different Venice" (Diaries, p. 963); "We have had a fortnight of unbroken sunshine" (*Diaries,* p. 984); "Fog all day unbroken, and scum on lake" (*Diaries*, p. 1013). Because the third dimension is increasingly unavailable, a new territory is opened up, a territory that is neither in front of the observer nor to the side. It is not a territory that is perceived in three dimensions. With day transformed into night by the Master of the Reverse Creation, the nights become not only as active as the days but as "broken."

The nights are "broken" by dreams occuring behind Desiring Eyes that are separated from the objects of their desire by a "dome of Ashes": "Another good though much broken night of vain, partly melancholy dreams; one of finding a wrecked ship's mast; another of being turned back by snowstorm . . ." (*Diaries*, p. 937). But it is the "snowstorm" in front, and not the dream of one behind, that, breaking the optical affiliation with the third dimension, the space of the vanishing perspective, is responsible for the interior, broken topography of dream. Turned back by a "snowstorm," the self is caught in a collapsing space between an original landscape and one that imitates the original. Finally, what is behind the Desiring Eyes works no better than what is either in front or to the side. Dream topography, becoming a topography of imitation rather than compensation, is no more satisfactory than locations that are either recessional or peripheral:

> Very long it is since I've had so evil a night, of broken, feeble, disgusting tormenting dream, after a much fatigued, disappointed, and exerciseless day, and raisins and Marsala at dessert. One rather pretty bit of going home to Brantwood in violent rain and storm, our people looking out for the carriage, at a turn of the road as like Coniston as Walter Scott's Lucerne is like Lucerne— where the horses couldn't pull up the carriage; I wanting to get out—nothing

in the world would let me out. Another of a watchmaker—magnetist or mesmerist—looking into my mind as he held my hand, telling me "never for an instant to stop loving anybody." But most, merely disgustful or ominous, and I was waked at last, as I thought by a flash of lightning. . . . (*Diaries*, p. 936)

The dreams, "disgustful or ominous," do not function in terms of the "doubleness," the "biped" stance, that is always required. Mostly, the dreams are not antithetical. Fulfillment is not the organizing principle of Ruskin's dream topography. Only occasionally, does that territory offer a way out, a sense of release from collapsing space. And then the exit is swiftly shut, or the room, its window's blinds drawn, is without a view: ". . . I did a bit of beautiful fast running and spring up the stairs, the exact reverse of the laborious captivity of common nightmare. A dream followed, however, of extreme ghastliness, that I had holes opened through my hand (by frost or illness) through which I could see the light, from one edge of the hand across to the other" (*Diaries*, p. 938). More often, dream to-pography, shaped by the pressures of the inverted perspective, with the inevitable result being "the concentration of man upon himself," fails to reflect the "exact reverse," but, instead, the pressure itself—a pressure, be-yond words, that is worth forgetting: "Can't get stomach right, now. Woke at two again, after dreaming a horrid dream about restoration of a Gothic pinnacle and bracket; and another, more horrid yet and very memorable, yet so disagreeable that I can't write it, and ludicrous as loathsome, incon-ceivably. If I forget it, perhaps as well! But these bilious disgusts as op-posed to the dreams of pure body, how wonderful!" (*Diaries*, p. 937)

Yet the "bilious disgusts" occuring behind an optical system recording the failure of recessional space—"disgusts" occuring in the only arena left for performance—are not always unwritten in order to be forgotten. At times, Ruskin appears transfixed by dreams that seem the transforming equivalent of the Supper Guest's diary entry, which was written during a time of "excitement." An "eddying" mind, "unstable" as Reuben's water and including both water serpents, if not crocodiles, and supper, if not bacon, can be a subject of sinister fascination for Ruskin, as he observes a shifting topography that anticipates his own disintegration:

Nightmare in old way, but more grotesque. An entirely graceful lady began dancing a minuet to quick music, for a lesson, in company, all standing by to see, and it was entirely pretty for a few moments; and then in her quickest mo-tion she staggered, and one of her legs seemed to break, and we saw it was a wooden stilt, tied on with blue ribands, and she had to limp away to mend it, only in a tumultuous wild way the whole. Then of crossing a bridge and seeing that what I thought were weeds in the water were large green serpents; and I called Crawley to look and he wouldn't come, and then the serpents came out of the water and on the road to meet me, but I saw they were harmless, and they turned, and glided beside me, with large blunt heads, like dogs. Then of a most grotesque fight, between two large snails, rearing up like sea-horses, and one biting the other like a weasel, covering it with blood. Then of a dinner where I was talking a great deal and forgetting to see people who were close to me; and at last talking so fast that a bit dropped out of my mouth into a dish that was handed to me, and the kind waitress only seeing and pointing to me where it was, so that I could take it out. Then lastly, of some abominable cheat and imposter bothering me as I was arranging things. This is all vague and gone now—only I remember a vast plate of quartz with titanium which I was debating whether to give to a Museum, or keep for myself, and determined to keep. (*Diaries,* pp. 867–68)

The dream activity, the product of the pressures of collapsing space and an inverted focal point, takes place in a topography that is itself often without space—a topography in which objects are treated like the words of the young Ruskin who, interested in paginal conservation, spends his time "cramming and ramming, and wishing days were longer and sheets of paper broader . . ." (II, xxxii). But his paper is not "broader," his world is not larger, and it is not Ruskin who does the "cramming and ramming." Though unguided by Atropos, who is responsible for the discursiveness of the Third Style, Ruskin is not in control. His shrinking worlds, both the one in front, deprived of its third dimension, and the imitative dream world behind, feel the pressure of having run out of space—out of antithetical space, at the least, and perhaps out of any space at all. With the distance failing like the "outside" of parentheses, the dream world begins to cave in:

> Dreams become a wonderful study: the various ingenuities of their unpleasantness. Dreamed last night first of being in a street where the masons were unroofing all the houses, and showers of lime coming down, and broken slates to be avoided; secondly, of watching at a junction of two rails, a transit of a mass of native copper six feet high by more long, a mountain of solid copper, on a truck (classical more or less in wheel form—my dream did me so much grace) and another equally ponderous train coming up, not at any great pace but as fast as a horse trots; the two jamming together (by intention—not catastrophe) like two mountains, and I, dreaming, and looking at the copper, had only by a hairsbreadth, and by chance, drawn back from between as they met. Woke slowly with the sense of escape. (*Diaries,* p. 939)

At a premium, the space of dreams becomes crowded with a plenitude that is infernal, like a crowded parenthesis, with too much of the "outside" turned "in." Christ, no longer defined by the Robert Fludd of the *Mosaicall Philosophy,* is no longer involved in the act of filling. Instead, voids have become sacred. But without unused space, there is more immediate death than potential or future: "Nightmare of overflowed country; corpses built into walls like statues; crumbling backs. My mother to be guided. Both escaped, I hiding the dead bodies from her" (*Diaries*, p. 1086).

Without either significant distance or future before him and with a corpse-laden "over-flowed country" behind, Ruskin, trapped between closing perspectives, is in the prison that his instincts towards doubleness, the "biped," have so energetically attempted to avoid: "An extremely bad night after being indoors all day and it looks as if it meant the same to-day: sky black all over. It is really very difficult to live under such a heaven as we have, day after day, mercilessly getting darker every moment, and one feels like one of the spirits in prison" (*Diaries*, pp. 1040–41). In the closing arena between the inverted perspective and the country of the dead, "with corpses built into walls like statues," all that remains is the immediate, what is close at hand. The foreground has always been a poor version of the background, yet there is no other place to turn. But even the foreground, or the activities of the immediate, fail. The writer, passive in the face of invasion, cannot read. The "dome of ashes" leaves him without even the disdained proximate focus that would happily be sacrificed for distant vision: "Just as we got within four miles of Oxford, the north west black wind came up, filled the country with mist like burning manure; spread and carded down the clouds into one blackness; changed the soft air into a malignant chill; and when I got to Corpus, it was so black all over that after drawing up the blinds I could not read the titles of my books in bookcase" (*Diaries*, p. 846).

As recessional space fails him, Ruskin finds it difficult to make the distinctions that were modelled on spatial gradations. Eliminating the outside, much as the impulse towards the "collective aspect" eliminated the middle, the parenthetical self achieved the homogeneity of the interior. Everything was turned in. But now, with the confusion between outside and inside established, Ruskin, at least for a moment, inverts the process, turning the "inside out," as if in the act of creating a visionary landscape. Signaling the decline of an optical self with nothing left to "desire," blindness, at the least threatening reading, has become more cosmic than personal. The feared and advertised optical end, beginning with the specialized self of the Desiring Eyes, is now as public as that horizontal perspective which encompasses economics and society. In darkness, Ruskin finds himself watching the death of the world's eye: "The mornings always dark; no vestige of dawn ever coming to comfort me. Fire and candle only. Now, one does not *want* dawn in summer—it is too early—but just now, the one precious thing and eye of day taken out of it.—Blind, Blind, Blind, for ever . . ." (*Diaries*, p. 877).

That cosmic blindness is traced by Ruskin to the "diminution of snow on the Alps" (xxviii, 444) and the effect of melted snow on atmosphere.[2] It is part of the aging process of the world. Characteristically confusing auto-biography with history, Ruskin, with the inside "turned" out, reads history as a process of decline. He dramatizes the optical end in a diary entry later extracted for *The Storm-Cloud of the Nineteenth Century*. Organized about three temporal vantage points that keep updating the tense of the passage—"half past seven," "quarter to eight," and "half-past eight"—the passage is written with a sense of urgency that illustrates the pressures of existence within optically confining and reflexive structures, structures that might be a parenthesis, a room without a view, a collapsing world, or even a diary entry describing blindness:

> *August 13th, 1879.* BRANTWOOD. The most terrific and horrible thunderstorm this morning, I ever remember. It waked me at six, or a little before; then rolling incessantly, like railway luggage trains, quite ghastly in its mockery of them. The air one loathsome mass of sultry and foul fog, like smoke; scarcely raining at all, but increasing to heavier rollings, with flashes quivering vaguely through all the air, and at last terrific double streams of reddish-violet fire, not forked or zigzag, but rippled rivulets, two at the same instant some twenty to thirty degrees apart, and lasting on the eye at least half a second, with grand artillery-peals following: not rattling crashes or irregular cracklings, but de-livered volleys. It lasted an hour, then passed off, clearing a little, without rain to speak of; not a glimpse of blue, and now, half past seven, seems settling down again into Manchester devil's darkness.
>
> Quarter to eight, morning. Thunder returned; all the air collapsed into one black fog, the hills invisible and scarcely visible the opposite shore; heavy rain in short fits, and frequent, though less formidable, flashes and shorter thunder. While I have written this sentence the cloud has again dissolved itself, like a nasty solution in a bottle, with miraculous and unnatural rapidity, and the hills are in sight again. A double-forked flash—rippled, I mean, like the others—starts into its frightful ladder of light between me and Wetherlam, as I raise my eyes. All black above; a rugged spray cloud on the Eaglet. (The Eaglet is my own name for the bold and elevated crag to the west of the little lake above Coniston mines. It had no name among the country people, and is one of the most conspicuous features of the mountain chain, as seen from Brantwood.)
>
> Half-past eight. Three times light and three times dark since I wrote, and the darkness seeming each time as it settles more loathsome, at last stopping my reading in mere blindness. (*Diaries*, pp. 978–79)

[2] In a passage in *Fors Clavigera*, Ruskin explains this point: "One-third, at least in the depth of all the ice of the Alps has been lost in the last twenty-years; and the change of climate thus indicated is without any parallel in authentic history. In its bearings on the water supply and atmospheric conditions of central Europe, it is the most important phenomenon, by far, of all that offer themselves to the study of living men of science . . ." (xxvii, 635–36).

This optical apocalypse of self and world leaves no opening from the prison of blind eyes but the "bitter play" of language, Ruskin's "nothing but process" of survival that is employed in the face of spatial collapse: "*April 30th. Sunday.* KNARESBOROUGH. So ends 'the month of opening' with entirely clouded though not wholly black sky, inclining more and more to utter blackness" (*Diaries*, p. 896). Yet the function of Ruskin's immediate architecture has changed. Still Ruskin, requiring that his truths be "biped" and his architecture antithetical, is nothing if not adaptable. A blind world requires adjustment. Before, the prison, causing claustrophobia and an intensification of self-consciousness for an autobiographer who would be pseudonymous, compelled Ruskin to annihilate his foreground in order that he might move along a vanishing perspective towards the background of his landscape. But now, without a third dimension for optical release and self-annulment, without even significant vision, Ruskin would turn an imprisoning foreground into a fortress, like a Neapolitan prison, a medieval castle before the opening up of space, or an early parenthesis used as a version of pastoral. Conventional responses to "outside" and "inside" are inverted. And the prison is turned to advantage, in an effort to prevent the invasion of reflexive space, the invasion of the plague cloud that rides a cold wind: "Y[esterday] entirely horrible, one bitter, searching, all but freezing wind under unbroken vault of coalpit dust—frown of heaven. Yes, and now it darkens every moment as I write, and I have to stop the chink in my window—jam it close, I mean, with paper—because the loose old frame admits a stream of cold air, enough to drive me from the light" (*Diaries,* p. 896).

The invasion of reflexive space yields to bombardment. It is as if atmosphere, the dense *Storm-Cloud of the Nineteenth Century,* had been condensed into an object. Further, with a distance that has failed and an "outside" that has become increasingly aggressive, it is as if the focal point were assaulting the vantage point, a vantage point that at all costs must be fortified: ". . . all my friends are throwing stones through my window, and dropping parcels down the chimney, and shrieking through the keyhole that they must and will see me instantly, and lying in wait for me if I want a breath of fresh air, to say their life depends on my instantly superintending the arrangements of their new Chapel, or Museum, or Model Lodginghouse, or Gospel steam engine. And I'm in such a fury at them all that I can scarcely eat" (XXXVII, 388). If Ruskin's surrounding architecture, reenforced by an invading world, is sound enough to keep him from getting out, it is not efficient enough to keep the outside where it belongs. Enclosed but issuing no invitations, unlike the parenthetical self who would turn the world "outside in," Ruskin, scarcely able to eat, unable to take a recessional "space" that doesn't exist for "food" (XXVIII, 19), would rather be the diarist's St. Crumpet than the Supper Guest. He would rather be digested than digesting. Still, given a choice, he might finally like to leave the table altogether. Avoiding friends who throw "stones," he might like to be left alone, or almost alone. He might like to be left with his past-tense self, whose eyes are still desirous, and some paper, "magnificently blank," rather than a filled mirror, for the long avoided "face to face" confrontation. Defensive and in a world of reflexive space, Ruskin can always be left to his own devices. And the final device, when friends are like a failing distance that has belligerently turned into a foreground, may prove to be the self-reliance of responding to the autobiographical impulse—an impulse that will be worked out not with mirrors or the canvas of self-portraiture, the tools of his favorite dimension, but with words, even the "fury" of print, that he has always considered overrated and forgettable. But for now, this is only speculation.

ASSAULTS: SPECTRAL VISION AND AUDIT

Unable to enjoy the optical release of sight in a third dimension that no longer exists, Ruskin becomes aware of other forms of sensory perception. The optical self, with function impaired by a blind world and an inverted perspective, develops a sense of hearing. But sound, which has had a vigorous and assaulting existence within the sealing parentheses of "broken" sentences, can provoke without rising to the shriek of a steam whistle. At times, almost anything is disturbing. And the ear, overly sensitive, seems to be a mere extension of an eye that has been rudely treated: "It seems to me the light a little dimmer than of old, but that may be in my own eyes. I am thankful they still see all they do, but I could well spare my ears, sometimes; a cow, calling to another, very steadily by the riverside, much disturbing the calm of the morning" (*Diaries*, p. 851). As sight fades into a blindness that is either personal or cosmic, Ruskin's hearing becomes painfully acute.

Yet the sound of a cow calling to another is only occasionally an affront to the ear. In "Notes and Correspondence," a catchall tacked on to an exploding *Fors* that can take only so much "cramming and ramming," Ruskin quotes from the letter of one E. L., whose version of what appears to be an approaching apocalypse differs from Ruskin's death of the "eye of day." Recalling a landscape of Tory pastoral, E. L. "hears" her present world destroyed, appropriately enough, by the "American Devil." And, as in the case of the bombarded Ruskin, whose friends shriek through the keyhole and drop parcels down the chimney, the inside, E. L.'s "innermost chambers," fail to defend adequately:

"I woke with an expectant heart. It was a bright May day, such as I re-membered twenty years before. The big church bell tolled nine, then came a pause, and my thirsty ears were strained to catch the first sounds of the dear old chimes. 'Ding' went a treble bell high in the air, the first note of "Tara's Halls," and then!—a hideous sound I cannot describe, a prolonged malignant yell, broke from the sky and seemed to fill the earth. I stopped my ears and ran indoors, but the sound followed to the innermost chambers. It gathered strength and malignancy every moment, and seemed to blast all within its reach. It lasted near two minutes, and ended with a kind of spasm and howl that made every nerve shudder. I do not exaggerate. I cannot adequately describe the hideous sound. When I had recovered my wits, I asked the meaning of this horrible noise. My informant, a rising young townsman of the new stamp, told me that it was the new steam-whistle at the foundry, commonly called the "American Devil"; that it was the most powerful in the West Riding, and could be heard five miles off. . . .'" (xxviii, 412)

The "American Devil" of Wakefield is also Ruskin's "Lucca devil"— an infernal whistle that punctuates the "broken" intervals of the present tense, disrupting Ruskin's maneuvering in roomy tenses that are virtually without sound, tenses less immediate and pugnacious than those underscored by the devil's whistle:

I am writing my account of Giotto's "Poverty," for you and for others who care for it—and was getting into some feeling and power with it, when I was entirely stopped and paralyzed by a steam whistle at the railway, sent clear through intensely calm and watery air at intervals of about a quarter of a minute for the last quarter of an hour—a sharp, intense, momentary explosive whistle, like a mocking Devil playing the "Lucca trumpet" in a high key—the most torturing and base thing that in all my St. Anthony times has happened to me. It comes every morning at my best worktime, and at midnight—it is a luggage train which can't make up its mind to anything, and whistles at every new idea that strikes it. . . . And the whistle of the Lucca devil is going on *all this time.* (xxxvii, 129–30)

Yet even as sound, like sight, forces his consciousness towards a sense of immediacy that is without release, Ruskin can conceive of a pastoral of noise. Still, despite Ruskin's capacities for adjustments, it is not his pastoral. Instead, it is that of an "active and prosperous man of business," who, first crowning the landscape with a "dome of ashes," suffers from silence the way the early Ruskin, with space to waste and seeking after plenitude, suffered from visions of the void. But alternative pastorals do not supply "biped" relief, the relief of "doubleness": ". . . I knew also that what appeared in their way of life painful to me, might be agreeable to them; and it chanced, indeed, a little while afterwards, that an active and prosperous man of business, speaking to one of my friends of the disappointment he had felt in a visit to Italy, remarked, especially, that he was not able to endure more than three days at Venice, because there was no noise there" (xxii, 163). Ruskin's man of business, his "traffic interrupted," is compared by Ruskin to Goethe's Mephistopheles who, hearing the song of the angels, seems to hear something else: "Discord I hear, and intolerable jingling" (xxII, 165). The absence of sound in Venice, which encourages the play of an alert mind, almost as if the void of noise were empty space to be filled with ideas instead of objects, cannot buoy Ruskin's man of business, whose present tense is made "vital" by complex cacaphony and discordant invasion. For without the noise that Ruskin attributes to the devil, Ruskin's man of business is deprived of the only tense he knows, a present tense defined by discord. And without discord, like the optical self investigating the vanishing perspective, the man of business ceases to exist, perhaps swallowed not by recessional space but by the past and future tenses that Ruskin's exploratory mind would fill.

But all sounds are not discordant. And Ruskin is not without musical ambitions, ambitions that reduce themselves to a simplicity that is close to sacred: "For the present, therefore, not abandoning the hope of at last attaining a simple stringed instrument, I have fallen back—and I think, probably, with final good reason—on the most sacred of all musical instruments, the 'Bell'" (xxIX, 500). The sacred simplicity of bells creates a pastoral of the ear that has nothing to do with the infernal discord of the man of business, an aural pastoral that has the same sense of equilibrium and felicitous immediacy as Ruskin's early landscape of immanence: "Whether the cattle-bell of the hills, or, from the cathedral tower, monitor of men, I believe the sweetness of its prolonged tone the most delightful and wholesome for the ear and mind of all instrumental tone" (xxIX, 500).

Unsurprisingly, Ruskin's responses cannot be reduced to formula. And this version of the "song of angels" does not require either the syntactic sealing of "broken" sentences or the defensive architecture of E. L.'s "innermost chambers." But it is interesting to note that the most prolonged celebration of that "most sacred of all instruments" occurs in a description of the Valley of Cluse, which is topography not very different in function from those "innermost chambers." Still, with angelic song inside, instead of infernal shrieks assaulting like the "dome of ashes," the structure of the closed valley discourages transitional movement back and forth, the homogeneous movement that is like the ingestion of both the Supper Guest and the parenthetical self. At least momentarily, the boundaries between inside and outside, foreground and background, are reestablished, and the result is the "biped" equilibrium of "useful truth":

> But presently, as I walked, the calm was deepended, instead of interrupted, by a murmur—first low, as of bees, and then rising into distinct harmonious chime of deep bells, ringing in true cadences—but I could not tell where. The cliffs on each side of the Valley of Cluse vary from 1500 to above 2000 feet in height; and, without absolutely echoing the chime, they so accepted, prolonged, and diffused it, that at first I thought it came from a village high up and far away among the hills; then presently it came down to me as if from above the

cliff under which I was walking; then I turned about and stood still, wondering; for the whole valley was filled with the sweet sound, entirely without local or conceivable origin. . . . Perfectly beautiful, all the while, the sound, and exquisitely varied,—from ancient bells of perfect tone and series, rung with decent and joyful art. (xxvi, 152)

The separation is complete if fleeting. It is too good to last. The Valley of Cluse, as a version of enclosed pastoral, is not only aurally different from what lies outside, but, "unchanged since I knew it first, when I was a boy of fifteen, quite forty years ago" (xxvi, 151), its tense is not that of the belligerent present, the tense of claustrophobia and self-consciousness. But outside, away from "doubleness," even the sacred becomes devilish. The bells of an uncensored present, bells that are outside, do not possess the "true cadences" of a protected, enclosed past tense. Preventing the free play of the mind, they participate in the movement towards homogeneity and inertia. "Restless discord," the product of infernal energy, leads to paralytic contemplation. At times, there is nothing to do but listen to the destruction of God's "harmony": ". . . clashing of church bells, in the morning, dashed into reckless discord, from twenty towers at once, as if rung by devils to defy and destroy the quiet of God's sky, and mock the laws of His harmony: filthy, stridulous shrieks and squeaks, reaching for miles into the quiet air, from the railroad stations at every gate: and the vociferation, endless, and frantic . . ." (xxvi, 151).

The cosmic blindness of the "dome of ashes" that seals off the vanishing perspective of the third dimension is the spatial and public analogue of the personal deafness that the optical self, having recently learned to "hear," is forced to seek: "I write this morning, wearily, and without spirit, being nearly deaf with bell-ringing and bawling . . ." (xxvii, 355). But, at this point, deafness, unlike the blindness of Desiring Eyes that is a prison, is part of a defensive posture towards the assaults of a claustrophobic present tense: ". . . gambling boys shrieking, howling, swearing, in the sweet field of the cloister, and beside the cypresses of Turner's view—so that deafness would now be a mercy to me in Italy" (Diaries, p. 806). With recessional space cut off, Ruskin turns to the only space at hand, proximate space, and, in his version of "innermost chambers," simulates a deafness that is as satisfactory as blindness can never be: ". . . nearly every word anybody says, if I care for them, either grieves or astonishes me to a degree which puts me off my sleep, and off my work, and off my meat. I am obliged to work at botany and mineralogy, and to put cotton in my ears . . ." (xxxvii, 294).

Still, there are times when blindness might be as satisfactory as deafness. More precisely, there are times when blindness might be a relief. There is a visual effect closer to the infernal, aural assaults than the cosmic blindness of the "dome of ashes." Further, if the assaulted ear causes pain and paralysis, a paralysis that may be countered by the mathematical "play" of measuring the length of the assault, that ear, perhaps stuffed with "cotton," is at least not as vulnerable as the eye: "Remember that the eye is at your mercy more than the ear. 'The eye, it cannot choose but see.' Its nerve is not so easily numbed as that of the ear, and it is often busied in tracing and watching forms when the ear is at rest" (VIII, 156). The roots of the visual equivalent of dissonance are described by Ruskin, as he analyzes a passage from Milman's *History of Latin Christianity*:

> The last sentence—equally, and violently, foolish and false—I must put well out of the reader's way. Whatever these phenomena [i.e., religious visions at the time of St. Gregory] were, they were not poetry. They might have been insanity, or the reports of them may be folly, but they were neither troubadour romances nor Newdigate prize poems. Those who told them, believed what they had seen,—those who heard them, what they had heard; and, whether sane or insane, some part of the related phenomena is absolutely true, and may be ascertained to be so by any one who can bear the trial. And this I know simply because I have been forced myself to bear it not once nor twice, and have experienced the two forms of state, quickening of the senses both of sight and hearing, and the conditions of spectral vision and audit, which belong to certain states of brain excitement. (XXXIII, 198)

The origins of the visual equivalent to spectral audit can be seen in Ruskin's early attitudes towards chiaroscuro. Nature's chiaroscuro, which is based on a delicate distribution of contrast, of lights and shadows, is entirely acceptable to Ruskin. Avoiding extremes, nature reduces her landscape to a middle that is like the coiling and digressive aspects of the Third Style, Ruskin's style of survival that, seemingly employed to prevent conclusions, the arrival at a preconceived "point" (revenons à nos moutons), acts as both a cushioning middle between origins and endings, the extremes of argument, and the angelic tendency towards "mosaic." But nature's chiaroscuro is radically different from that of conventional artistic representation which mechanically leads to the "point" of darkness, the death and end of the "eye of day":

> Now it is a curious thing that none of our writers on art seem to have noticed the great principle of nature in this respect. They all talk of deep shadow as a thing that may be given in quantity; one fourth of the picture, or, in certain effects, much more. Barry, for instance, says that the practice of the great painter, who "best understood the effects of chiaroscuro," was, for the most part, to make the mass of middle tint larger than the light, and the mass of dark larger than the masses of light and middle tint together, *i.e.* occupying more than one half of the picture. Now I do not know what we are to suppose

is meant by "understanding chiaroscuro." If it means being able to manufacture agreeable patterns in the shape of pyramids, and crosses, and zigzags,
into which arms and legs are to be persuaded, and passion and motion arranged, for the promotion and encouragement of the cant of criticism, such a
principle may be productive of the most advantageous results. But if it means,
being acquainted with the deep, perpetual, systematic, unintrusive simplicity
and unwearied variety of nature's chiaroscuro; if it means the perception that
blackness and sublimity are not synonymous, and that space and light may
possibly be coadjutors; then no man who ever advocated or dreamed of such a
principle, is anything more than a novice, blunderer, and trickster in chiaroscuro. (III, 311–12)

But the lowest stunt performed by the trickster in chiaroscuro is neither
the visual dissonance of the juxtaposition of light and shadow, nor the sacrifice of light and an intervening middle tint to a growing darkness that is
not sublime. Instead, it is a visual invasion similar to the aural assault of
shrieking "devils" and cacophonous bells. This form of chiaroscuro, with
shapes closing in upon the spectator, reverses expectations of painting as a
model of recessional space. The spectator of chiaroscuro might as well be
sitting in E. L.'s "innermost chambers," with, if not cotton in his ears, at
least a handkerchief over his eyes:

> Finally, far below all these [uses of light and shade] come those particular
> accuracies or tricks of chiaroscuro which cause objects to look projecting from
> the canvas, not worthy of the name truths, because they require for attainment
> the sacrifice of all others; for not having at our disposal the same intensity of
> light by which nature illustrates her objects, we are obliged, if we would have
> perfect deception in one, to destroy its relation to the rest. . . . And thus he who
> throws one object out of his picture, never lets the spectator into it. Michael
> Angelo bids you follow his phantoms into the abyss of heaven, but a modern
> French painter drops his hero out of the picture frame. (III, 164)

Already bombarded by friends "throwing stones through the window, and
dropping parcels down the chimney," Ruskin suggests the further possibility of being optically assaulted by the painter who, anticipating the
inverted perspective of reflexive space by employing cheap tricks of chiaroscuro, throws his subject at the spectator.

Yet if the nameless French painter, as anonymous as the optical self exploring the vanishing perspective, is adept at the tricks of chiaroscuro, the
painter whose work comes closest to the "spectral vision" that Ruskin has
noticed in "certain states of brain excitement" is Rembrandt. References to
Rembrandt run through Ruskin's work with the harsh consistency of a
dissonant symphony. And what Ruskin particularly objects to in Rembrandt is his chiaroscuro: "Among the etchings and drawings of Rem-

brandt, landscape thoughts may be found not unworthy of Titian, and studies from the nature of sublime fidelity; but his system of chiaroscuro was inconsistent with the gladness, and his peculiar modes of feeling with the grace, of nature; nor, from my present knowledge, can I name any work on canvas in which he has carried out the dignity of his etched conceptions, or exhibited any perceptiveness of new truths" (III, 186). The ingredients of Rembrandt's chiaroscuro not only include too much darkness, but also the use of a secondary light source: ". . . it must be evident to the reader, that in the same way, and in a far greater degree, those masters are false who are commonly held up as the great examples of management of chiaroscuro. All erred, exactly in proportion as they plunged with greater ardour into the jack-a-lantern chase. Rembrandt most fatally and consistently . . ." (III, 317).

Rembrandt's chiaroscuro, if not actually participating in the "jack-a-lantern chase," is at least usually involved in a variation of that chase, a variation that approaches the condition of "spectral vision and audit." In the "Portrait of a Burgomaster," it is the light, "rejoicing in darkness," that disconcerts Ruskin: "You cannot see a finer work by Rembrandt. It has all his power of rendering character, and the portrait is celebrated through the world. But it is entirely second-rate work. The character in the face is only striking to persons who like the candlelight effects better than sunshine; any head by Titian has twice the character, and seen by daylight instead of gas. The rest of the picture is as false in light and shade as it is pretentious, made up chiefly of gleaming buttons, in places where no light could possibly reach them . . ." (XXII, 47).

But if Rembrandt, "rejoicing in darkness," reverses creation, his appeal is compared by Ruskin to the appeal of light—an interior light that makes attraction to Rembrandt, illuminating by his rushlight, a "jack-a-lantern chase" and the spectator a moth: ". . . there are attractions, and attractions. The sun attracts the planets—and a candle, night-moths; the one with perhaps somewhat of benefit to the planets;—but with what benefit the other to the moths, one would be glad to learn from those desert flies, of whom, one company having extinguished Mr. Kinglake's candle with their bodies, the remainder, 'who had failed in obtaining this martyrdom, became suddenly serious, and clung despondingly to the canvas'" (XIX, 107–8). Rembrandt's version of light is the "lamp-light upon the hair of a costermonger's ass" (XIX, 109). His rushlight that summons, even if it does not effect, martyrdom, is a "more active kind of darkness"—a light of darkness that is also within the self, "in the inner world of man" (XIX, 109). Just as the sun is transformed into rushlight, so the "soul's light" is transformed, by Rembrandt, into a "guttering, sputtering, ill-smelling" "*tallow* candle" (XIX, 109).

Rembrandt's light, when not inside, "guttering, sputtering," is not far

outside. Describing the lighting effects of Cagliari and Rubens, Ruskin op-
poses them to Rembrandt's effects: "We have no lantern-lights in their
works, all is kept chaste and shed equally from the sky, not radiating from
the object . . ." (III, 317). Yet even if the light source does not radiate from
the object, but comes from the sky, the observer of Rembrandt's lighting,
who possesses Ruskin's requirements, is not released to that sky. Com-
menting on R. N. Wornum's remarks on Rembrandt in *Epochs of
Painting,* Ruskin significantly locates the vantage point for the model of
Rembrandt's light effects:

> . . . we find that our author, after expatiating on the vast area of the Pantheon,
> "illuminated solely by the small circular opening in the dome above," and on
> other similar conditions of luminous contraction, tells us that "to Rembrandt
> belongs the glory of having first embodied in Art, and perpetuated, these rare
> and beautiful effects of nature." Such effects are indeed rare absolutely. The
> sky, with the sun in it, does not usually give the impression of being dimly
> lighted through a circular hole; but you may observe a very similar effect any
> day in your coal-cellar. (XIX, 108)

As if he were either in a "coal-cellar" or the "defiled den" of a "strong
and sullen animal" (XIX, 111), Ruskin's spectator of Rembrandt is without
the recessional space of anonymity. And as a painter of the Reverse
Creation, the value of whose etchings are in "inverse ratio of the labour
bestowed on them," Rembrandt, painting "the lamp-light upon the hair of
a costermonger's ass," also manufactures backgrounds that are inversions of
the open-ended distances that encourage the penetration of space.
Decidedly, Rembrandt is not the painter for the traveler who decides to stay
home, in his foreground, because of his awareness of the possibility of attaining a focal point that is also a vanishing point—a vanishing point that is
located in a distant and illuminated background: ". . . I know not any truly
great painter of any time, who manifests not the most intense pleasure in
the luminous space of his backgrounds, or who ever sacrifices this pleasure
where the nature of his subject admits of its attainment; as, on the other
hand, I know not that the habitual use of dark backgrounds can be shown
as ever having been coexistent with pure or high feeling except in the case
of Rembrandt (and then under peculiar circumstances only), with any high
power of intellect" (IV, 81–82). The judicious Ruskin of the second volume
of *Modern Painters,* then under less pressure than later because he is still
able to organize converging orthogonals in recessional space, understands
that occasionally Rembrandt is able to open up his architecture of the
"coal-cellar," as in the etching of the "Presentation of Christ in the
Temple," "where the figure of a robed priest stands glaring by its gems out
of the gloom, holding a crozier. Behind it there is a subdued window-light,
seen in the opening between two columns, without which the im-

pressiveness of the whole subject would, I think, be incalculably brought down" (IV, 82).

But the Spectral Vision of the "jack-a-lantern chase" does not often lead to an exit from Rembrandt's "coal-cellar." The anterior lighting of "rushlight," "jack-a-lantern," "or gleaming buttons, in places where no light could possibly reach them," is like the lighting of the night that plagued the traveler who would stay home—the lighting which appears to be, "though we know it boundless," "a studded vault that seems to shut us in and down . . ." (IV, 81). Rembrandt's close, interior light that radiates from gleaming buttons which are like small stars, becomes an inversion of the focal point that is a vanishing point for the penetration of space. What on the "outside" was the light of an exit, having shifted "inside," as if to illuminate a prison or a "defiled den," has lost its characteristics of "Escape, Hope, Infinity" (IV, 83). Simply, in order to avoid both claustrophobia and the spatial self-consciousness of the autobiographical impulse, which is a "face to face" art form of enclosure, light must be exterior, where the important distinctions can be made, the distinctions between foreground and background, vantage point and focal point, self and other. Light must be "beyond," instead of either immediate or "behind," where distinctions collapse towards a dreaded sameness: "Neither will any amount of beauty in nearer form make us content to stay with it, so long as we are shut down to that alone; nor is any form so cold or so hurtful but that we may look upon it with kindness, so only that it rise against the infinite hope of light beyond" (IV, 83). That "infinite hope of light beyond," inverted to the finite "rushlight" within a "coal-cellar," signals the beginning of an assault far more sinister than either Ruskin's bombarding friends or the nameless French trickster in chiaroscuro, who hurls his subject at his audience. This becomes the final assault of the Spectral Vision, the final failure of what was once anonymous and recessional space—a space that had the distance to lose an undesired autobiographical impulse along a vanishing perspective.

SPECTRAL VISION CONTINUED: FROM STEREOSCOPICS TO PSEUDOSCOPICS

The regression of the focal point is the dark side of the penetration of space—just as Ruskin's discussion of Rembrandt in *The Cestus of Aglaia* is the dark side of the chapter "Of Typical Beauty" of *Modern Painters* II. But that location of light and dark, of positives and negatives, is considerably less complicated than the location of the contrasting light and dark elements of Ruskin's landscapes. Furthermore, as we shall see, it is less complicated than the location of his foregrounds and backgrounds, which prove to be as mobile as the elements of light and dark.

In "The Law of Contrast," Ruskin point out the cognitive significance of juxtaposition: "Of course the character of everything is best manifested by Contrast. Rest can only be enjoyed after labour; sound to be heard clearly, must rise out of silence; light is exhibited by darkness, darkness by light . . ." (xv, 191). But if contrast is important, it can also be difficult to portray. Early in his *Diaries,* Ruskin suggests his problems with contrast: ". . . and, later, a most wonderful bit of effect to the north, which I have been trying to note, but cannot, because I find it impossible to give the effect of very white cloud in very dark twilight—(think of this with respect to some of Turner's effects: they are perhaps intended for greater gloom than I have supposed) . . ." (*Diaries,* p. 286). Yet the effect of the relief of light against dark is an effect Ruskin sees everywhere. Having studied the Louvre drawings, he decides that "all great men *incline* to draw the dark outline towards the light, and light towards dark. Though there are many exceptions to this, it is clearly the tendency, and vice versa of the inferior men" (*Diaries,* p. 521). Even in darkness without apparent light, Ruskin sees relief, "The Law of Contrast," in operation: ". . . all natural shadows are more or less mingled with gleams of light. In the darkness of ground there is the light of the little pebbles or dust; in the darkness of foliage, the glitter of the leaves; in the darkness of flesh, transparency; in that of a stone, granulation: in every case there is some mingling of light . . ." (xv, 37).

Yet when the contrast is too extreme, like the chiaroscuro of Rembrandt, whose contrasting patterns of light and dark are without middle tints, the result is painful. If great painters, creating relief, draw dark and light outlines towards each other, they nevertheless inject Rembrandt's missing middle, his intervening tints: "Great painters do not commonly, or very visibly, admit violent contrast. They introduce it by stealth, and with intermediate links of tender change; allowing, indeed, the opposition to tell upon the mind as a surprise, but not as a shock" (xv, 191). In an exercise in *The Elements of Drawing,* Ruskin warns beginning draftsmen against the "violent contrast" that, modified, obsesses Ruskin's own vision: "Choose any tree that you think pretty, which is nearly bare of leaves, and which you can see against the sky, or against a pale wall, or other light ground: it must not be against strong light, or you will find the looking at it hurts your eyes . . ." (xv, 39). Understanding the need for those "intermediate links of tender change," Turner, Ruskin is pleased to point out, employs middle tints even outside of chiaroscuro: "Turner hardly ever, as far as I can remember, allows a strong light to oppose a full dark, without some intervening tint. His suns never set behind dark mountains without a film of cloud above the mountain's edge" (xv, 191). Like Ruskin's intervening space that separates the self from the perceived object, while at the same time permitting the affiliation of the Desiring Eyes, the "intervening tint" separates, even as it supplies the transitional space of Rembrandt's missing middle to the violence of extreme contrast—a violence that, even in the angelic and hovering juxtapositions of *Fors* in its "collective aspect," must be tamed by the serpentine and linear digressions of the "nothing but process" style that Ruskin takes for existence.

Ruskin's contrasts depend not only upon light but location. And light has a location. In the orthodoxy of Ruskinian relief, light is behind darkness. Establishing position in a world of recessional, rather than peripheral, space, the key word to contrast is "behind": "His suns never set behind dark mountains without a film of cloud. . . ." And again: ". . . after glorious clear evening with delicate cirri in light behind Old Man summit: unbelievably radiant" (*Diaries,* p. 1074). Contrast, beyond the lateral comparisons of the museum, is rarely made on the same depth plane. Ruskin has virtually no sidestep: "Avoid, as much as possible, studies in which one thing is seen through another. You will constantly find a thin tree standing before your cottage, or between you and the turn of the river; its near branches all entangled with the distance" (xv, 108). Without the middle, what is distant can be brought near and what is near can be distanced. This inversion is what Robert Shattuck, writing about a temporal and mnemonic equivalent to what is an essentially optical organization, calls a "pseudoscopic effect." Shattuck, concerned with Proust, quotes a passage from *The Notebooks of Leonardo da Vinci* that is as important to the understanding of spatial and temporal locations in Ruskin, as in Proust:

> Our judgment does not reckon in their exact and proper order things which have come to pass at different periods of time; for many things which happened many years ago will seem nearly related to the present, and many things that are recent will seem ancient, extending back to the far-off period of our youth. And so it is with the eye, with regard to distant things, which when illuminated by the sun seem near to the eye, while many things which are near seem far off.[3]

But with Ruskin, there is an enormous difference between spatial and temporal pseudoscopics. Temporal pseudoscopics—the past taking the place of the present—can offer a momentary release from pressures. John Rosenberg has noted the occasional confusion of tenses in *Praeterita*.[4] Writing an

---

[3] *The Notebooks of Leonardo da Vinci,* translated by Edward MacCurdy (New York, 1947), I, 67. Quoted in Robert Shattuck's *Proust's Binoculars* (New York, 1963), p. 149.

[4] John Rosenberg, *The Darkening Glass* (New York and London, 1961), p. 251, note.

autobiography that is dependent upon the mnemonic distance for control, Ruskin, attempting to retrieve what he has lost, is at times overwhelmed by his find. In autobiography, his dead father can be treated with an immediacy that is fiction: "Papa cannot bring himself to think of anybody in Irish-like costume as Conservative" (xxxv, 590, note 1.) And Rose La Touche, long since dead at the time of autobiography, appears in the present tense: ". . . Paradisiacal [walks] with Rosie, under the peach-blossom branches by the little glittering stream which I had paved with crystal for them. . . . 'Eden-land' Rosie calls it" (xxxv, 561). The invasion of the past, if only possible momentarily, is a return to paradise.

Yet the pseudoscopic entanglement and rearrangement of landscape, connected with an inverted perspective and the failure of the distance, is more infernal than paradisiacal. Even the ecstatic confusion of tenses is not part of a syntax that is built to last. Nevertheless, the retrieval of the past is attractive in a way that the invasion of the background is not. But the coming close of space has never been the same as the immediacy of time. There has always been a difference between looking at oneself in a mirror and writing about oneself. The page is not a mirror and the working-out of the autobiographical impulse is, in each case, different. The act of "looking," causing pressure, is undispersed. But the writer, refracting the pressures of the autobiographical impulse, is not necessarily the reader. And if he is, like the diary reader, he is a later self. Further, the autobiographer's subject, discovered in the past, is neither the writer nor the reader. At the least, unlike the man of mirrors (or the spectators trapped in Rembrandt's "coal-cellar" and his "defiled den," all of whom are confined to the stifling immediacy of reflexive space), the writer of autobiography has a triangulation of selves involved in dispersing the burden of pseudoscopic confrontation. In any case, the Ruskin whose fundamental movement is the stereoscopic penetration of recessional space attempts to avoid the confusion of certain kinds of spatial entanglements, the entanglements of "near branches . . . with the distance."

Still, when Kate Greenaway, an artist who is either beyond or before the tensions of contrasts, avoids the entanglements of reverse relief by reducing her drawings to a single plane—a technique that would condense Ruskin's world of converging orthogonals to a horizontal dimension—Ruskin protests against this solution to the dangers of potential inversion: "And you must give up drawing round hats. It's the hats that always save you from having to do a background—and I'm not going to be put off with them any more" (xxxvii, 495). With Kate Greenaway, there is no chance for either contrasting entanglement or spatial inversion, because what might be "behind" has been eliminated. The single plane she employs is the horizontal plane of the foreground, which is the only available topography for a Ruskin without a third dimension. In his models, which, after all, do not have to be imitative, Ruskin would rather not be deprived of the only spatial options available.

Both the entanglement of the background with the foreground and the loss of a background entirely, along with Ruskin's energetic attitude towards Rembrandt's "jack-a-lantern chase" that occurs within confined, interior spaces, reflect Ruskin's distress over the rearrangement of his landscape. Once, the lights in Ruskinian topography had been beacons charting distant territories, not highlighting interior and impenetrable objects. Essentially, the emphasis had been on escape, not containment: "And I think if there be any one grand division, by which it is at all possible to set the productions of painting, so far as their mere plan or system is concerned, on our right and left hands, it is this of light and dark background, of *heaven light* or of *object light*" (IV, 81). Later, deprived of a background, Ruskin, confirming this point in a note, elaborates on it: "This quite true conclusion reaches farther than I knew, or at least felt clearly enough to express. Not only light *in* the sky, but light *from* it, is essential to the greatest work; the diffused light of heaven on all sides, as distinguished from chiaroscuro in a room" (IV, 81, note). The need is for that familiar "luminous distant point as may give to the feelings a species of escape from all the finite objects about them" (IV, 82). But the lights that had marked spaces of release beyond the incipient reflexive design, beyond recognition and autobiography—those lights that designated, finally the focal point as vanishing point, begin to move in reverse relief towards the single plane of Kate Greenaway, or, more emphatically, towards a "closed room," which is the "coal-cellar" of chiaroscuro.

This spatial, pseudoscopic movement towards reverse relief is part of the dark side of the penetration of space that ends in spectral assault. Contrasted with deep shadow, Ruskin's lights of pain, no longer in the luminous background or connected with the "extreme felicities of life" (XXXV, 22), fall like the "stones" and "parcels" that bombard Ruskin, whose version of "innermost chambers" might now prove a fitting setting for the interior lights of an actively offending chiaroscuro. Animated, with a vitality and immanence of their own, the "good" lights are weightless, applying no pressure, while lights that are "bad," assaulting like falling "parcels" or "stones" that are "hailstones," are dead weights incapable of dispersion: "The broken lights in the work of a good painter wander like flocks upon the hills, not unshepherded, speaking of life and peace: the broken lights of a bad painter fall like hailstones, and are capable only of mischief, leaving it to be wished they were also of dissolution" (XV, 200). The "luminous distant point," once providing a "species of escape" but now no longer located in recessional space, no longer performs the function of an exit. Instead, as weighty and oppressive as an inverted focal point, it seals off potential escape into optional space, like the prison bars of the corrupt Dungeon of *Me*-ology, which is a most "unpoetical" and hardly pseudonymous architecture of an offending autobiography: "Fierce black sky and storm, after a warm gleam of sunshine in setting out. Here round abbey utterly in whirlwind, and black without break all the evening, and now, in wretched little bedroom with nasty iron bedstead. A little light coming through at 1/2 past six. (That gleam of light closing in hopelessly in worse blackness characteristic of this frightful time: vacillation always.)" (*Diaries,* p. 893)

But not only is the "luminous distant point," now a closing gleam, no longer "distant," it is no longer "luminous." If background competes with foreground in the contrasting entanglement of locations, varieties of light are also in competition. Fundamental to lighting is surface, and what is most important is the difference between penetrable surface and reflective surface: "It is necessay . . . carefully to distinguish between translucency and lustre. Translucency, though, as I have said above, a dangerous temptation, is, in its place, beautiful; but lustre, or *shininess* is always in painting, a defect" (xv, 138). Yet even with penetrable surfaces, the surface of "varnish," the painter is led into a room like Rembrandt's "coat-cellar":

> The habit of depending on varnish or on lucid tints for transparency, makes the painter comparatively lose sight of the nobler translucence which is obtained by breaking various colours amidst each other: and even when, as by Corregio, exquisite play of hue is joined with exquisite transparency, the delight in the depth almost always leads the painter into mean and false chiaroscuro; it leads him to like dark background instead of luminous ones, and to enjoy, in general, quality of colour more than grandeur of composition, and confined light rather than open sunshine. . . . (xv, 138–39)

The route of transparency to confinement is indirect. Still, "lustre, or *shininess*," reflecting and reflexive—the surface of spatial autobiography, the undispersed, mirrored autobiography of immediacy—refers back to the self and the Dungeon of *Me*-ology. If the distant focal point is "luminous," like the light of Turner—"Severn comparing Turner to the old Italian school, for his luminous feeling, as opposed to Rembrandt" (*Diaries,* p. 220)—the focal point of the inverted perspective is "lustrous." The luminous light of Turner, which is a vanishing point, is at the least pseudonymous, like the tentative *The Poetry of Architecture*. At the least, it permits an approach towards self-annulment. But the light of "lustre," like the Spectral Vision of Rembrandt's "jack-a-lantern chase," returns the self to a space with no more potential for release than that "coal-cellar" or "defiled den." "Closing in hopelessly" towards reverse relief, the gleam that is the focal point of the failing distance finally invades the "intellectual lens and moral retina" of the optical self. The dark side of the penetration of space is complete. And curiously, the end of the autobiography of spatial pseudo-scopics leaves the optical self without even a mirror. But then a mirror isn't necessary. The Desiring Eyes are as blind as the "eye of day." Finally, the Spectral Vision is the vision of Nothing: "Just before dinner, zigzag frameworks of iridescent lights fluttered in my eyes, and I could not see even to read large print . . ." (*Diaries,* p. 834).

But once things were different. Before the regression of the focal point and the attendant loss of the third dimension, those spectral "zigzag frameworks of iridescent light"—with little apparent potential for the invasion and internalization that virtually turns consciousness into a "coal-cellar"—elicited more awe than anguish. They were like the bells that were sacred before they were profane:

> The "Girandola" has got its reputation, and is performing somewhat shabbily under the protection of past years, people still giving it the preference over far finer explosions bestowed constantly on the populace of Paris, but the whole effect of the twenty minutes' burst of changing fire, taking place, as it does, among the architectural outlines of the noblest scale and character, and assisted by the roar of the artillery of the fortress, is still unequalled, and I never expect to see any piece of mere spectacle produced by human art fit to be named in the same day with the illumination of St. Peter's. (I, 389)

The young Ruskin, with a recessional space that is as well-charted and distant as his future, applauds those same aural and visual effects that, later, intensify the burden of selfhood beyond "due relation." Still, the most effective illumination is that in which the contrast of light and darkness is cushioned by the intervening tint that permits the eye to see things in serial, extensive, and orthodox perspective: "Illumination above all conception, showing the beauty of design of cupola infinitely better than the lines of stones, and thrilling as a piece of splendour. Nothing can possibly equal it in its way in the world. . . . As a piece of elegant design it was best when there was darkness enough to give brilliance to the lamps, yet light enough to leave the building some of its principal shadows, its larger features and aerial perspective" (*Diaries,* p. 172).

Given shape by "aerial perspective," the illumination, without the pressures of a proximate and closing background, is nevertheless as oppressive as the dead weight of the "bad lights." But Ruskin, only intimating the "state of brain excitement" of Spectral Vision and Audit, is controlled enough to enjoy the burden: "The burst of fire as the bell tolled eight, at the second stroke, is almost oppressive with its wonder. I am afraid the impression will wear off, for I was afraid of the night air, and could not watch it long for my eyes, but I know it was such as no other spectacle of human contrivance will I believe, ever excite in me" (*Diaries*, p. 172).

Susceptible to being excited by a "spectacle of human contrivance," which is composed of exploding lights punctuated by tolling bells, Ruskin begins *Modern Painters* as a defense of a painting by Turner that is close to being an analogue of the "Girandola": "His [Turner's] freak of placing Juliet at Venice instead of Verona, and the mysteries of lamplight and rockets with which he had disguised Venice herself, gave occasion to an article in *Blackwood's Magazine* of sufficiently telling ribaldry, expressing, with some force, and extreme discourtesy, the feelings of the pupils of Sir George Beaumont at the appearance of these unaccredited views of Nature" (xxxv, 217). Significantly, Ruskin's response to the attack on Turner's version of Spectral Vision is the same as his later response to Spectral Vision itself. The attack anticipates the Vision: "The review raised me to the height of 'black anger' in which I have remained pretty much ever since" (xxxv, 217).

But nature's equivalent to Spectral Vision, unattacked, needs no defense. As with chiaroscuro, at least at first, nature, always possessing the ominous potential of closing in "hopelessly," can do no wrong. Simply, there is no "black anger": "I have just come in from an evening walk among the stars and fireflies. One hardly knows where one has got to between them, for the flies flash, as you know, exactly like stars on the sea, and the impression to the eye is as if one was walking on water. I was not the least prepared for their intense brilliancy. They dazzled me like fireworks, and it was very heavenly to see them floating, field beyond field, under the shadowy vines" (xxxv, 562). Like both stars and fireworks, fireflies present a contrast of light and shadow without that middle of intervention. Still, Ruskin's reaction, unlike his reaction to Rembrandt's "jack-a-lantern chase," is more ecstatic than agitated: "I hope, wherever you are, that this weather has found you still in Italy; and that you will outstay the firefly time. I always think that nothing in the world can possibly be so touching, in its own natural sweetness, and in the association with the pensive and glorious power of the scene, as the space of spring time in Italy during which the firefly makes the meadows quiver at midnight" (xxxvi, 527).

In the same way that "broken lights painted by a good painter," which speak of "life and peace," are weightless, Ruskin's fireflies, "very heavenly," float freely, "field beyond field," like reflections on a body of water. But if Ruskin's focused attention can penetrate space by observing the floating fireflies, those fireflies also plunge themselves and observer into Rembrandt's imprisoning interior lighting. To watch Ruskin's fireflies is to alternate between maneuvering in "heavenly" space and confinement within the infernal "coal cellar" of Rembrandt's chiaroscuro. Incorporating opposites, Ruskin's firefly is closer to the spatial versatility of Tintoretto than the obsessive enclosure of Rembrandt: "But among the greater colourists of Italy the aim was not always so simple nor the method so determinable. We find Tintoret passing like a firefly from light to darkness in one oscillation . . . one moment shutting himself into obscure chambers of imagery, the next plunged into the revolutionless day of heaven, and piercing space, deeper than the mind can follow or the eye fathom . . . " (XII, 289).

Capable of both plunging into confined space and floating in open-ended space, those fireflies are also described as if in competition with other light sources that lack their versatility: "Last night the air was quite calm, the stars burning like torches all over the sky, the fireflies flying all about, literally brighter than the stars" (XX, liii). When Ruskin's fireflies are not merely likened to stars, but become the most significant object in the comparison, "brighter than the stars," the emphasis is on the nearer at the expense of the farther, the foreground at the expense of the background. Ruskin's "gleam of light," no longer "luminous" or "distant," is swiftly closing down on the observer. And fireflies, participating in the inversion of the observer's perspective, the reversal of relief that is part of the failure of recessional space, are no longer the heavenly lights similar to those which speak of "life and peace": ". . . with only the somewhat to me awful addition of fire-flies innumerable, which, as soon as the sunset is fairly passed into twilight, light up the dark ilex groves with flitting torches, or at least, lights as large as candles, and in the sky, larger than the stars. We got to Siena in a heavy thunderstorm of sheet-lightning in a quiet evening, and the incessant flashes and showers of fire-flies between, made the whole scene looking anything rather than celestial" (XX, liv).

The confusion between the lesser and the greater, the nearer and the farther, which predicts the problem of reverse relief, is a confusion that fails to distinguish between significant objects of attention and those that are somehow unworthy of visual pursuit. In a dialogue dealing with his illuminated entrance into Siena, Ruskin explains the meaning of fireflies: "Well, May, you never were a vain girl; so could scarcely guess that I meant them [fireflies] for the light, unpursued vanities, which yet blind us confused among the stars. One evening, as I came late into Siena, the fireflies were flying high on a storm sirocco wind,—the stars themselves no brighter and all their host seeming, at moments, to fade as the insects faded" (XVIII, 368). Symbols of "unpursued vanities" that are "confused among the stars," fireflies, participating in a scene that is "anything rather than celestial," are also components, at least by comparison, of that form of assaulting perception which includes Spectral Vision and Audit. Ruskin, often reducing perception to gastronomics, dream to indigestion, reduces the performance of Spectral Vision and Audit to the condition of the liver:

> Now this power of visionary sight and hearing is absolutely healthy, when the flesh through which it works is healthy; and absolutely diseased, when the flesh is diseased.

> 24. You will understand this best by the properly Socratic method of examining it first in simplest things.

> One day in the spring of 1863 I got a great fright about my eyes. I had eaten rather a large breakfast, and climbed the limestone mountain between Annecy and the Tournette rather fast. At the top I was stooping down to look at the lichens of it for about ten minutes, and when I raised my head, behold all the sky was covered with stars flying about like fireflies, only brighter than fireflies, very bright indeed, and immensely pretty. This unexpected illumination lasted about half a minute, and then, to my great satisfaction, faded away. But I got a terrible fright, and thought I was going to have amaurosis.

> I have since to my much comfort ascertained by experience that this phenomenon is only a particular and brilliant form of biliousness. (xxii, 502)

But the discomfort of this "visionary sight and hearing," which is Spectral Vision and Audit, is more likely the result of psychic disequilibrium than a malfunctioning liver. And that disequilibrium is illustrated by the relation between stars and fireflies. Fireflies can be compared with stars, the lesser with the greater, the nearer with the farther, but stars, compared with fireflies, not only suggest the reversal of relief, the invasion of the background, but also a world that is out of control, a world capable of no astronomical and orchestrated movement. Rather, the comparison of stars to fireflies describes a world of agitated instability with no more design or harmony behind it than the flitting of flies—a world, finally, of careless vanity, of self-indulgence that anticipates an autobiographical confrontation that would be avoided, instead of a world of significance, permanence, and coherence.

Despite Ruskin's defense of Turner's Spectral Vision—a defense, we recall, that was engaged in with an anger that was "black"—and despite Ruskin's enjoyment of the "Girandola," which excited him like no other human contrivance, Ruskin's response to the contrasting of light and dark, without an intervening tint of gradation, is rarely happy. An early passage from Ruskin's diaries, shortly after the "black anger" elicited by the review in *Blackwood's,* indicates more mental pain than indigestion:

> I went up Vesuvius to day . . . and lay among the ashes in the sun . . . they [the guides] little thought of the dark ashes my spirit was lying in. It was a bright day and I worked hard to keep my thought among the black lava and

along the pleasant shore. They went a little, however, back to that evening in Ch. Ch. when I first knew of it—oddly enough the 12th—and went staggering down the dark passage through the howling wind, to Child's room, and sat there with him working through long interminable problems, for what seemed an infinite time, without error, without thought, all confusion and horror in eyes and brain. How well I remember how my feet slipped on the smooth pebbles as I staggered on, and the stars danced among the dismal clouds above me like fire-flies! (*Diaries*, p. 165)

The imbalance of the diary entry, which is produced by Ruskin's discovery of the marriage of Adele Domecq, and which is illustrated by a description of dancing "stars" as unstable as those fanciful "fireflies" unworthy of "pursuit," is the same disequilibrium that causes the assault of Spectral Vision and Audit. Still, what produces the later disequilibrium— those "certain states of brain excitement"—is not the marriage of Adele, but the pseudoscopic inversion of locations, an inversion resulting from the failure of the recessional space that had separated Ruskin from his world, giving him neither a sense of "elbow room" nor a place to spatially "vanish." And the importance of that failure is demonstrated by Ruskin's excessive response to the missing middle of Rembrandt—a middle that, before it was lost, had prevented relief from being reversed and the self from having an exaggerated notion of density and importance. Those lost intervening spaces and tints had allowed Ruskin to hold the world at a controlling distance, instead of being confined in it, like a spectator in the "coal-cellar" of chiaroscuro. Pseudoscopic effect, turning the world "outside in," which is the solution of the avaricious parenthetical self, leads towards an unreadable but inescapable autobiography, and an autobiography, "face to face" with the self, of undispersed, spatial confrontation— the world as self, instead, perhaps, of pseudonymous biography. At this point, Ruskin would prefer his story told by a reluctant third person instead of an advertised autobiographer. But then Ruskin, even as he writes *Praeterita*, will be engaged in a form that is part biography and part fiction.

Finally, Ruskin insists upon playing all the roles. Losing himself in self-annulment at the borders of his sight, he later finds a version of himself in the carefully censored autobiography of *Praeterita*. Penetrating space, he later back-pedals through it, in order to recreate, as we shall see in the next chapter, a temporal version of the foreground he had earlier sacrificed. More important for present purposes, the "black anger" that the Ruskin who could appreciate the "Girandola" felt when faced with the criticism of Turner's painting, which included the then celestial "mysteries of lamplight and rockets," shifts from a defensive "black anger" to an offensive rage. But then Ruskin has always been "biped," intrigued by doubleness. He has always wanted to be at both ends of London Bridge at the same time. Once situated at the vantage point, he has moved towards the focal point. With Ruskin, seeing is becoming. And his shift from one version of "black anger" to another is a shift of roles that is no less spectacular than the "Girandola."

Doubtless, Turner is not Whistler, and Turner's Spectral Vision of mysterious "lamplight and rockets" is not Whistler's "Nocturne in Black and Gold (the Falling Rocket)." But Whistler's Spectral Vision of the fireworks at Cremorne turns Ruskin into the *Blackwood's* reviewer he had attacked. Attacking Whistler, Ruskin is attacking an early version of himself. To be enraged by Whistler's "Falling Rocket" is to feel "black anger" when "face to face" with the signs of autobiographical confrontation, an inevitable confrontation that is presented with the spatial immediacy of a relief that is now reversed.

R. H. Wilenski's contention that Ruskin's judgment of Whistler is distorted by a fear of lights against a dark background is a valuable perception—just one of many that Wilenski makes—and it takes on considerable significance when examined in the context of theories of selfhood, the heretical but inevitable impulse toward autobiography, and the arrangement of spatial and temporal coordinates.[5] Just as Ruskin's discussions of Rembrandt's chiaroscuro show that Ruskin's Rembrandt, "rejoicing in darkness," is effecting a Reverse Creation involving the manufacture of an advancing space, instead of Turner's recessional space, so Ruskin's Whistler reverses the orthodox positions of light and shadow, positions that had been established by Ruskin in the crucial chapter "Of Typical Beauty" of *Modern Painters* II. Whistler paints what amounts to a photographic negative of Ruskin's theory, illustrated by Turner, that a painting requires a "luminous distant point" to provide a "species of escape" from what is often a dark foreground. Whistler's painting, like many of Rembrandt's, is a pseudoscopic inversion of Ruskin's requirements. Instead of self-annulment in a light that is "distant" and "luminous," the spectator of Whistler meets himself in a light that is more reflexive than extensive.

Whistler's spatial pseudoscopic effect—the inversion of the locations of background light and foreground darkness, creating a space, "closing in hopelessly," that predicts the painful self-consciousness of undispersed autobiographical confrontation—is as infernal for Ruskin as the occasional temporal equivalent ("'Eden-land' Rosie calls it.") is agreeable. Just as *The Cestus of Aglaia* is the reverse relief of the "Of Typical Beauty" chapter, so Whistler's "Falling Rocket" is the reverse relief of the censored autobiography of *Praeterita*. And Ruskin, observing Whistler's Spectral Vision, is not merely engaged in a kind of generalized autobiographical confrontation,

---

[5] R. H. Wilenski, *John Ruskin: An Introduction to Further Study of His Life and Work* (London, 1933), pp. 138–143.

but, specifically, he is looking at the Spectral Vision of himself. Never painted, it is nevertheless an internalized self-portrait, a portrait of a self-as-world. But it is a world gone mad: ". . . last year, at this very time, I saw the stars rushing at each other—and thought the lamps of London were gliding through the night into a World Collision. . . . Nothing was more notable through the illness than the general exaltation of the nerves of sight and hearing . . . " (XXXVII, 442). Ruskin's autobiographical Spectral Vision is a vision undefined by distance and separation, a claustrophobic vision of disorder and collapse in which the lights of coherence, now rushing stars and gliding lamps, have broken loose in spatial confusion and entanglement, even as those stars that danced like fireflies, when he discovered the marriage of Adele Domecq. His madness is his world's failure of distance and discrimination. And his "World Collision," suggesting the disintegration of space and matter into the inert rubble of a world reduced to absolute sameness, recalls his dream of collapsing space and nightmarish compression: "Dreamed last night . . . of watching at a junction of two rails, a transit of a mass of native copper . . . on a truck . . . and another equally ponderous train coming up, not at any great pace but as fast as a horse trots; the two jamming together (by intension—not catastrophe) like two mountains, and I, dreaming, and looking at the copper, had only by a hairs-breadth, and by chance, drawn back from between as they met. Woke slowly with a sense of escape" (*Diaries,* p. 939). But the "species" or "sense of escape" begins coming for shorter times and at greater intervals as dream, no longer left behind by waking, becomes the Spectral Vision of madness.

Beginning in the public arena of "loyal noise, and fancies of fire"—the human contrivance of the "Girandola"—and ending in private, interior apocalypse, the Spectral Vision is finally not only inside Ruskin, with the assault of the inverted perspective, but emanates from him. Carlyle, in a letter to Emerson, describes Ruskin as a manufacturer of explosive light, amidst contrasting shadow: "There is nothing going on among us as notable to me as these fierce lightning balls which Ruskin copiously and desperately flings into the black world of anarchy all around him" (XXX, 327). And Ruskin, himself, warns a friend that, writing *Fors Clavigera,* he is mixing gunpowder: "You'll have such an explosion of fireworks . . . next month if I keep well . . . " (XXIV, xxxvi).

The shift from creator of components of the Spectral Vision to a participant in the Spectral Vision is a transformation accomplished first by Ruskinian personae. In the same way that Tintoretto passes "like a fire-fly from light to darkness in one oscillation," so Ruskin's Ulysses plays that spectral and unforgettable role which an awed, then anguished, Ruskin has watched all his life: "In hell, the restless flame in which he is seen, from the rocks above, like a firefly's flitting to and fro . . . " (XXII, 177). Ruskin might well have been talking about his own feared spectral ambitions, instead of Adele Domecq, when, in an early and entirely unsuccessful work of fiction, *Chronicles of Bernard,* he describes Ada: "'Nay, Ada,' said Velasquez, 'it is such a heaven as this which should be the home for one so beautiful as thou; in thine own clime thou wert like a thing of light in a dwelling of darkness'" (I, 540). The personae prefigure the real thing. Predictably and disastrously, Ruskin becomes what he watches. The background becomes the foreground. And the description of others becomes the description of himself. Claustrophobic sameness prevails. As the inverted perspective focuses on what were once Desiring Eyes, Ruskin is himself transformed into a firefly: "Heard from Mrs. Ackworth . . . the most overwhelming evidence of the other state of the world that has ever come to me; and am this morning like a flint stone suddenly changed into a firefly, and ordered to flutter about—in a bramble thicket" (*Diaries,* p. 876).

The transformation becomes a form of multiplication. Playing all the roles, the spectator who had at first sought self-annulment becomes larger than life, beyond "due relation." The undispersed autobiographical pressures of spatial pseudoscopics are too much for one self. And that self who would cease to exist becomes, instead of nothing at all, a small society. Still, fearing homogeneity and the collapsing space that might lead to a "World Collision," Ruskin has always had the impulse towards "doubleness," the impulse towards the "biped" stance. Once intrigued by the idea of being "in two places at once" (xxxvii, 242)—of stereoscopically seeing, if not painting, St. Paul's from both ends of London Bridge simultaneously—he now views a world populated by undifferentiated multiples of a single self with horror. Excessive self-consciousness may be unfortunate, but a plenitude of selves involved in perpetual multiplication creates an infernal population: ". . . a society in which every soul would be as the syllable of a stammerer instead of the word of a speaker, in which every man would walk as in a frightful dream seeing spectres of himself, in everlasting multiplication, gliding helplessly around him in a speechless darkness" (xv, 117). Even though appalled by multiplicity, the plenitude of selves, Ruskin, rather like the multiple or condensed meanings of *Fors Clavigera,* would characteristically have it both ways. At times the population explosion at the focus of the inverted perspective—the self as focal point—comes closer to division than multiplication: "I have not written to you, because my illness broke me all to pieces, and every little bit has a different thing to say . . ." (xxxvii, 248). In any case, beyond the "due relation" of tolerable awareness of self, of acceptable autobiographical confrontation, Ruskin is either multiple fragments of a single self, or multiple selves: ". . . I am, as far as I can make out, quite myself again, and for the present *one* self only, and not one—beside myself. I never understood the meaning of that phrase before, but indeed I was a double, or even treble, creature through part of that dream" (xxxvii, 246).

CHAPTER VI The Peeled Self:
The Desiring Eyes of
Time

THE ART OF THE NEST: THE FOREGROUND MADE
LIVABLE

The background has lost its magic, as a failing recessional space, turned "outside in" as if by that avaricious and destructive parenthetical self who has made ambitious plans for the interior, is organized along a perspective that is now inverted. Creation, along with relief, has been reversed. Encyclopedic to the point of becoming, under the stress of being pinned down, of being confined to a single space or a single definition, a "double, or even treble creature," he has cultivated, as he does in almost all the structures of his consciousness, an alternative attitude towards foreground and immediacy. This attitude looks back to a present that is vital and forwards to the focal point of the first person, which is the autobiography of *Praeterita*. It also recalls a fiction that Ruskin has been fond of: "We have only to attend to what is happening here—and now" (xxix, 60).

The environment of that self, who, as the subject of the inverted focal point, has run out of space, is the foreground that has a history of eliciting claustrophobic response, the inability to make discriminations. And if that foreground is to be made habitable, as both the "defiled den" and "coal-cellar" of chiaroscuro are not, reflexive space must be made as agreeable as

158

that early space within the walls of the Herne Hill garden. The efficacy of the foreground, which is the environment of the self both before and after the penetration of space, expresses itself in a phenomenology of the home. It is a phenomenology that unravels through Ruskin's work as a self-referring, autobiographical design that is opposite in every way to the anonymous movement through recessional space. As early as *The Poetry of Architecture* (1838), Ruskin had considered analyzing livable space in terms of psychic requirements: ". . . at some future period we hope to give a series of essays on the habitations of the most distinguished men of Europe, showing how the alterations which they directed, and the expression which they bestowed, corresponded with the turn of their emotions, and leading intellectual faculties" (I, 78). Although this project is not carried out, the relation between habitable space and psychic requirements is never forgotten.

Behind the utility of the foreground is the assumption that the background, the transcendental frontier, is a better place to visit than live. Certainly no place to write an autobiography, the background arrived at by the vanishing perspective, makes demands that a potential habitant cannot meet. Essentially, it is a place of anonymity and transcendence. But living space requires more "recognition" than "surprise." The creation of a foreground of living space is a preparation for the writing of autobiography, if not the reading of it. Still, autobiography can only come after life, and living is an act of "restraint," of coming to terms with the near, the "humble," and what lacks "violent stimulus":

> So that it is, in reality, better for mankind that the forms of their common landscape should offer no violent stimulus to the emotions,—that the gentle upland, browned by the bending furrows of the plough, and the fresh sweep of the chalk down, and the narrow winding of the copse-clad dingle, should be more frequent scenes of human life than the Arcadias of cloud-capped mountain or luxuriant vale; and that, while humbler (though always infinite) sources of interest are given to each of us around the homes to which we are restrained for the greater part of our lives, these mightier and stranger glories should become the objects of adventure,—at once the cynosures of the fancies of childhood, and themes of the happy memory, and the winter's tale of age.
>
> Nor is it always that the inferiority is felt. For, so natural is it to the human heart to fix itself in hope rather than in present possession, and so subtle is the charm which the imagination casts over what is distant or denied, that there is often a more touching power in the scenes which contain far-away promise of something greater than themselves, than in those which exhaust the treasures and powers of Nature in an unconquerable and excellent glory, leaving nothing more to be by the fancy pictured, or pursued. (VI, 167–68)

The instincts for something other than "present possession" are rarely missing. Almost always, Ruskin would rather be both outside and elsewhere, in the world of the vanishing perspective. And even the home permits the "restrained" resident the alternatives of both looking backwards, in an act of "happy memory," and forwards, to "scenes which contain far-away promises of something greater than themselves." Nevertheless, the attention to the immediate has a utility that goes beyond the dubious value of simply being without "violent stimulus." To accommodate the immediate with a "recognition" untrammeled by contempt is an act of life, an act that is itself a preparation for a readable autobiography. It is the acceptance of an existence in which one can, touching time, also hope to touch objects, if not the first person, without contamination. And if there is no one to be touched, including himself, in Ruskin's solipsistic world of voyeurism and eavesdropping, perhaps there is a first person who is neither pseudonymous or invisible. Perhaps, in autobiography, Kata Phusin has become an unnecessary fiction.

In a discussion of Gothic, as opposed to modern, ornamentation, Ruskin makes a case for the Gothic by pointing out its attention to optical limitation. Carved to be seen, Gothic ornamentation is ornamentation of the immediate: "Now, the Gothic builders placed their decoration on a precisely contrary principle, and on the only rational principle. All their best and most delicate work they put on the foundation of the building, close to the spectator . . ." (xii, 58). But more important to the efficacy of the near is the source of Gothic design, a source that is traced to a re-decorated Dungeon of *Me*-ology:

> But the main thing I wish you to observe is, the complete *domesticity* of the work; the evident treatment of the church spire merely as a magnified house-roof; and the proof herein of the great truth of which I have been endeavouring to persuade you, that all good architecture rises out of good and simple domestic work; and that, therefore, before you attempt to build great churches and palaces, you must build good house doors and garret windows. (xii, 42–43)

But the acceptance of a home, even though it possesses both memory and hope, is no easier than the acceptance of the autobiographical impulse. Ruskin is involved in endless vacillation, the vacillation, finally, of someone who would be in two different places at two different times, avoiding both homogeneity and simultaneity. Still, against his transcendental instincts, he goes about making a case for the "here—and now." He complains that "Rome should go on sending missionaries to China, and, within a thousand yards across the water of St. Carlo's isle, leave the people of her own Italy's Garden of Eden in guilt and misery" (xxxv, 331). But Ruskin, who becomes the object of his own "black anger," is like Rome. A reader of *Fors Clavigera* points out the difference between places and homes. Making the most of little, she gardens, as Ruskin in the beginning, enclosed by the Edenic walls of Herne Hill, could not. She understands that a home does not require distance, that to have a home, you don't have to be away from it. With a home, there is no such thing as collapsed space:

> Thirdly (and this is wherein I fear to offend you), *I will join St. George's Company whenever you join it yourself.* Please pardon me for saying that I appear to be more a member of it than you are. My life is strictly bound and ruled, and within those lines I live. Above all things, you urge our duties to the land, the common earth of our country. It seems to me that the first duty any one owes to his country is *to live in it.* I go further, and maintain that every one is bound to have a home, and live in that. You speak of the duty of acquiring, if possible, and cultivating, the smallest piece of ground. But (forgive the question) where is your house and your garden? I know you have got *places,* but you do not stay there. Almost every month you date from some new place, a dream of delight to me; and all the time I am stopping at home, labouring to improve the place I live at, to keep the lives entrusted to me, and to bring forth other lives in the agony and peril of my own. And when I read your reproaches, and see where they date from, I feel as a soldier freezing in the trenches before a Sebastopol might feel at receiving orders from a General who was dining at his club in London. If you would come and see me in May, I could show you as pretty a little garden of the spade as any you ever saw, made on the site of an old rubbish heap. . . . (xxviii, 249–50)

But Ruskin is not to be "restrained" to anything that lacks "violent stimulus" so completely as a "little garden of the spade" that was once a "rubbish heap." The impulse is to avoid one home by having two houses. Ruskin protests that he does not like to "leave." Still, his houses are "wherever": "Wherever *my home is,* I shall stay much more quietly than you might think. Indeed I never was a rambler in the common sense. My delight was always to *stay* in places that I loved; and I am sure that neither my mother nor you can recollect my wishing to leave *any* place when I was comfortably settled among hills" (xiii, xlviii). Ruskin's affections for the domestic are confused by his attitudes towards mobility. His houses are "wherever," but his "sympathy" is not with people who want to "*go* anywhere." It would seem that houses should be mobile but not ships: "Of the larger and more polite tribes of merchant vessels . . . I have nothing to say, feeling in general little sympathy with people who want to *go* anywhere; nor caring much about anything, which in the essence of it expresses a desire to get to other sides of the world; but only for homely and stay-at-home ships, that live their life and die their death about English rocks" (xiii, 26).

Tracing the source of Gothic design to domesticity, Ruskin traces the source of modern architecture, which he is certain is bad architecture, to the mobility to those who, like "Rome," or the "larger and more polite tribes of merchant vessels," sacrifice the immediate for the "other sides of the world." The problems of architectural wandering are compounded by a social mobility that separates the self from those roots with which Ruskin would be in touch:[1]

> . . . I believe that the wandering habits which have now become almost necessary to our existence, lie more at the root of our bad architecture than any other character of modern times. We always look upon our houses as temporary lodgings. We are always hoping to get larger and finer ones. . . . It is not for me to lead you at present into any consideration of a matter so closely touching your private interests and feelings; but it surely is a subject for serious thought, whether it might not be better for many of us, if, on attaining a certain position in life, we determined, with God's permission, to choose a home in which to live and die,—a home not to be increased by adding stone to stone and field to field, but which, being enough for all our wishes at that period, we should resolve to be satisfied with forever. (XII, 72)

There is a need for permanence, without the ultimate immobility of the "collective aspect." And permanence means satisfaction, the trading of perpetual "surprise" for "recognition." The need for permanence is an acceptance of the autobiographical impulse, an acceptance of the condition of living "face to face" with one's self. To stay home requires that the home be transformed from the conventional Dungeon of *Me*-ology. It must have something like the "nerves" of the classical landscape, a sense of an animated interior. If it lacks "vital stimulus," it may provide a kind of peace, like E. L.'s defensive "innermost chambers." That peace is a domestic variation of the transcendental species of "Escape." Instead of escaping by going out the window of the room with a view, the domestic Ruskin, no avaricious parenthetical self, draws the blinds, shutting the outside out. And this is at least a possibility because Ruskin, by an act of the imagination, has made the foreground as "vital" as the background, the inside, once a "defiled den," as "sacred" as the outside:

> This is the true nature of home—it is the place of Peace; the shelter, not only from all injury, but from all terror, doubt, and division. In so far as it is not this, it is not home; so far as the anxieties of the outer life penetrate into it . . . it ceases to be home; it is then only a part of that outer world which you have roofed over and lighted fire in. But in so far as it is a sacred place, a vestal temple, a temple of the hearth watched over by Household Gods, before whose faces none may come but those whom they can receive with love,—so far as it is

---

[1] Ruskin's concern with source, points of origin, "roots," "The Roots of Honour," which is the first chapter of *Unto This Last,* is everywhere apparent. The *Index* of the Library Edition has a substantial listing.

this, and roof and fire are types only of a nobler shade and light,—shade as of the rock in a weary land, and light as of the Pharos in the stormy sea;—so far it vindicates the name, and fulfils the praise, of Home. (xviii, 122)

Home-space as uncontaminated foreground, as shelter rather than prison, is further defined by Ruskin's need for something more than a Biedermeier ideal of space that is livable. From Denmark Hill, in a letter to Rawdon Brown, Ruskin complains: "I have no house of my own—not even rooms; and living with two old people, however good, is not good for a man" (xxxvi, 407). For a while, he decides to make his background the foreground. He will live at the transcendental edge. More accurately, he decides to live on the frontier arrived at after the actual penetration of space. He will make his home among the mountains that, like clouds, are heavenly "thrones": "To-morrow I leave England for Switzerland; and whether I stay in Switzerland or elsewhere, to England I shall seldom return. I must find a home—or at least the shadow of a roof of my own, somewhere; certainly not here" (xxxvi, 407). But Ruskin does not find a "shadow of a roof" in Switzerland. Later, from his rooms in Corpus Christi, he again refers to his problem in a letter to Carlyle: ". . . the loss of my mother and my old nurse leaves me without any root, or, in the depth of the word, any home; and what pleasant things I have, seem to me only a kind of museum of which I have now merely to arrange the bequest . . ." (xxxvii, 72).

The search is not so much for a house as it is for that ideal he had imaginatively constructed—a home that would approach the condition of domestic immanence created by the presence of the watchful "Household Gods." But he is left, instead, with a museum. Still, the museum that leaves Ruskin "without any root" provides him with something more than the "shadow of a roof." At its most exaggerated, the will towards the museum-home expresses itself in Ruskin's attitude towards his Guild Museum at Sheffield: "I wonder if it will give you any pleasure to hear that my museum is fairly now set afoot at Sheffield, and that I am thinking of living as much there as possible. The people are deeply interesting to me, and I am needed for them and am never really quiet in conscience, elsewhere" (xxxvii, 299).

If the search for a "shadow of a roof" is the tentative acceptance of the autobiographical impulse, of being able to live "face to face" with one's self, the creation of a space of possession is largely the result of a desire not merely to accept but to preserve. Among other things, he would now preserve the notion of "present possession." More specifically, he would hold onto the present tense, or at least memoranda of the present. Even in his early diaries, the fear of a lost present is apparent. To forget is to lose time: ". . . forgot something which I wished particularly to note. I think it will come into my head again, but it is stupid to forget it, and loses time" (*Diaries*, p. 265); "A good day because wet. I wish Sunday were always wet; otherwise I lose the day" (*Diaries*, p. 266); ". . . a complete day of lassitude and lost time" (*Diaries*, p. 269). Against this sense of loss, the need for possession as a form of preservation is strong. And lost space is like lost time. He fears losing things just as he fears losing days. The museum curator, as versatile as Ruskin's selves are encyclopedic, is also a fireman: "My time is passed in a fierce, steady struggle to save all I can every day, as a fireman from a smouldering ruin, of history or aspect" (xxxvii, 136).

Holding things in "present possession," instead of allowing them to slip into the past like lost days, becomes an obsession. From Venice, hearing of Turner's death, Ruskin exhorts his father to buy some sketches he thinks will be made available. Predictably, the desire for possession, for gathering objects "here" in an act of consolidation, is mingled, like the "near branches all entangled with the distance," with the desire to have paintings of what is "there." He will collect mountains, bringing transcendental topography home: ". . . the chief thing is to get mountains. A mountain drawing is always, to me, worth, just three times one on any other subject . . ." (xiii, xxiv). And again, in the same letter: "Buy *mountains,* and buy *cheap,* and you cannot do wrong. I am just as glad I am not in England. I should be coveting too much—and too much excited—and get ill. I must now go to my work, and keep my thoughts away from these things" (xiii, xxv). Possession becomes conditional biography, the anticipation of autobiography. With Ruskin, it is always the third person first. Writing about Sir Walter Scott, Ruskin wrote an early version of *Praeterita.* Now, he considers how he would occupy himself if he were to live life over again. He decides he would possess everything about a man who himself possessed a world in a memory of "first vision." Perhaps he would "collect" Turner himself. With this compounding of possession, nothing would be forgotten and days would not be lost: "Were my life to come over again, for these last ten years, I would devote my self altogether to Turner—the man, I mean, recording every sentence that he spoke, and collecting every picture that came in my way" (xiii, xlvii).

Unable to get the man, he settles for the paintings. And most intense with the collecting of Turners, Ruskin's avidity for possession, which is memory made concrete, approaches the fervor of the glutton. As if in preparation for autobiography, for a foreground of Household Gods, he will refurbish a "nerveless" interior with museum pieces. The foreground and the inside will become as special as vast "storehouses." Always concerned with gastronomics, he is like the Supper Guest of the diaries: ". . . I am always laying up for myself treasures upon earth, with the most eager appetite . . ." (xxvii, 425). With Ruskin, the primary aesthetics are those of "numerical superiority," the aesthetics of plenitude. More, at least until the point of "Illth," is better than less. At its most ambitious, the autobiographical instinct goes far beyond either the supper table or the museum. Possession becomes conservation. It is as if, faced with the prospects of "World Collision," the failure of a recessional space that has been turned "outside in," and the general movement towards the homogeneity and simultaneity of no movement at all, he has decided to save the world from disintegrating into a heap of indistinguishable rubble, a heap that may be the world-as-self, the world as a self-portrait of madness. At the least, preserving the potential for discrimination, if not the random travel of a casual sacrifice of foreground for a background that no longer exists, he will save the Rhone Valley from collapse: "You know I'm going to redeem that Valley of the Rhone. It's too bad, and can't be endured any longer. . . . And before I die I hope to see a rampart across every lateral valley holding a pure quiet lake full of fish, capable of six feet rise at any moment over as much surface as will take the meltings of the glaciers above it for a month. And if I don't master the Rhone that way, they shall shut me up in Chillon for the rest of my days if they like" (xxxvi, 569).

If Ruskin's version of conservation suggests excessive pride, his methods of possession indicate a "covetousness which is idolatry." He writes to his father about his instincts for acquisition—a gathering of possessions that intensifies that same selfhood the transcendent consciousness would lose:

> . . . My love of art has been a terrible temptation to me, and I feel that I have been sadly self-indulgent lately—what with casts, *Liber Studiorum*, missals, and Tintorets, I think I must cut the whole passion short off at the roots, or I shall get to be a mere collector, like old Mr. Wells or Redleaf, or Sir W. Scott, or worst of all Beckford or Horace Walpole. I am sure I ought to take that text to heart, "covetousness which is idolatry," for I do idolize my Turners and missals, and I can't conceive anybody being ever tried with a heavier temptation than I am to save every farthing I can to collect a rich shelf of thirteenth-century manuscripts. There would be no stop to it, for I should always find the new ones illustrating all the rest. I believe I shall have to give up all ideas of farther collection, and to rest satisfied with my treasures. (xii, lxviii–lxix)

Self-indulgence leads to self-consciousness. But the glutton, as "biped" as "useful truth," wants neither indigestion nor a gain of weight. Indulging himself, he would at the same time forget himself. If the glutton writes autobiography, he will not read it. He will not be reminded of himself. In order to justify self-indulgence, to tame the explosion of selfhood, Ruskin's home becomes a public place: the act of possession, beginning privately with minerals at Herne and Denmark Hills, ends publically, at his Sheffield museum. As his space becomes public, so he, as "dream-gifted" curator, becomes plural. He decides to delegate authority to assistants such as William Ward and Charles Fairfax Murray, who, as extensions of the Master, possess and sketch for a museum that is Ruskin's public home.[2] Collecting everything, Ruskin has come too far to want to "lose" himself. If he doesn't want either to read autobiography or look in mirrors, he no longer concerns himself with the vanishing perspective. Still, by multiplying himself to the point of public dissolution, he can reach a condition of centrifugal fragmentation where self-indulgence is public spirited. Possession becomes civic duty, and the autobiographical impulse is justified.

Gathering objects into a foreground that is being redecorated in order that it may be made livable, the act of collection engages both the world of objects and the self in a relation that is close to satisfactory. The inevitable movement towards autobiographical confrontation is also a movement towards domesticity. Although it is a version of Gothic architecture that finds greatness in domesticity, modern art also finds one of its chief characteristics in domesticity. But the domesticity of modern art, providing a comfort that is not entirely commendable, is not so much the source of art, as the end of it:

> . . . the second characteristic is Domesticity. All previous art contemplated men in their public aspect, and expressed only their public Thought. But our art paints their home aspect, and reveals their home thoughts. Old art waited reverently in the Forum. Ours plays happily in the Nursery; we may call it briefly—conclusively—Art of the Nest. It does not in the least appeal for appreciation to the proud civic multitude, rejoicing in procession and assembly. It appeals only to Papa and Mama and Nurse. And these not being in general severe judges, painters must be content if a great deal of the work produced for their approbation should be ratified by their's only. (xix, 200–201)

Both the problems with Domesticity and its virtues are part of Ruskin's third characteristic of modern art: "Connected with this Domestic character is the third, I am sorry to say now no more quite laudable, attribute of modern work—its shallowness. A great part of the virtue of Home is actually dependent on Narrowness of thought. To be quite comfortable in your nest, you must not care too much about what is going on outside" (xix, 201). The appetite within the Home has to be restrained. One cannot collect too much without turning Nest into Museum. Unlike either the devouring parenthetical self, who turns the "outside in," or the Supper Guest, who would go so far as to participate in self-cannibalization, the modern artist, depending on shallowness and narrowness, keeps the outside

[2] Wilenski makes the point that Ruskin's assistants are proxy selves (*John Ruskin: An Introduction*, p. 149).

out, as if he were E. L., hiding in "innermost chambers." Recessional space—all that either is or once was "outside"—cannot fail when virtue is found in a shallowness that precludes distance. With Ruskin, to employ this characteristic of domestic limitation is to return to a vision before the public, horizontal perspective, a perspective that included the troublesome problems of economics, architecture, and society. It is a return to a world that is censored, a world of the self, without "Collision," as the self would have it. The Nest is a fitting place to write *Praeterita*. The shallowness and narrowness of the Nest eliminate both the private problems of a failing distance and the public problems of the horizontal perspective.

But Ruskin begins to develop his version of Nest Art long before he ever worries about the failure of the distance or the burden of an inclusive vision. As a child, his foreground, which is a space of enclosure, is made livable by virtue of a scrutinizing focus that only takes into account what is "here." Attaining "serene and secure methods of life and motion," the child passes his days "contentedly in tracing the squares and comparing the colours of my carpet;—examining the knots in the wood of the floor, or counting the bricks in the opposite houses. . . . But the carpet, and what patterns I could find in bed-covers, dresses, or wall-papers to be examined, were my chief resources . . ." (xxxv, 21). Later, released from confined space, the space of walls, Ruskin is dispossessed of that peace which attends a focus that is without the complication of either the "outside" or peripheral extension. To leave closeness that is not claustrophobic—space in which objects can be manipulated and catalogued, without outside interference—is to enter an open space of controversy that is without shelter: "I had begun my studies of Alpine botany just eighteen years before, in 1842 . . . and should have made a pretty book if I could have got peace. Even yet, I can manage my point a little, and would far rather be making outlines of flowers than writing; and I meant to have drawn every English and Scottish wild flower. . . . But *Blackwood's Magazine,* with its insults to Turner, dragged me into controversy; and I have not had, properly speaking, a day's peace since . . ." (xxv, 204–205).

Ruskin's time "outside," which has become a time without either future or recessional space, is also without peace. Withdrawing into something like the walled spaces of his childhood, he can examine possessions, entirely his own, that are without the pretense of the museum's public accommodation: "My only way of being cheerful is precisely the way I said, to shut myself up and look at weeds and stones; for as soon as I see or hear what human creatures are suffering of pain, and saying of absurdity, I get about as cheerful as I should be in a sheepfold strewed hurdle-deep with bloody carcases, with a herd of wolves and monkeys howling and gibbering on the top of them" (xxxvi, 417–18). The Art of the Nest is an art of withdrawal that transforms the foreground into a heterodox, interior version of pastoral—a defensive pocket of space into which the consciousness retreats in order to maintain a hold on an infirm equilibrium: ". . . sleeping, only to dream of finding the dead body of a child in a box, a little girl whom I had put living into it and forgotten. Fought through it all by keeping my mind on geology" (*Diaries,* p. 1099).

Yet the escape into immediacy is often ignored, even at the risk of Ruskin's sanity. The movement back and forth between the "bloody carcases" of the engaged self and the pockets of space that are an interior version of pastoral becomes a tightrope performance between breakdown and that domination of limited areas of space which passes for equanimity. When the space becomes too large, the control vanishes. Having attempted to expand centrifugally his area of control through St. George's Guild, to enlarge controlled museum-space beyond the confining architecture of Sheffield's, to turn his Inside into an Outside in an untypical act of visionary performance, Ruskin, failing even as the outside is turned in, is finally pleased to require little—an enclosed center in which he can be ignorant of the outside circumference that will not have his St. George's pastoral imposed upon it:

> The amount of subscriptions [for the St. George's Fund] received, during the four years of my mendicancy, might have disappointed me, if, in my own mind, I had made any appointments on the subject, or had benevolence pungent enough to make me fret at the delay in the commencement of the national felicity which I propose to bestow. On the contrary, I am only too happy to continue amusing myself in my study, with stones and pictures; and find, as I grow old, that I remain resigned to the consciousness of any quantity of surrounding vice, distress and disease, provided only the sun shine in at my window over Corpus Garden, and there are no whistles from the luggage trains passing the Waterworks. (xxviii, 202)

The shallowness and narrowness of Nest Art, the art of the foreground, are utilitarian dimensions because they engage only a limited portion of the self, a portion that can be "amused" inside, without having ambitions to devour, or even deal with, an outside composed of "surrounding vice, distress and disease." Before, what was inside intensified a sense of selfhood, an incipiently autobiographical impulse that Ruskin would stifle. There was no vanishing perspective in the "coal-cellar." But now, the inside, instead of compounding the autobiographical impulse beyond "due relation," keeps it tamed. To be inside is to be humiliated in the right way. And the right kind of humiliation, keeping Ruskin inside, keeps him out of Bedlam:

> . . . it has been the result of very steady effort on my own part to keep myself, if it might be, out of Hanwell, or that other Hospital which makes the name of

Christ's native village dreadful in the ear of London. For, having long observed that the most perilous beginning of trustworthy qualification for either of those establishments consisted in an exaggerated sense of self-importance; and being daily compelled, of late, to value my own person and opinions at a higher and higher rate, in proportion to my extending experience of the rarity of any similar creatures or ideas among mankind, it seemed to me expedient to correct this increasing conviction of my superior wisdom, by companionship with pictures I could not copy, and stones I could not understand. . . . (xxviii, 202–203)

Confined to the shallowness and narrowness of Nest Art, Ruskin takes as few chances as possible. He will avoid Bedlam. He has seen the "bloody carcases." The "green tide . . . full of floating corpses" has cost him his sanity. He has seen and felt too much. Now, he will stay home, "amusing" himself in order to protect his precarious sanity. Keeping his vision deliberately shallow and narrow, he will forget the outside, the world of both horizontal perspective and a recessional space that has turned "outside in": "Here is a little grey cockle-shell, lying beside me, which I gathered, the other evening, out of the dust of the Island of St. Helena; and a brightly-spotted snail-shell, from the thirsty sands of Lido; and I want to set myself to draw these, and describe them, in peace" (xxviii, 757). The snail shell offers peace. It is fit material for Nest Art. Yet the distance fails, and we know that Ruskin often "becomes" what he "regards." With Ruskin, not only is seeing the essence of existence, but he later "is" what he has already "seen." Finally, the vantage point becomes the focal point. He will not only paint the snail shell, he will live in it, perhaps painting it from the inside. His Nest will be a shell: "The lectures are coming nice; though they're giving me sad trouble—and, in fact, I oughtn't to be teased to talk about any more at my time in life, but should be left to paint snail-shells—and live in a big one . . ." (xxxvii, 4).

INCIPIENT AUTOBIOGRAPHY

A good many of the descriptions of Ruskin's early activities, now seen from the far and dark side of life—*The Cestus of Aglaia* side of the chapter "Of Typical Beauty" of *Modern Painters*—appear to possess only the accuracy of a photographic negative. Playing all the roles, even as he has used up the "magnificent blank" of both paper and space, Ruskin has assumed most positions. He has seen St. Paul's from both ends of London Bridge. Certainly, his selves are encyclopedic. At times, it would appear that Ruskin is doing something only in preparation for an opposite performance later on. Often, it seems that he is saying something so he can later contradict himself. But then, playing with options, doubleness, and paradox, Ruskin has always been as "biped" as "useful truth." At best precariously balanced between sanity and insanity, Ruskin is now also balanced, as if supported, between apparent contradictions that are like the spidery, yet buttressed, cathedrals that fascinate him.

Still, one of the most persistent characteristics encountered in Ruskin's work—a characteristic complicated by his attitudes towards the vital present, which is a tense of public engagement, the tense of the "bloody carcasses"—is his reluctance to respond to the autobiographical impulse, his reluctance to show himself. When he does emerge, he not only shows himself, but often shouts. After all, he is the Master. And as the Master, he can be dogmatic, pontifical. But there is always the problem of "due relation." And when Ruskin emerges, that sense is often lost. His early pseudonymous existence as Kata Phusin anticipates the outward-bound movement, beyond both pseudonymity and invisibility, towards the vanishing point. Ruskin has always been more comfortable as a voyeur than a performer; he has always preferred the starting point to the finish line, the vantage point to the focal point. We recall his comments about Carlyle's letter to Emerson—comments that suggest all the emotive involvement of the Camera Lucida, the sympathy and self-consciousness of a piece of optical equipment:

> In the beginning of the Carlyle-Emerson correspondence, edited with too little comment by my dear friend Charles Norton, I find at page 18 this—to me entirely disputable, and to my thought, so far as undisputed, much blameable and pitiable, exclamation of my master's: "Not till we can think that here and there one is thinking of us, one is loving us, does this waste earth become a peopled garden." My training, as the reader has perhaps enough perceived, produced in me the precisely opposite sentiment. *My* times of happiness had always been when *nobody* was thinking of me. . . . My entire delight was in observing without being myself noticed,—if I could have been invisible, all the better. (xxxv, 165–66)

Yet in a letter to a good friend, Dr. John Brown, Ruskin introduces a shadowy figure, as problematical as the audience of *Fors Clavigera*. The figure, unnamed, is nevertheless familiar: "I like the passage very much about self-forgetfulness, but how is this virtue to be gained? Happy those whose sympathies stretch out like gold leaf until their very substance is lost. But there are others—not unprincipled men—who yet cannot make themselves to themselves transparent nor imponderable. They overbalance and block out everything with their own *near* selves . . ." (xxxvi, 85). Ruskin's invisible man is not a fact. More accurately, he is not an excluding fact. There is always the "buttress" of apparent contradiction. Attempting to move towards the vanishing point, the "lost" self, whose "happiness had always been when *nobody* was thinking of me," calls into existence its own opposite, a self who would, reversing normal optical procedures, focus on the vantage point. Opaque and weighty, with no aspirations to leave either the inside or the foreground, this other self sympathizes with the autobiographical impulse. This aspect of Ruskin may even engage in self-portraiture. For a time, he may flirt with mirrors.

Once invisible but seeing, Ruskin, as this new portrait self, learning to act, learns the attractions, if not the dangers, of the mirror. As opposed to, say, the detached Camèra Lucida, the empathizing portrait self would rather live at Warwick Castle than look at it—to perform rather than observe.[3] The focal point has become the Nest of a first person who had once been an invisible man. Vantage point and focal point, once assiduously separated by recessional space, have become indistinguishable. Still, all this has happened before when the spectral "gleam," the infernal focal point of the inverted perspective, closed in "hopelessly." But now things are different. Enclosed space is not the space of an unsought self-consciousness. The "coal-cellar" or "defiled den" has become a Nest. Putting himself where his eyes were once focused, Ruskin, learning that the attraction of mirrors can overcome the fear of reflexive space, decides that if there is one thing better than being a curator, it is being catalogued: ". . . if we are not buried in a respectable way—if we tumble down Niagara, or sink in an Irish bog, or get lost in a coal-hole, or smothered in a sand-pit—the earth takes care of us, and bitumenises, or carbonises, or calcines, or chalcedonises, until we are as durable as rock itself; and then, if we have the luck to get picked up and put in a museum, we may stay there and grin out of the limestone with quite as good a grace as a mammoth or ichthyosaurus" (I, 415).

But the movement towards the museum, towards density and opaqueness, is slow, tentative. Banished towards the vanishing point by a transcendental impulse that is connected with the will-towards-objectification, Ruskin, despite his self-indulgences as collector—indulgences that anticipate the movement towards autobiography—does not have a history of self-cultivation. Or more specifically, indulgence has always been qualified by the repression of self-awareness: "Choose, then, a subject that interests you; and so far as failure of time or materials compels you to finish one part, or express one character, rather than another, of course dwell on the features that interest you most. But beyond this, forget, or even

---

[3] For reference to Warwick Castle, see "Camera Lucida" section of the first chapter; and also XXXV, 16.

somewhat repress yourself. . . . You are not to endeavour to express your own feelings about it; if anything, err on the side of concealing them. What is best is not to think of yourself . . ." (xxii, 28). Ruskin's invisibility, as an object of pride, comes close to a paradoxical materialization, a museum piece. The first person enters, boasting about his repressed self: "I hear it often said by my friends that my writings are transparent, so that I may myself be clearly seen through them. They are so, and what *is* seen of me through them is truly seen, yet I know no other author of candour who has given so partial, so disproportioned, so steadily reserved a view of his personality" (xxxv, 628).

But in the 1881 "Epilogue" to *The Stones of Venice,* Ruskin suggests that his invisibility, his reticence, cost him those converts who, involved in a love-affair with themselves, could not understand his reluctance to emerge in the role of a self-advertising first person: ". . . I think I can now see a further reason for their non-acceptance of the book's teaching, namely, the entire concealment of my own personal feelings throughout, which gives a continual look of insincerity to my best passages" (xi, 232). Yet it was not for Ruskin the readers of *Stones* were looking, but themselves, or rather themselves in Ruskin. The failure of "recognition"—the absence of the mirror that Ruskin, up until this point, has assiduously avoided—disappointed readers in search of themselves: "If . . . I had written quite naturally, and told, as a more egoistic person would, my own impressions as thinking *those,* forsooth, and not the history of Venice, the most important business to the world in general, a large number of equally egoistic persons would have instantly felt the sincerity of the selfishness, clapped it, and stroked it, and said, 'That's me'" (xi, 232). Failing to provide "recognition," an invisible Ruskin, happiest "when *nobody* was thinking of me," wrote neither the biography of his own readers nor his own incipient autobiography. It is a failure, coming with the failure of the distance, that he will correct.

Once lost and "repressed," but now prompted by a desire to endure, to avoid the world of the vanishing perspective, Ruskin allows himself, almost as a possession—at times becoming a "bitumenised" collector's item—to be found. At first, in this role, Ruskin is shy. The reluctant first person, this portrait self, enters, from his previous condition of translucent pseudonymity borne by syntactic politesse: "The reader must pardon me a momentary allusion to work of my own . . ." (xiv, 75). Or again: "I cannot help what taint of ungracefulness you or other readers of these letters may feel that I incur, in speaking, in this instance, of myself. If I could speak with the same accurate knowledge of any one else, most gladly I would . . ." (xvii, 412). The first-person intrusions—"To me, personally (I must take your indulgence for a moment to speak wholly of myself)"—lead into embryonic autobiography, vignettes of the first person, which occur in the present tense, the tense of incipient, though not final, autobiography: "I am writing on St. John's day, in the monastery of Assisi; and I had no idea whatever, when I sat down to my work this morning, of saying any word of what I am now going to tell you" (xxii, 444).

Even as Ruskin, with a diminishing future, is forced back into the present tense, the first person drops the delicacy that surrounds his intrusions. He becomes familiar with his own voice: "How garrulous one gets, talking about myself!" (xxxvi, 155). His letters, once extensive, encompassing public material, now become as reflexive as the space outside his Nest: "So there's a letter—about myself and nothing else. I wonder I have the face to send it . . ." (xxxvi, 357). And that first person, once invisible or at least pseudonymous, becomes defiant, if not as aggressive as the Spectral Vision and Audit that, anticipating autobiography, created the necessity of a defiant first person: "I am fifty-seven to-day; and may perhaps be allowed to talk a little of myself" (xxviii, 545). In the Nest, he writes not only of himself, but for himself. With his impulse to play all the roles, his world becomes a solipsistic reflection of himself. Yet he is not dissatisfied. In the Nest, there is no "World Collision" because there is no outside. Space is already both shallow and narrow. Like his Supper Guest, he is both digested and digester. Like his diarist, who writes about himself for himself, Ruskin is both performer and audience. And both performer and audience are pleased by his enclosed aspect of doubleness, an aspect that predicts a dangerous union that can lead to the immobility of the angelic "collective aspect": "If I get tiresome, the reader must skip; I write, for the moment, to amuse myself, and not him" (xxxv, 347). Yet amusing himself, he can still announce that, having created an agreeable interior, as well as an agreeable foreground—an area for potential autobiography—his scrutiny of that first person is not entirely satisfactory. Some of the old qualms of being "face to face" (iv, 176) remain: "several letters from pleased acquaintances have announced to me, of late, that they have obtained quite new lights upon my character from these jottings, and like me much better than they ever did before. Which was not the least the effect I intended to produce on them; and which moreover is the exact opposite of the effect on my own mind of meeting myself, by turning back, face to face" (xxxv, 279).

Still, occasional displeasure is only a passing fancy. For the most part, "face to face" with himself, Ruskin is no longer dismayed. His attitude towards the first person has changed and his ultimate role as his own focal point is inevitable: "In the autobiography which will develop, I hope in *Fors,* into something more interesting than I had expected (for as I think over it much becomes interesting to myself which I once despised), I am perhaps going to try to give a portrait or two, and may end with myself" (xxxvii, 160). With surprising alacrity, he turns attack to his own autobiographical advantage. Speaking of "you," he is determined to speak of himself. And attack becomes confession: "Who am I, that should challenge *you*—do you ask? My mother was a sailor's daughter, so please you; one of my aunts was a baker's wife—the other, a tanner's; and I don't know much more about my family, except that there used to be a greengrocer of the name in a small shop near the Crystal Palace. Something of my early and vulgar life, if it interests you, I will tell you in next *Fors* . . ." (xxvIII, 147–48). Certainly, Ruskin's role as collector, or curator, is as tinged with incipient autobiography as his highly visible performance as "bitumenised" museum piece. The act of possession, of bringing objects into foreground space, is the substantiation of the self's identity through its possessions. And possession becomes a form of narcissism: ". . . we centre our affections too much on our own possessions—whether of things, or souls . . . it seems to me that the forms of affection which thus occupy us wholly must really be ranked as one of the more amiable conditions of self-love . . ." (xxxvII, 228–29).

Confession, coupled with the autobiography of possessions, leads to a kind of economic autobiography—a skeletal and dehumanized account of Ruskin's formerly "despised," but now "interesting" self. Under the "Affairs of the Master," in *Fors,* the Master, now as opaque as he once was transparent, considers a chronicle of economic exhibitionism: "I do not suppose that any of my readers—but there is a chance that some who hear and talk of me *without* reading me—will fancy that I have begun to be tired of my candour in exposition of personal expenses. Nothing would amuse me more, on the contrary, than a complete history of what the last six months have cost me . . ." (xxIx, 140). But this autobiography of "personal expenses" is, in theory, not to be limited to the Master. Just as Ruskin has imitated what he has seen, so the Companions of St. George are to imitate the Master. Everyone is to participate. The movement towards candour and density, which is to be a public, centrifugal movement away from privacy and secrecy, includes having transparent pockets: "I am surprised to find that my Index to Vols. I. and II. of *Fors* does not contain the important article 'Pockets': and that I cannot therefore, without too much trouble, refer to the place where I have said that the Companions of St. George are all to have glass pockets; so that the absolute contents of them may be known of all men. But, indeed, this society of ours is, I believe, to be distinguished from other close brotherhoods that have been, or that are, chiefly in this, that it will have no secrets . . ." (xxvIII, 528).

Ruskin's economic autobiography, the exhibition of the contents of his "glass pockets," occurs in "Notes and Correspondence" at the end of "Letter 76" of *Fors.* In it, the collector, the possessive curator, who once suffered from a *horror vacui*, attempts to create what amounts to a vacuum of "personal expenses"—to die, his "glass pockets" empty, "as poor as possible" (xxIx, 102). Having written a miniature autobiography of possessions, a tale of covetous self-indulgence, he will now set about writing a negative addendum to his life as collector—an autobiography of dissolution. The sleight of hand is characteristic of Ruskin's "biped" instincts. The first person has entered, opaque, weighty, and for all the world to see. But he has entered in order to empty his "glass pockets," to rid himself of the possessions that were an "amiable" form of "self-love." The autobiographical impulse is undercut by the dispersal of possessions, which is a disclaimer of even "amiable" narcissism.

Still, the "glass pockets" reveal only economics as those economics, as if on a vanishing perspective, reduce to nothing. Essentially, it is an autobiography of Nothing. But "face to face" confrontation is a more delicate matter. If the first person, tantalized by the mirror, does not return to the invisibility of the contents of empty pockets, there are nevertheless aspects of that first person which do. In the same way that the Art of the Nest eliminates the problems of both an inverted distance and the horizontal inclusion of "bloody carcases" by promoting shallowness and narrowness, so an editorial process is introduced that presents the self on its own terms. This editorial process is part of the return to a private, though visible, perspective—a mnemonic perspective rather than a spatial perspective. The Desiring Eyes will penetrate the distance of time. Before, attacking Whistler with "black anger," Ruskin was attacking his past-tense self, whose own "black anger" had been elicited by a defense of what was later to become Spectral Vision. But now he resurrects that past-tense self, censored and filtered by the cleansing depths of memory. In the manufacture of a livable foreground, a Nest that will lose its possessions as Ruskin, "bitumenised," becomes the main exhibit, a first person is created, who, opaque without overbalancing and blocking out everything with its own "*near*" self, will sit happily, "face to face," in a condition of autobiographical confrontation.

Attempting to construct livable space, an arena of sanity—of "innermost chambers" that will preclude both the assaults of Spectral Vision and Audit and the demands of a "green tide" of floating corpses—Ruskin employs not only the private dimensions of shallowness and narrowness, but also the perspective of memory. But memory, itself a form of visualization and fixed by the sight of "first vision," is transformed by autobiography into words that are no longer a "quack's drug for memorandum." And a special kind of language must be employed. Fundamentally, there are two kinds of language. The distinction, like the distinctions between "good" and "bad" lights, as well as heavenly and infernal sounds, is by now familiar: "'Blasphemy.'—If the reader can refer to my papers on Fiction in the *Nineteenth Century,* he will find this word carefully defined in its Scriptural, and evermore necessary, meaning,—'Harmful speaking'—not against God only, but against man and against all the good works and purposes of Nature. The word is accurately opposed to 'Euphemy,' the right of well-speaking of God and His world; and the two modes of speech are those which, going out of the mouth, sanctify or defile the man" (xxxiv, 72). Censoring the assertions of an overbalancing, "*near*" self, the language that Ruskin will use for autobiographical exploration is the pastoral language of "Euphemy." Further, even beyond autobiographical reporting, he will speak kindly, avoiding what he calls the "Cathedra Pestilentiae," or "seat of the scornful" (xxix, 365). It is as if, speaking kindly of others, he will become "good" himself, the kind of person who might best be described in language that is euphemistic. Or more accurately, instead of becoming "good," he might, for a while, remain sane. In any case, Ruskin's Nest, his arena of sanity, will employ memory shaped by a severely limited dictionary, something he could not do before: "I thought to have finished my blameful work before now, but *Fors* would not have it so;—now, I am well convinced she will let me follow the peaceful way towards the pleasant hills. Henceforth, the main work of *Fors* will be constructive only; and I shall allow in the text of it no syllable of complaint or scorn" (xxix, 294).

A portion of this "constructive" but exclusive work of limited vision is the manufacture of models, which are imaginative worlds for occasional respite and habitation. The *Fors* that contains proclamations from the "seat of the scornful" also contains Marmontel's *Contes Moraux,* in which models of livable space are retrieved and filtered by memory. Little else, Marmontel's models are products of the language of "Euphemy." Verbal equivalents to the drawings of Kate Greenaway, they have the excuse of being oases in a desert of "bloody carcases." They provide the perfect climate for temporal autobiographical confrontation. They are, Ruskin announces, "Real, but only partially seen; still more partially told. The rightness only perceived; the felicities only remembered . . ." (xxvii, 255). Ruskin insists upon the actuality of the recalled model, which is constructed by a memory that will only "partially" recall. Unsurprisingly, summoning "realities that are to last for ever," Ruskin will have it both ways: "He is not remembering his native valley as a subject for fine writing, but as a beloved real place, about which he may be garrulous, perhaps, but not rhetorical. But *is* it, or was it, or could it ever be, a real place indeed?—you will ask next. Yes, real in the severest sense; with realities that are to last for ever, when this London and Manchester life of yours shall have become a horrible, and, but on evidence, incredible, romance of the past" (xxvii, 255).

Still, the final euphemistic model that is to be retrieved by memory is not Marmontel's world that is "real" in "the severest sense," if no other. *Fors,* containing periods of rest that are pockets of pastoral dealing with idealized agricultural economy, in the midst of the destructive, anti-language of Blasphemy, also contains a euphemistic model that is especially good practice for autobiography. It is a model that will show him "the peaceful way towards the pleasant hills," where, instead of losing himself, he will find himself, or at least an edited version of himself that will permit him an amiable "face to face" confrontation. There, autobiography will become the right kind of self-awareness, rather than the claustrophobic self-consciousness of the "defiled den" or "coal-cellar."

Ruskin prepares for this condition of autobiographical confrontation—of the existence of subject and autobiographer in apparent immediacy—by engaging in *Fors* in the felicitous biography of Scott. Surrounded by the "blameful work" of *Fors,* Ruskin, describing the "quietude" of Scott's home when he was a child, not only creates an apt, euphemistic model—a snail-shell into which he can retreat—as opposed to the Blasphemy of the "outer" text, but also practices for the autobiographical description of the silence of his own home: "I never heard my father's or mother's voice raised in any question with each other. . . . I had never seen a moment's trouble or disorder in any household matter . . ." (xxviii, 349). The difference between Blasphemy and Euphemy is often a matter of tense. Ruskin's memory, if not silent, is rarely discordant. And that first person, summoned by the act of memory, will be incapable of the present-tense "scorn" of Ruskin's *"near"* self.

But even autobiographical confrontation requires a distance. After all, the Desiring Eyes, still farsighted, now see through time. And the mnemonic distance between a past-tense first person and the writer of autobiography is virtually the same as the distance between Ruskin and the Scott of his biography. The movement towards "face to face" confrontation started, without much promise, at the vanishing point. That movement had to overcome topographical entanglements that anticipated infernal self-consciousness, possession as "amiable" narcissism, and economics, after "Illth," as indulgence. But in his pastoral biography of Scott, in Scott's third person, he finds, as if with a telescope, his own first person. And that first person, separated from the autobiographer by an appropriate mnemonic distance, is Ruskin's final focal point. Accurately, it is not the spatial "face to face" confrontation of mirrors. That is too immediate. With the failure of the distance, the instincts towards spatialization and the "collective aspect" have become suspect. Instead, it is a confrontation refracted by time, a confrontation that is also an escape into a censored self, who is the "biped" alternative to the dreamer of "World Collision."

THE PEELED SELF: SELF-APPLAUSE TAKEN MEDICINALLY

With no future—the days of his potential life having been subtracted until minus categories represent the only available plenitude—and a recessional space that has been turned "outside in," Ruskin, looking behind to all that now remains, turns to his own version of that retrospective sight which he had explored earlier with Turner: "It is very strange to me to feel all my life become a thing of the past, and to be now merely like a wrecked sailor, picking up pieces of his ship on the beach. This is the real state of things with me, of course, in a double sense—People gone—and things. My Father and Mother, and Rosie, and Venice, and Rouen—all gone . . ." (xxxvii, 183). Everything is gone, and the future will never "be." There is still the present tense, but that, with the important exceptions of the vital present and the bitterly playful digressions of the Third Style, has rarely been satisfactory. And with everything gone, Ruskin shuffles in and out of sanity. The best sense he can make is that he should "go" too. His breakdowns, intensifying his need for retrospective sight or movement, create a self and world apart: ". . . *both* these illnesses have been part of one and the same system of constant thought, far out of sight to the people about me, and of course getting more and more separated from them as they go on in the ways of the modern world, and I go *back* to live with my Father and my Mother and my Nurse, and one more,—all waiting for me in the Land of the Leal" (xxxvii, 348).

Yet even that land which is not "Leal"[4]—a land eliciting by landscape association a past tense that is autobiographical history—recalls a world close to the "Leal" of Ruskin's Tory pastoral: "Above written before coffee—after coffee, walk for two glorious hours over all my old haunts—from the church I drew when I was fourteen to the balconies you know so well. It's all safe—and lovely and delicious beyond words, and I've come home to write the end of II. *Praeterita* . . ." (xxxvii, 607). If Ruskin's past-tense landscape is a matter of sanity and insanity, it is also a matter of life and death. The "Land of the Leal," behind the association of landscape—his "old haunts"—is food for a futureless Ruskin, whose only distant landscape is behind him: "I believe it was the damp and absence from my old haunts that nearly killed me at Brantwood . . ." (xxxvii, 607–608).

Just as memory is a form of sight, so Ruskin's sight becomes mnemonic—the "dream vision" of "Turnerian Topography." Spatial perspective in front is transformed into the perspective of memory behind. Ruskin's retrospective sight, moving both backwards and inwards, towards the autobiographer's history, is a mnemonic version of Ruskin's "immaginative penetrative," which, in *Modern Painters* ii, is directed towards the middle, the heart of things. What might be called Ruskin's "menmonic penetrative" moves towards the heart of a self who is not close enough to

---

[4] "I know not how it may be in the south; but I know that in Scotland, and the northern border, there still remains something of the feeling which fastened the old French word 'loial' among the dearest and sweetest of their familiar speech; and that there are some souls yet among them, who, alike in labour or in rest, abide in, or will depart to the Land of the Leal" (xxvii, 601).

the autobiographer to redecorate his foreground. If the Art of the Nest, advertising shallowness, precludes distance, it does not preclude the distance of memory. The newly discovered first person is an old self at an early age, or rather a new self at the source of his life. The autobiographer is reborn in the depths of his own memory. He takes his subject out of an oppressive present tense and examines him in a context that is historical. He is "face to face" with himself, but the tenses are different. What was once a separating space between vantage and focal points—a space that collapses with the coming of the inverted perspective—has been replaced by separating tenses. The intrusions of incipient autobiography, which were once present-tense intrusions, are now distanced.

But if that first person, who, as he becomes the subject, is located in a past that is the equivalent of a distant focal point, the impulse of the autobiographer is nevertheless to write that first person into the present tense by using up all the available material, which is the material of the distance. The desire, which is reminiscent of the parenthetical self's avaricious appetite, is to recall "all" that is "gone." If that is done, the autobiographical impulse can only feed off experience of the present. And present-tense autobiography, like the intrusions that lead into first-person vignettes, is an act of total immediacy. If "all" that is "gone" is recalled, the two selves become one. And the final distinction fails. The final distance collapses.

Yet even without attending to the possibility of writing the first person into the present tense, the enjoyment of what lies in the past is not always easy for Ruskin. He writes to a friend: "The things I fancy we are both wanting in, is a right power of enjoying the past. What sunshine there *has* been even in this sad year! I have seen beauty enough in one afternoon, not a fortnight ago, to last me for a year if I could rejoice in memory" (xxxvii, 292). Ruskin's description of that memory he is not always able to rejoice in is characteristically contradictory. On the one hand, he can say that he possesses a "good quick and holding memory" (xxxv, 83), and, on the other, that his "memory was of average power" (xxxv, 51). In any case, recalling the past, if not rejoicing in it, he suffers from a kind of mnemonic vertigo. It is as if the past, like the outside which is turned "in," is closer than the present: ". . . am giddy with the lot of things that focus, now, out of past work" (xxxvii, 194).

To recall what is "gone," he must first forget. At least, he must forget the "all." He must have a sense of separation between autobiographer and recollected image. He must forget the serial transition, the "mnemonic distance," that links him to a past-tense self who is a fitting subject for autobiography only as long as he remains in the past. Curiously, Ruskin's necessary relation with his young first person is the antithesis of the ideal relation he observes in Europe between the people of the Continent and their own past: ". . . on the Continent, the links are unbroken between the past and present, and, in such use as they can serve for, the grey-headed wrecks are suffered to stay with me; while, in unbroken line, the generations of spared buildings are seen succeeding each in its place" (vi, 12). Instead, looking at his former self—"looking back from 1886 to that brook shore of 1837" (xxxv, 220)—Ruskin is looking at a self from whom he is separated by an abyss of time, a temporal equivalent to the intervening space of the optical self. The "unbroken line" must be broken. The autobiographer, observing his young, past-tense self, must maintain, even as he looks "back from 1886 to that brook shore of 1837," his new distance. If Ruskin is going to look at a mirror, the mirror must be on the far shore. The distance keeps the retrospective autobiographer, who has been born again in his own first person, from sullying that earlier self with precisely those problems that drive the autobiographer to both his Nest and his art. Further, keeping the focal point of the first person from the autobiographer's vantage point, the mnemonic distance also keeps the writer of *Praeterita,* whose food is the past, the world summoned by "old haunts," from ingesting the future St. Crumpet on his inviolate "brook shore." The first person must maintain his autonomy. The "face to face" confrontation cannot be a marriage.

The distance over the brook, the mnemonic distance, which is the reason for both the lack of contamination on the far "brook shore" and the intensity of the sympathetic identification, provides a control that is opposite to the "nothing but process" of the Third Style—that style which depends for its success, which is Ruskin's survival, upon the fact that it is composed without an interval of "mature consideration," a consideration that, as a variation of the distance that no longer exists except in time, now leads to the Spectral Vision of "World Collision." The recalled world of *Praeterita* has some of the sharpness of Turner's "first vision," though Ruskin's act of memory is often an act of revisitation and metamorphosis. Still, there is the control of the "brook," which, uncursed by Reuban and unvisited by crocodiles that might be transformed into either swine or dragons for St. George, is no "green tide." And the "bloody carcases" lie on the near shore, out of the first person's view, by the feet of an autobiographer whose sanity is his art. *Praeterita,* begun in *Fors Clavigera,* is not the product of *Fors'* peregrinating consciousness, which has no notion of the future, no idea where it is going—no plans at all. Instead, *Praeterita* is blocked out in advance.[5] Writing *Praeterita* is more an act of filling an already existing container than tracing a syntax of consciousness. It is as if, in the act of efficacious autobiography, with the new-found mnemonic distance of the "brook," Ruskin has returned to an empty world that only requires

---

[5] Showing E. T. Cook his elaborate plans for *Praeterita,* Ruskin, according to Cook, pointed out that "everything is written except for the chapters themselves" (xxxv, liv).

the digging of Faust and the filling of Christ. Writing *Praeterita,* Ruskin
has returned to his Herne Hill garden. But this time, along with his spade,
he has brought a sense of economy, which is to say a sense of boundaries:
"The thirty-six chapters of *Praeterita* being already arranged to the end,
require extreme care in packing their contents, so as to keep what I have
called essentials only. Far more interesting things might be told, in every
case; but not the cardinal ones . . ." (*Diaries,* p. 1136).

If Ruskin writes with the freshness of a "first vision," he has
nevertheless learned his lesson the second time around. Packing, or writing,
"all" that is "gone," everything that is on the far "brook shore," would
lead to the intense claustrophobia that has driven him towards his censored
self. Further, he has come to understand that if "all" is packed, if
everything is filled with the retrieved "all," the past-tense self is no longer
censored and the autobiographer no longer has his functioning art, which is
itself an art of discrimination. Employing the conventional dimensions of
shallowness and narrowness, Ruskin supplements his newly discovered
brook distance of memory by creating a new kind of horizontal space, a peripheral area that does not include the surrounding "bloody carcases" of
slaughtered sheep. Next to the empty structure of *Praeterita,* with its thirty-
six compartments that are, finally, only filled to twenty-eight chapters, is
another structure, a lateral addendum, that is for the accomodation of
"interesting things . . . but not the cardinal ones": "It [at first *Manentia*
and finally *Dilecta*] is to be a supplement to *Praeterita,* giving friends' letters, and collateral pieces of events or debate for which there is no room in
the closely packed story, or which would make me jealous of their branching
and often livelier interest. I shall be able thus to give pieces for reference
out of diaries, and sometimes a bit of immediate Fors-fashion talk—which
will be a relief from the please-your-worship and by-your-leave style of
Praeterita" (xxxv, liii).

Dilecta, an addendum for "branching" digression, is designed to release
Ruskin's instincts for present-tense maneuvering—the intricate turns, close
to consciousness, of epistolary, diary, and parenthetic thought (xxxv, 572).
With his collateral extension, Ruskin moves the "by-ways" of digression,
which in *Fors* threatened to push "mature" thought, editorial thought, the
thought of distance, right off the page, back towards the peripheral areas
where those "by-ways" were born. In the face of a necessary autobiographical narrowness, it is an assertion of an obscured horizontal impulse.
What Ruskin establishes with his collateral structure is room for digressive
instincts to branch, so that *Praeterita,* as an autobiography and not as a
"new book on the trotting of Centaurs and Lapithae, or the riding of Bellerophon, or the crawling of the Tortoise of Aegina, or the flying of Harry
the Fifth's tennis balls," does not "overlap into the next planet or nebula"
(*Diaries,* p. 1136). Like the perspective study that charts the penetration of

space, *Praeterita,* because of the room provided by *Dilecta,* is a straight line.

Praeterita and collateral environs are constructed about division and separation. This is apparent in the space between the autobiographer of *Praeterita* and his subject, who, standing on the "brook shore of 1837," is himself a potential autobiographer. It is apparent in the stylistic difference between the "please-your-worship and by-your-leave style" of *Praeterita,* which with obvious charm but a sense of insistent progression, is determined to fill *Praeterita's* thirty-six chapter molds, and the wandering, exploratory style of *Dilecta,* which, closer to the "immediate Fors-fashion talk," would branch peripherally and infinitely beyond molds and towards no conclusion at all, no ultimate point of punctuation. In the same way, in *Praeterita* itself there is in operation a separating and excluding process that performs surgery on even "cardinal," autobiographical points. The world of *Praeterita* is censored by the act of recollection which is the backward counterpart—"I transpose myself back through the forty years . . ." (xxxv, 368)—of the forward penetration of space. Both mnemonic and distant perspectives are essentially private and exclusive. Neither perspective takes into account peripheral areas of complication. To do so, would be to move laterally, like *Manentia* and *Dilecta,* towards the "next planet or nebula," instead of ahead through space, or backwards through time.

Like the distant perspective, the mnemonic perspective, penetrating the distance of memory, the brook distance, organizes what it chooses to deal with—never "all"—on its own terms. Ruskin's autobiographically recalled self leaves behind, forgotten, a complex private self, the writer of the Forsian periphery, who is as invisible in *Praeterita* as he has been outside diaries, parentheses, and occasional first-person intrusions. Significantly, Ruskin writes to Kate Greenaway, whom he had scolded for censoring backgrounds, about a process that is no less editorial: "I am so very glad you like *Praeterita,* for it is, as you say, the 'natural' me—only of course, peeled carefully. It is different from what else I write—because, you know, I seldom have to describe any but heroic, or evil, characters, and this watercress character is so much easier to do, and credible and tasteable by everybody's own lips" (xxxv, lii). "Peeled," made "tasteable," Ruskin markets himself, or at least a public version of himself, for general consumption. But it is not merely the recalled self who has been edited by the private, mnemonic perspective. The entire world of *Praeterita* has been filtered. As opposed to the aural assaults in *Fors* that Ruskin has attempted to compartmentalize, Praeteritan sound, transmitted over the brook distance that separates the first person from his autobiographer, is either muffled or harmonious. A form of visualization even as it is transformed into a euphemistic lexicon, memory, crossing water, tames cacophony. The infernal, what was often in "first vision" devilish, becomes something quite different. Now, the autobiographer not only hears charming sound but sees it. But of course the "now" is "then": "After all, the chief charm of it [the Belfry of Calais] was in being seen from my bedroom at Dessein's, and putting me to sleep and waking me with its chimes" (xxxv, 416).

After the approach to silence, there is the fact. Even more than devilish sound, emotional discord is smothered by the brook distance. Censoring as he "packs," Ruskin reduces dissent to a condition of "total silence": "I have written them [the sketches that compose *Praeterita*] therefore, frankly, garrulously, and at ease; speaking, of what it gives me joy to remember, at any length I like—sometimes very carefully of what I think it may be useful for others to know; and passing in total silence things which I have no pleasure in reviewing . . ." (xxxv, 11). A "joy to remember," Ruskin's edited, mnemonic world offers pleasure beyond the peripheral complexity of the Third Style's "bitter play." Writing *Fors* with an inclusive vision, a vision without narrowness, Ruskin turns to the brook distance of an autobiographical memory for rest, a memory designed to forget: "there is much casual expression of my own personal feelings and faith together with bits of autobiography, which were allowed place, not without some notion of their being useful, but yet imprudently, and even incontinently, because I could not at the moment hold my tongue about what vexed or interested me, or returned soothingly to my memory" (xxxv, 384–85).

Looking with the Desiring Eyes of time at a "peeled," "watercress" version of a self he would once have rather annulled than either retrieved or visited, Ruskin, having found himself, as St. Crumpet, good enough to eat, now prescribes himself for medicinal purposes: ". . . having already prepared for this one ["Letter 51"], during my course of self-applause taken medicinally, another passage or two of my own biography . . ." (xxviii, 271). Ruskin has become his own best exit from himself. Without possessing the characteristics of Infinity, his first person—the subject of his autobiography—has been transformed into a white light of the past tense: "My described life has thus become more amusing than I expected to myself, as I summoned its long past scenes for present scrutiny . . ." (xxxv, 11). But if, as Poulet maintains, both Bergson and the romantics discover themselves in the depths of their own memories,[6] Ruskin, reborn in that first person, discovers himself, perhaps tastes himself, certainly applauds himself—all in order to lose himself in a past-tense version that has a future, a fresh sense of distance that the autobiographer only possesses "outside in," or retrospectively. The world of *Praeterita* is Ruskin's most

[6] Georges Poulet, *Studies in Human Time* (Baltimore, 1956), p. 34.

extended example of options, doubleness or antithetical architecture. Censored, edited, a world of Euphemy, it provides a target for sympathetic identification that the world described by the "bitter play" of *Fors* cannot. The first person whom Ruskin discovers on the "brook shore of 1837" annuls the agonized existence of the writer of *Fors,* who stands "hurdle-deep" amid slaughtered sheep, more effectively than the vanishing point ever could. But the autobiographer remains, and remaining, he is dependent upon, though separated from, his recent discovery—his first person.

Yet the essential problem persists, the problem of an autobiography that is necessarily structured about discriminations: the young first person on the far "brook shore," who is also a past-tense self, his future before him like a distance that has yet to fail, will eventually indulge in the same art as the autobiographer and for the same reasons. The distinction between selves cannot be maintained. The furnishing of the empty chapters of *Praeterita* is the construction of a bridge over the brook distance. And the construction of the bridge is the act of writing, which is an act of censored recollection. The success of autobiography is in the Forsian "nothing but process" of the act of writing (though the style fails to approach the immediacy of *Fors*) and not the filled page, the furnished and finished chapter. And the failure is in the completed bridge, the mastery of a brook distance that is a forgetful memory. To escape into the first person by writing an autobiography that only works because it is, in fact, biography—the two selves being separate except for the seeds of anticipation in the first person—is eventually, in the process of writing, to use up the "all" that was "gone." And using up what was "gone" is to make it present and available for the reader, which is the writer's death. Then, the bridge is built, the brook distance traversed, and all that was selectively forgotten is remembered. The two selves become one and neither is as "biped" as "useful truth." In the movement towards homogeneity, as two worlds and times fuse until there is nothing "apart," biography becomes autobiography.

But then, as if this were intuited, *Praeterita* never reaches the proposed thirty-sixth chapter, appropriately entitled "Calais Pier." The bridge is never entirely finished. The brook distance is never completely filled in by the act of memory. Something is forgotten. And if at times tenses are confused and the past becomes the present ("'Eden-land' Rosie calls it"), the first person of 1837 never greets the autobiographer of 1889. The separation is fortunate. And the ending is the only ending possible—or, more accurately, the ending is one that cannot be followed. The twenty-eighth chapter, "Joanna's Care," concludes masterfully, punctuated by ecstatic exclamation points, with a triumph over the infernal effect of spatial pseudoscopic inversion. It is a triumph, after the failure of the distance, over the inversions of foreground and background that, in embryonic form, may have contributed to the "black anger" directed towards the *Blackwood's* critic of Turner, a critic whom Ruskin, always engaged in acts of metamorphoses, becomes in 1877 as he observes Whistler's "Falling Rocket" at the Grosvenor Gallery. It is a triumph over an effect that an unhappy Ruskin, as the "stars danced among the dismal clouds above me like fire-flies," associated with Adele Domecq's marriage. And it is a triumph over an effect, anticipated by his response to both Rembrandt's "jack-a-lantern" chase and his illuminated "costermonger's ass," that may have provided the energy for Ruskin's own assault on what he considered to be Whistler's assaulting Spectral Vision.

Finally, Spectral Vision is mastered by the distinction of tenses, the mnemonic brook distance that has been reduced to eight empty chapters. The past in which the first person operates is never made "tangible" for the autobiographer, as was the child's present tense in the Herne Hill garden. The past tantalizes, flirts, just out of reach, but, with those rare exceptions in which tenses are "entangled" like foregrounds and backgrounds, does not cross a bridge that is never recalled into completion. And because the past remains where it should, as opposed to the invading "outside" of recessional space, what had elicited "black anger" can be described with felicity. Once, in a letter of July, 1870, only two weeks after the fact, he had described his entrance into Siena, an entrance that had been either close to infernal or "anything rather than *celestial*": ". . . while Siena, in a hill district, has at this season a climate like the loveliest and purest English summer, with only the somewhat, to me, awful addition of fire-flies innumerable, which, as soon as the sunset is fairly passed into twilight, light up the dark ilex groves with flitting torches, or at least, lights as large as candles, and in the sky, larger than the stars. We got to Siena in a heavy thunderstorm of sheet-lightning in a quiet evening, and the incessant flashes and showers of fire-flies between, made the whole scene look anything rather than *celestial*" (xx, liv). But now, in the depths of his memory, he has discovered a first person who can transform the autobiographer's infernal experience into an experience that is paradisiacal.

The triumph of *Praeterita*—the triumph of an autobiography that, created between the interplay of first person and autobiographer, is like a biography—is actually a triumph of fiction and time. But it is a fiction that is not always recorded by the autobiographer. Avoiding mirrors, he comes close to avoiding the page. If language, with the exceptions of those words transcribed by the ornate script to be taught at the St. George's school, or the "fossilized" language that becomes a substitute for St. Mark's, is a cheap "quack's drug for memorandum," and if the "eye is a nobler organ than the ear," the autobiographer nevertheless speaks his memorable fiction, dictating most of the closing "Joanna's Care" to Joan Severn's sympathetic and attentive ear.[7] With the introduction of an amanuensis, confrontation between autobiographer and first person is dispersed to triangulation. In any case, fiction, time, and sequence—all disdained by the Ruskin whose early impulse is towards the angelic "collective aspect" of spatial, "fossilized" form—succeed where the truth of space fails. Ending where it must, *Praeterita* closes with an opening, an opening that is an imaginative recreation of recessional space, the lost third dimension. The cleansing brook distance, which is the distance of a forgetful memory and so a distance of fiction, transforms a sky of gleams closing in "hopelessly" into an "openly golden sky," a sky that is a species of infinite "Escape." What passes for autobiography is only possible with the imaginative recreation of a distance that long ago failed. And if Ruskin's world is built upon discriminations that would avoid the "face to face" movement towards claustrophobia and homogeneity, which is the ultimate condition of metamorphosis (all the transformations having been made, all the roles having been played), those fireflies, once infernal, "anything rather than *celestial*," but now "rising and falling, mixed with lightning and more intense than the stars," orchestrate a vision that is the closest that Ruskin can come to harmonious union, a "Marriage in Cana," the "binding and blending of all things"—and this without the collapsing space of "World Collision":

> How things bind and blend themselves together! The last time I saw the Fountain of Trevi, it was from Arthur's father's room—Joseph Severn's, where we both took Joanie to see him in 1872, and the old man made a sweet drawing of his pretty daughter-in-law, now in her schoolroom; he himself then eager in finishing his last picture of the Marriage in Cana, which he had caused to take place under a vine trellis, and delighted himself by painting the crystal and ruby glittering of the changing rivulet of water out of the Greek vase, glowing into wine. Fonte Branda I last saw with Charles Norton, under the same arches where Dante saw it. We drank of it together, and walked together that evening on the hills above, where the fireflies among the scented thickets shone fitfully in the still undarkened air. How they shone! moving like fine-broken starlight through the purple leaves. How they shone! through the sunset that faded into thunderous night as I entered Siena three days before, the white edges of the mountainous clouds still lighted from the west, and the openly golden sky calm behind the Gate of Siena's heart, with its still golden words, "Cor magis tibi Sena pandit," and the fireflies everywhere in sky and

---

[7] It should be noted that Ruskin, entering Siena the second time around, is "face to face" with both his first person and his page. That last triumphant section is composed on paper. But, reversing the process of normal dictation, it virtually demands to be read aloud, and with no inaudible murmuring of reticent lips. The end, appealing to the ear, may appeal to an organ that was once less than noble.

cloud rising and falling, mixed with the lightning, and more intense than the stars. (**xxxv**, 561–62)

And if the autobiographical triumph, which is the triumph of forgetfulness and fiction, is tainted by the eleven years that follow his second and ecstatic vision of the entrance into Siena, an entrance that is also an exit—eleven years of madness and a silence far greater than either the "quietude" of Herne Hill or the harmonious act of selective autobiographical recollection, a madness and silence that accompany him until his death—it is nevertheless a triumph that is as real as any possible for someone who had long ago adopted the "biped" stance of "useful truth" (a stance of alternatives that has now become a "useful fiction"), for someone whose self-awareness, tempered by self-forgetfulness, is only possible with a first person who is no more than a prediction of his autobiographer. The intensity of the triumph is the result of having felt and having failed to forget that original "black anger." And the felicitous entrance into Siena, the second time around, in the guise of that "peeled," fictive first person, requires that he neither crosses the bridge nor disembarks at the Calais Pier, where self-portraiture is an infernal act, a "uniped" art of debilitating truth, and where all things fall into one, as if in a spectral and cosmic collision of rushing stars and gliding lamps, with the dancing fireflies, no "unpursued vanities," the largest and most awful of all, and hardly celestial.

The Johns Hopkins University Press

This book was composed in Baskerville text and display
type by the Maryland Composition Company, Inc., from a
design by Victoria Dudley Hirsch, and printed on 60-lb.
Warren 1854 Regular paper. It was printed and bound by
Universal Lithographers, Inc.